The university in the digital age

Mario Torres Jarrín (ed.)

The university in the digital age

PETER LANG

Berlin - Bruxelles - Chennai - Lausanne - New York - Oxford

Library of Congress Cataloging-in-Publication
A CIP catalog record for this book has been applied for at the
Library of Congress.

**Bibliographic information published by the Deutsche
Nationalbibliothek**
The Deutsche Nationalbibliothek lists this publication in the Deutsche
Nationalbibliografie; detailed bibliographic data is available on the
Internet at http://dnb.d-nb.de.

*This publication is a collaborative effort between university scholars and
international experts, developed within the research group "EU & Ethics
Governance of Artificial Intelligence" led by the Institute of European
Studies and Human Rights at the Pontifical University of Salamanca.*

Universidad
Pontificia
de Salamanca

Institute of
European Studies
and Human Rights

ISBN 978-3-631-93820-1 (Print)
E-ISBN 978-3-631-93722-8 (E-PDF)
E-ISBN 978-3-631-93723-5 (E-PUB)
DOI.10.3726/b22511

© 2025 Peter Lang Group AG, Lausanne
Published by Peter Lang GmbH, Berlin, Deutschland

info@peterlang.com - www.peterlang.com

Contents

Chapter 1

The university in the digital age: Rethinking its future and the return to its origins

MARIO TORRES JARRÍN

Abstract: The emerging technology in fields such as artificial intelligence, quantum computing, the Internet of Things, nanotechnology, biotechnology, etc. is changing the way we think, produce and communicate. According to Klaus Schwab, the world lives in a new age, which he has named the 'Fourth Industrial Revolution', characterized by a fusion of technologies between the physical, digital, and biological spheres. As societies we live a changing world and as humanity a new stage. This chapter examines the role of the university in the digital age.

Keywords: university, digital age, Fourth Industrial Revolution, big tech companies, disruptive technologies

Introduction: The university as an architect of the development of societies

Nowadays, when we refer to a university, we define it as an institution of higher education that issues academic degrees, which enable those who hold such degrees to exercise a profession and, consequently, to access the sector of the labour market corresponding to some of the areas of knowledge of their degree. At the same time, it is assumed that having a university degree gives one a better chance of success in finding a good job and developing as a professional. In reality, however, these assertions are not entirely accurate and correct. However, the argument that having a university degree will give more chances to get a job has been the main argument for people to choose to study at a university. This reality means that people often study by 'choice' (to get a job) rather than by 'vocation' (a person's natural inclination or predilection for a specific field of work).

The process of urbanization of cities, the growing population and competition in the labour market has led to an increase in the number of universities in urban areas, which has led to a massification of higher education (Addie, 2016). These facts have led to education being seen as an industry, and a university industry has been created, which produces professionals with technical skills, but not necessarily people with a universal vision of things and committed to the development of their societies.

Of course, there are still universities that are aware of their commitment to being agents of development in their societies and committed to building a better world, training leaders with positive action, with values and principles, and with a universal vision of the world. But for many universities, education is not seen as a service, but as a product. This has contributed to the development of a mercantilist vision of education, a vision characterized by an emphasis on economic models of scale and commercial aspects of education, a vision that is detrimental to the quality of teaching (Segovia-García & Martín-Caro, 2023). For many universities, students are no longer citizens to be educated and trained, but customers to satisfy a need and to be paid.

If we take any city in the world as a reference, we look at the number of inhabitants and map the professional needs of that city: teachers, doctors, nurses, lawyers, economists, etc. We would see that the demand for jobs in that city does not correspond to the academic offer provided by the number of universities in that city. On the one hand, because all the universities have the same academic offer. On the other hand, with all of them together, they will offer the market a higher number of graduates than the number of jobs that the city requires. In commercial terms, we could say that there is misleading advertising on the part of the universities, which already know from the outset that there are not that many jobs or, even worse, that the courses they offer will not guarantee their graduates a job.

The first role of a university is to understand its time, to study the social, economic and cultural phenomena that may have an impact on its societies and to try to respond to the challenges that a society faces in a given period of its history. The essence of a university is to be a centre of thought, reflection and knowledge, a generator of new ideas that contribute to the development of its societies.

Since their origins, universities have used research as a working method in order to teach on the basis of the results of this research, only what is known can be taught, and this knowledge is provided by research and study. However, under a business and mercantilist vision, many universities are created only to teach, without research, and what is even worse, they are not committed to the development of societies but to the development of their shareholders of the business group that owns them. This vision has not only damaged the image of the university but has also brought certain professions into disrepute and has led to low salaries, generated by an excess of job seekers compared to the supply of jobs.

There are an estimated 25,000 universities in the world and an average of 254 million university students, a figure that has doubled in the last 20 years and is set to increase; but despite booming demand, the overall enrolment rate is 42 % with large differences between countries and regions (UNESCO, 2024). Among the top 10 countries with the highest number of universities are:

Table 1. Ranking of the countries with the largest number of universities in the world

Countries	Number of universities
1. India	5.288
2. United States	3.216
3. Indonesia	2.595
4. China	2.565
5. Brazil	1.297
6. Mexico	1.173
7. Japan	1.063
8. Russia	1.058
9. Iran	704
10. France	617

Own elaboration. *Source:* Statista 2024.

As can be seen, if we take as a reference only the first 10 of the 193 countries, we can conclude that, of the 10 countries with the most universities in the world, 9 belong to the G20 and 4 to the G7, and in all cases they are regional powers. If we were to take into account the geographical location, we would say that, of the five continents, there are mainly three continents with the highest number of universities world-wide: Asia, America and Europe.

Asia is the continent with the most universities in the world, with 18,555 universities (including the universities of India, Indonesia, China, Japan and Iran). This figure would be higher if we consider Russia, which is always in doubt as to whether it is a European or Asian country. In this study, we have considered Russia as a European country. The second continent with the most universities is America with 5,686 universities (United States, Brazil and Mexico), and in third place would be Europe with 1,675 universities (adding the universities of Russia and France).

It is not surprising that Asia is the continent with the most universities in the world, considering that developing countries in East Asia and the Pacific are growing faster than the rest of the world (World Bank, 2024), which translates into more companies in that region, and therefore more labour supply. World Trade Organization forecasts for 2024 estimate that Asia will contribute more to global trade growth than in the past two years (World Trade Organization, 2024), and by 2023 Asia is expected to account for two-thirds of the global middle class (KPMG, 2019).

If we take as indicators two of the main international rankings: Shanghai & *Times Higher Education, we* find the following universities as the best in the world:

Table 2. Academic ranking of world universities

Top 10 ranking universities	Country
1. Harvard University	United States
2. Stanford University	United States
3. Massachusetts Institute of Technology	United States
4. University of Cambridge	United Kingdom
5. University of California, Berkeley	United States
6. Princeton University	United States
7. University of Oxford	United Kingdom
8. Columbia University	United States
9. California Institute of Technology	United States
10. University of Chicago	United States

Own elaboration. *Source:* Shanghai Ranking 2023.

Table 3. World University Ranking 2024

Top 10 ranking universities	Country
1. University of Oxford	United Kingdom
2. Stanford University	United States
3. Massachusetts Institute of Technology	United States
4. Harvard University	United States
5. University of Cambridge	United Kingdom
6. Princeton University	United States
7. California Institute of Technology	United States
8. Imperial College London	United Kingdom
9. University of California, Berkeley	United States
10. Yale University	United States

Own elaboration. *Source:* Times Higher Education 2024.

Looking at these figures, we can conclude the following points:

1. That the most prestigious universities worldwide are those that continue to apply the essential or traditional model of a university, in terms of knowledge generation and dissemination: first step, research; second step, creation of academic offerings based on the research developed.
2. The universities that lead the academic world are those that invest the most in research. Each of these universities has departments, institutes and research centres with large resources, both human and financial. They attract the best talent to their universities, researchers of recognized national and international prestige, who are usually at the forefront of generating ideas and knowledge.
3. These universities are the trendsetters in the academic world (the ones that create new lines of research and the ones that create new careers).
4. The university world is led by American and British universities, and consequently, the reference model for academic excellence at the international level is the Anglo-Saxon university model.
5. The language of academia is English. Just as Latin was at the origin of universities in Europe in the Middle Ages.

The Anglo-Saxon vision of the university is mainly oriented towards a special emphasis on research, institutional autonomy, promotion of interdisciplinarity, global vocation, and a focus on employability.

The concept of the university as we know it today originated in the Middle Ages, with institutions born under the influence of scholastic thought, which played an important role in the construction of Western academic discourse. The Middle Ages saw the emergence of the first universities, which were the main bastions of scholasticism, where it was taught and developed through a rigorous curriculum based on a *trivium* (grammar, logic and rhetoric) and a *quadrivium* (arithmetic, geometry, music and astronomy). Teachers and students used the scholastic method as a teaching and learning technique through *lectio* (reading), *question* (question) and *disputatio* (dipsuta). These in turn were structured in *positio* (position), that is, an affirmation or thesis was presented, then *objectiones* (objections) were presented, presenting arguments against the thesis, and then proceeding to a *respondeo* (answer), which consisted of presenting arguments in favour of the thesis, refuting the objections. This was followed by a *conclusio* (conclusion) based on the arguments presented.

Scholastic debates, academic disputes and the analysis of texts were common practices in the first universities, whose roots are to be found in the cathedral and monastic schools of the early Middle Ages, and on these schools were built the first universities in Europe and in the Western world: Bologna, Paris, Oxford and Salamanca.

The University of Bologna, created by Irnerius of the Carmelite Order as *Alma Mater Studiorum*, was born from the will of the students and for the students when teachers of grammar, rhetoric and logic began to apply themselves to law. The date of its foundation is not clear. On the one hand, it is believed that in 1158 the Holy Roman Emperor Frederick I Barbarossa granted the university *Authentica habita* (charter of foundation). On the other hand, in the nineteenth century, a committee of historians traced the foundation of the university back to the year 1088, making the University of Bologna the oldest university in the world in terms of uninterrupted operation. This university specialized in Roman law, creating the school of the 'glossators' who were jurists who studied and commented on *Justinian's Corpus Juris Civilis*, creating the 'glosses' which were the commentaries they created to explain and adapt the Roman laws to the realities of their societies.

There are no founding references to Oxford University, however, its creation dates back to 1096, making it the second oldest functioning university in Europe and the world, and the first in the English-speaking world. Although it was recognized by the Pope as a *universitas* in 1231.

When Roger Bacon used observation and experimentation as fundamental methods of knowledge, it was the germ of what would later be called empiricism. Realism and nominalism were also debated at this university, which laid the foundations for many later metaphysical debates in European and universal philosophy.

The University of Paris, also called the Sorbonne, because its founder was the Bishop of Paris, Robert de Sorbon, who was also confessor to the King of France Louis IX (Saint Louis). The original name of the University of Paris was 'Congregation of the very poor masters of the Sorbonne' (*Domus magistrorum pauperrrima*). It was created under the reign of Louis IX and was declared useful for religion by Pope Alexander IV in 1259.

The University of Salamanca was founded in 2018 by the King of León, Alfonso IX as *Scholas Salamanticae* and in 1255 Pope Alexander IV published the papal bulls recognizing the universal validity of the degrees taught at the university and granting it the privilege of having its own seal. This university created a school of thought called the 'School of Salamanca' which gave rise to disciplines such as international relations, economics, moral theology and natural law.

These early European universities were centres of thought and intellectual innovation that gave rise to several influential schools of thought in the history of knowledge, which not only contributed to philosophy, theology, law or medicine but also to the natural sciences, humanities and politics.

Medieval universities began to train the first professionals such as lawyers, doctors, theologians and philosophers, who contributed to the consolidation of professions that are still fundamental today. The schools of thought generated in these universities shaped European intellectual culture and laid the foundations for future scientific, philosophical and political developments that followed in later centuries.

Today, when we think of new technologies, we think of technologies such as artificial intelligence, *big data* or robotics, etc. But we have forgotten that technologies such as the compass (second century), the printing press (1439), the steam engine (1712), the automobile (nineteenth century), the telephone (1854), the light bulb (1879), television (1926), the aeroplane (1903), the computer (1940) or the development of the Internet (1969–1989) were also unprecedented technological advances at a time in history, and many of them were even disruptive technologies, because they meant major transformations and changes in all areas of societies: legal, economic, social and cultural. The emergence of these new technologies generated the need to create new norms, establish rules, mechanisms, instruments and institutions to ensure that these technologies serve the population as a whole and avoid the least possible negative impact on society as a whole.

The university and the Fourth Industrial Revolution

The world is currently experiencing a change of era, where technological advances are producing many disruptive technologies, which are changing the way we think, create, produce and communicate. Consequently, societies are being transformed. The digital era, driven by companies in the *Industry 4.0* sector (Federal Ministry for Economic Affairs and Climate Action & Federal Ministry of Education and Research, 2024) are leading the so-called Fourth Industrial Revolution (Schawb, 2015), which consists of the merging of the physical, digital and biological worlds (Schawb, 2016). Technologies such as biotechnology, robotics, quantum computing, artificial intelligence, virtual and augmented reality, among others. They are transforming the economy, the labour market and societies themselves.

The university is thus faced with multiple challenges at the same time. On the one hand, it must carry out research that studies the impact of these technologies on societies, the economy, politics, the law, but also on a cultural and even environmental level. But since we live in a global world, research must necessarily be carried out by a group of researchers from different countries and regions. The challenges are global, so the solutions must also be global. The diagnosis of the state of the art on a given issue must also be approached and studied globally.

Another major challenge is to adapt many curricula to the digital age. Most university degrees have been designed with reference to a world that no longer exists. One of the criticisms levelled at universities is that their academic offer is anachronistic, and that there is an over-supply of training that the market will not be able to absorb. The value of a university degree is no longer determined only by the university that issues it, but by the company that hires it, and which needs professionals for the digital era.

In 2018, Facebook, now Meta, presented a project to create a new university, a university that meets the needs of the digital era. With this initiative, Facebook sought to respond to the criticisms of today's universities: a mercantilist vision, anachronism in their academic offerings and a gap between the academic world and the labour market. Within this framework, Meta-University was launched in 2020 as an alternative to traditional face-to-face universities, and its objectives include working on youth participation, intercultural dialogue and global citizenship in the midst of the COVID-19 pandemic (Council of Europe, 2024).

At the time of the launch of the new university in 2018, Facebook representatives defended the creation of a new university because 'traditional universities don't teach what you need to know'. Laszlo Bock, vice president of Google, claimed that in today's world 'academic certification is useless' (Ramos, 2018). That same year, Google launched a set of courses whose certificates were issued by Google itself, many of the courses cost 300 US dollars, do not require a university degree, are 100 % online and can be completed in three to six months. Also called 'Google Career Certificates'. Google started its academic offerings with its first programme 'Google IT Support Professional', and later expanded its offerings with 'Data Analytics', 'Project Management' and 'User Experience'. In addition, as part of its marketing strategy, it offered 100,000 scholarships for students and indicated that, for the company, those who take these training programmes will be equivalent to a four-year university degree (Pastor, 2020).

How will universities be able to compete with the academic offerings of big tech companies?

Today's universities, just like the first universities, have the mission of studying the impact of disruptive technologies, analysing their advantages and disadvantages, as well as their repercussions on the political, economic, social and cultural life of countries. Even more so if we take into consideration that big tech companies are de facto political actors and economic agents on a global level (Torres Jarrín & Riordan, 2023). To put these assertions into perspective, if we only consider the capital of the Top 3 big tech companies (Microsoft, Apple and Nvidia) they have 7,771 U.S. dollars, compared to the GDP of Germany and France, the two main economies of Europe and two of the world's major economic powers, which together have a total GDP of 6,681 U.S. dollars. These figures are evidence of the power of these companies.

The irruption of big tech companies in the education sector represents the greatest challenge for the survival and future of the university. We can enter into the debate that these degrees will never be like those offered at university, that the face-to-face nature and the interaction between teacher and student will never be surpassed by virtual education or put forward other arguments. All right, they are all valid, but what is also true is that the big tech companies are providing answers to a labour market, from which the university is in many cases disconnected from reality and not adapted to the digital era, led by the big tech companies.

According to the International Monetary Fund (2024), Artificial Intelligence will affect 40 % of jobs worldwide. According to the International Labour Organization, the changing world of work will require the development of new skills and lifelong learning, therefore education and training systems will need to equip the workforce with the skills and competencies needed in the future, policy measures will need to be taken to strengthen the links between training institutions and enterprises, and to strike a balance between the quality of training and meeting the demand for more flexible and shorter training programmes (International Labour Organization, 2024).

In 2023, UNESCO produced a report entitled 'Technology in education: A tool on whose terms?', in which it stated that the countries should implement new education policies on the way technology is designed and used in education so that it never replaces in-person, teacher-led instruction and, supports the shared objective of quality education for all (UNESCO, 2023).

All these facts and figures show that higher education institutions need to be redefined. In 2050 there will be a variety of higher education institutions with new meaning, new processes, new students and new teachers (Rukspollmuang, 2021).

The impact of disruptive technologies and universities

One of the main challenges for universities is to adapt their academic offer to the current demand (Torres Jarrín, 2018), a product of the digital era. In 2017, the World Economic Forum published a report entitled '10 professions that will be most in demand in the future (but do not yet exist)'. This report highlighted that universities were not doing anything to respond to the demand for new professional careers demanded by the labour market (WEF, 2017). The lines of research that universities as a whole are focusing on are not focused on the digital era either.

COVID-19 triggered an acceleration in the process of digitalization at work (European Parliament, 2022), the use of tools, applications and programs, using different disruptive technologies such as artificial intelligence, robotics, *big data*, among others, generated a change in the way we work, since then there has been an increase in remote work, the use of online collaborative work platforms and the way we communicate.

Disruptive technologies are transforming higher education, driving significant changes in the way research is conducted, teaching methods and ways of assessment. For example, there are tools using artificial intelligence that can find bibliographic citations of academic texts, summarize books and articles, and even produce academic texts, with a certain degree of originality. On the other hand, technologies such as augmented and virtual reality offer the opportunity to create more interactive and hands-on learning. Artificial intelligence facilitates the personalization of teaching according to the individual needs of learners. Big data makes it possible to track academic performance, analyse student behaviour, optimize resources and improve institutional decision-making.

The importance of developing technological skills is mentioned, that is, the relevance of integrating advanced technologies into the curriculum is highlighted in order to better prepare students for the digital world in which we live, so that students have better access to the labour market. Emphasis is placed on the sciences, thinking that in the digital era only the sciences are necessary, however, degrees such as history, philosophy, literature, which are part of the humanities, are the disciplines that encourage critical analysis, reflective thinking, it is important to understand the world, the historical and cultural context in which we live, in order to solve the great challenges presented by the digital era. In addition, the study of the humanities helps people to explore fundamental and transcendental questions about life, identity, values, and so on. Disciplines such as religion and ethics guide people on the importance of having and applying moral principles, both personally and socially.

Although the predominant focus in the digital age has been on the so-called STEM (Science, Technology, Engineering and Mathematics) disciplines (UNESCO, 2019), the contribution of the humanities (philosophy, history, literature, linguistics, arts, etc.) in the digital age are crucial to address the ethical, cultural, social and philosophical challenges arising from technological advances, as well as offering the intellectual capacity to provide contextual understanding, critical insight and moral direction in an increasingly digitized and unequal world.

We usually talk about 'social inequality', but the digital age is creating another type of inequality, 'digital inequality'. This consists of a lack of access to technology and connectivity, both of which are creating inequality between countries. If we used to talk in economic terms about 'developed countries' and 'developing countries', we are likely to have the same definitions, but this time taking into consideration their levels of technological development and their access to internet connectivity, which could generate new categories of countries: 'technologically advanced countries', 'technologically developing countries' and 'technologically underdeveloped countries'.

Economic crises, social injustices, human rights violations, wars or the deterioration of the environment are political crises, which in reality are crises of values of people who exercise politics in an inhuman way. Inhuman, because it cannot be morally or ethically acceptable to generate poverty, famine, inequality, create conflicts or wars, or to violate people's human rights, whether because of religion, race, gender, etc.

The social sciences (sociology, anthropology, economics, political science, etc.) are also more than ever needed to understand and address the complex problems and challenges facing modern societies.

University governance in the digital age

The pandemic caused by COVID-19 highlighted how far countries were lagging behind in digital issues, as well as the problems of digital equity and inclusion in areas of education (OECD, 2023). Universities had to transform and adapt to the digitalization era in one year, despite the fact that most major international agencies had been telling governments to invest in digital-focused education for years.

Transformation must not only be made in curricula, teaching methods, student support and research; changes must also be made in management, the operating model, and fundamentally in the sum of capabilities working in the organization (KPMG, 2023).

The management and administration processes of a university also face great challenges in the digital era, and even more so with the technological advances, now through artificial intelligence, decisions can be made without following established rules, it is possible to work with unstructured environments and data, and a number of jobs can be automated, which used to take up a lot of time, resulting in expenses in human resources and financial resources (OECD, 2024). Not only because jobs may disappear, which can be automated using certain technological advances, but also because the main challenge for an organization is not only to design a strategic plan but to have the human resources to implement it.

During the 1990s many universities developed strategic plans that included internationalization strategies (Knight, 1994). Many of these so-called internationalization strategies focused on participating in international university fairs, seeking partnerships with other universities abroad, or having an academic offer in another language, mainly English. In most cases, these strategies and work plans failed. Because they did not consider the importance of having trained human resources to carry out all the new initiatives, projects and international programmes, whether academic or research. Either it was as basic as their academic and administrative staff not knowing languages, or in other cases they did not understand the vision and organizational culture of the foreign universities they were dealing with.

Conclusions

We are living through a change of era, in multiple senses and at multiple levels. In the past, technological advances produced changes in societies, but only gradually, and for disruptive technologies to affect the use and consumption of these technologies worldwide, it took decades or even centuries before they came to be used globally. However, in the current times, there has been an explosion of technological advances, and many of these are disruptive technologies, and never in history has the world been faced with assimilating so many disruptive technologies at once.

For some years now, technology has been seen as a source of disruption in our lives, communities and civilisations, causing changes at all scales, from the everyday activities of individuals to the dramatic competition between global superpowers (European Parliament, 2023). Most disruptive technologies have taken months to go global, posing a challenge for the public sector, the private sector and academia.

The answer to all the challenges presented by the digital age in the field of education is to strive for academic excellence. To achieve this, actions need to be implemented at multiple levels and approaches:

Return to the origins of the university: Mission A centre of thought & knowledge and service to society

- To return to the essence and origins of the university, that is, to be centres of thought, reflection and knowledge generation committed to society and seeking through its research to contribute to a better world. The academic offer of any university must be based strictly on its main areas of research. Research equals scientific production, which is then transformed into lessons and thus into teaching. As in ancient times, universities that were prestigious were so because they had the best, intellectually prestigious scholars, which is why students from all over the world travelled to study at the place where the master's they had met by reading the books of those scholars were.

- Re-emphasizing the importance of the social sciences and the humanities: There was a time when many universities provided within their curricula, whatever the degree or degree, a semester or two of 'general studies', in which philosophy, literature, history, rhetoric, etc. were studied. Students who go to a university must have a greater intellectual and cultural background than in any other institution of higher education. The vision of universality must be inherent in the vision of a student who has studied at a university.

Internationalization and strategic alliances: Global vision & global actors

- Universities as global players: Universities need to participate more actively in international forums and specialized meetings organized by regional integration bodies, as well as international organizations. It has to be present in decision-making on issues on the global governance agenda.

- Prioritize the creation of international research groups: This action allows multiple results: to carry out comparative studies with other countries, to have different perspectives and vision of the subject in question, to internationalize the research of academics, to create academic networks, which will then be translated into new international research projects, which will later be translated into the creation of new academic offerings.
- Seek research funds jointly with other universities, which forces them to be competitive and seek academic excellence with international standards.
- Create alliances and research consortiums between universities and big tech companies. So that universities can be at the forefront of technological trends and thus be able to carry out better research.
- To create international undergraduate and postgraduate programmes through the creation of consortia of universities from different regions of the world.

New curricula and academic programmes that are more flexible and open

- Offering short courses: Going for the implementation of microcredentials. There has always been a demand for refresher courses, continuing education and specialization, but today more than ever, the era of digitalization increases the needs of learners who are looking for a more interactive, collaborative and innovative learning experience that harnesses and develops their skills.
- Internships should be compulsory in all degree programmes.
- The level of demands placed on students should be raised, especially in the area of research work.
- Curricula should be designed under the 'triple helix' model of innovation: public sector, private sector and academia. By consulting and coordinating with the private sector and the public sector, there will be better information on the needs of society, and the academic offer of universities will be more realistic and adapted to the needs of their respective societies.
- Universities must abandon the mercantilist view of education. Education should be seen as a service, not as a commodity that can be produced.

- Research must be a *spillover* effect, that is, degrees are created on the basis of the spillover effect. Not the other way around.
- Encourage students to develop critical thinking: It is probably what differentiates us from certain disruptive technologies, our ability to understand the context, compare and project possible scenarios, based on critical thinking.
- Universities should provide their teachers with training programmes focused on the use of technologies and new teaching methods.
- Universities must be active players in the cultural, social and political life of their societies.
- Stimulate creativity and critical thinking.
- Careers in the digital age should combine natural sciences, social sciences, humanities and applied sciences.

University governance

The success of any project is the team. There is no point in universities investing in research, creating new education programmes, designing and implementing internationalization strategies, if the vision of the university's future is not shared by the university community as a whole. It is in this context that university governance plays an important role in the future of the university in the digital era.

Understanding university governance as the set of processes, structures and rules that guide decision-making and administration within a university, the university must face two challenges. The first is to return to governance as it was in its origins as a corporation of professors and students, that is, decision-making about the future of a university must be the result of a process in which all sectors and organizational structures of the university are involved. Often external companies or consultants are hired to design a strategic plan for a university. The question is, who are greater experts than those working in the university itself? This does not mean that studies can be commissioned on how to improve processes or how to be more efficient as an organization. But the future of the organization will always depend on its members. The members of the university community, be they teaching and research staff or administrative staff, must be trained. For example, an example of failure in the field of university internationalization is due to the fact that the universities that designed and implemented an internationalization strategy were only known and understood by a small part of the university, often by the authorities, but not by teachers, researchers, faculty managers or the university's service units as a whole.

In the digital era, administrative processes can be digitized, which will result in greater time efficiency, saving human and financial resources for the university. Automation through digital tools in enrolment management, course allocation, and even in human resources management, are some examples of the advantages of using new technologies in the education sector. This automation combined with *big data*, for example, can be used to make better decisions based on objective data.

Collaboration and communication platforms such as online forums, digital surveys or internal social networks allow for greater involvement of the university community in governance processes.

Digital inclusion needs to be considered, as not all members of the university community may have the same access to or competence in the use of digital technology.

In terms of internationalization, it is undoubtedly one of the sectors with the most advantages, considering that the different existing digital communication tools facilitate the creation of international networks and alliances, which allows universities to collaborate in research, teaching and management.

Finally, university governance also includes the need to develop digital governance, which consists of managing the university's academic activities and institutional image in the digital environment, using social networks and online platforms to interact with society.

Finally, it is curious to discover that, although we talk about disruptive technologies, changes of era, and unimaginable future scenarios, the answer to the future of the university is to return to its origins, to its essence, to its commitment to society, to be a centre of thought and generator of innovative ideas through research and study of historical events and social transformations that occur in society as a whole.

The university, unlike any other academy or centre of higher education that issues university degrees, is the architect of the development and construction of civilisations. Universal values and principles must be studied, defended and disseminated by universities. It must be understood that we are the architects of and responsible for the history of humanity. We are responsible for both the golden periods and the dark and chaotic periods, and the latter are caused by people who lack universal values and principles. The university is that beacon of knowledge and light that illuminates the paths of human history, and in order for there to be a more just world, it is necessary for the university to train and educate universal people of vision, with universal values and principles such as human dignity, freedom, justice, equality, solidarity, respect for human rights and the promotion of peace.

References

Addie, J. (2016). From the urban university to universities in urban society. *Regional Studies, 51*(7), 1089–1099. https://doi.org/10.1080/00343 404.2016.1224334

Council of Europe. (2024). *Meta-university.* https://www.coe.int/en/web/ north-south-centre/meta-university

European Parliament. (2022). *Digitalisation and changes in the world of work.* Study requested by the EMPL Committee. Policy Department for Economic, Scientific and Quality-of-Life Policies – Directorate-General for Internal Policies. https://www.europarl.europa.eu/RegData/etudes/ STUD/2022/733986/IPOL_STU(2022)733986_EN.pdf

European Parliament. (2023). *Disruption by technology. Impacts on politics, economics and society.* European Parliamentary Research Service. Authors: Boucher, P., Bentzen, N., Latici, T., Madiega, T., Schmertzing, L. and Szczepánski, M. https://www.europarl.europa.eu/RegData/etu des/IDAN/2020/652079/EPRS_IDA(2020)652079_EN.pdf

Federal Ministry for Economic Affairs and Climate Action & Federal Ministry of Education and Research. (2024). *The background to Plattform Industrie 4.0.* https://www.plattform-i40.de/IP/Redaktion/EN/Standard artikel/plattform-background.html

International Labour Organisation. (2024). *Chapter 9. The future of work.* https://webapps.ilo.org/100/en/story/future/

International Monetary Fund. (2024). *Artificial Intelligence. AI will transform the Global Economy. Let's make sure it benefits humanity.* https://www. imf.org/en/Blogs/Articles/2024/01/14/ai-will-transform-the-global-econ omy-lets-make-sure-it-benefits-humanity#:~:text=The%20IMF%20analy sis%20captures%20both,to%20impact%20high%2Dskilled%20jobs.

Knight, J. (1994). *Internationalization: Elements and checkpoints. CBIE Research*. Canadian Bureau for International Education. https://files.eric. ed.gov/fulltext/ED549823.pdf

KPMG. (2019). *Del Atlántico al Pacífico*. KPMG Tendencias. https://www. tendencias.kpmg.es/claves-decada-2020-2030/geopolitica-globalizac ion-asia/

KPMG. (2023). *The future of higher education in a disruptive world*. https:// assets.kpmg.com/content/dam/kpmg/xx/pdf/2020/10/future-of-hig her-education.pdf

OECD. (2023). *Digital equity and inclusion in education: An overview of practice and policy in OECD countries* (OECD Education Working Papers No. 299). https://www.oecd.org/content/dam/oecd/en/publications/repo rts/2023/08/digital-equity-and-inclusion-in-education_c56b91ad/7cb15 030-en.pdf

OECD. (2024). *OECD Social, Employment and Migration Working Papers N 282. What skills and abilities can automation technologies replicate and what does it mean for workers? New evidence*. OECD iLibrary. https://www. oecd-ilibrary.org/employment/what-skills-and-abilities-can-automation- technologies-replicate-and-what-does-it-mean-for-workers_646aad77-en

Pastor, J. (2020). *Universidad Google: por 300 dólares y en seis meses obtendrás un certificado que ellos equiparan al de una carrera universitaria*. Xataka. https://www.xataka.com/empresas-y-economia/universidad-google-300- dolares-seis-meses-obtendras-certificado-equivalente-a-carreras-univers itarias-cuatro-anos

Ramos, T. (2018). *¿Acabará Google con las universidades?* Elearning Coor- porativo. https://elearningactual.com/fin-universidad-por-grandes-empre sas-tecnologicas/

Rukspollmuang, C. (2021). *Futures of Higher Education in post-digital age*. UNESCO International Institute for Higher Education in Latin America and the Caribbean.

Schawb, K. (2015). The Fourth Industrial Revolution. What it means and how to respond. *Foreign Affairs*. Council on Foreign Relations.

Schawb, K. (2016). *The Fourth Industrial Revolution*. World Eco- nomic Forum.

Segovia-García, N., & Martín-Caro, E. (2023). Cost analysis in online teaching using an activity map. *Education Science, 13*(5), 506. https://doi. org/10.3390/educsci13050506

Torres Jarrín, M. (2018). La economía de América Latina y el Caribe en la era digital. In *Iberoamérica ante la era digital* (pp. 23–39). Fundación Carolina.

Torres Jarrín, M., & Riordan, S. (2023). *Science diplomacy, cyberdiplomacy and techplomacy in EU-LAC relations.* Springer.

UNESCO. (2019). *Exploring STEM competences for the 21st century.* In-Progress Reflection N30. On current and critical issues in curriculum, learning and assessment. https://unesdoc.unesco.org/ark:/48223/pf000 0368485

UNESCO. (2023). *Global Education Monitoring Report 2023. Technology in education: A tool on whose terms?* https://unesdoc.unesco.org/ark:/48223/ pf0000385723

UNESCO. (2024). *Higher Education.* https://www.unesco.org/en/higher-education

World Bank. (2024). *East Asia and the Pacific economic update.* https://openknowledge.worldbank.org/entities/publication/9776d 1e0-96e5-4582-bda4-863901333ce4

World Economic Forum. (2017). 10 profesiones que serán más solicitadas en el futuro (pero aún no existen). In *Empleos y el futuro del trabajo.* https:// es.weforum.org/agenda/2017/05/10-profesiones-que-seran-mas-solicita das-en-el-futuro-pero-aun-no-existen/

World Trade Organization. (2024). *World trade outlook and statistics.* https:// www.wto.org/spanish/res_s/booksp_s/trade_outlook24_s.pdf

Chapter 2

Building trusted AI through ethical governance in education: The impact of the EU Artificial Intelligence Act in literacy and training

Cecilia Celeste Danesi

Abstract: Artificial intelligence has become an essential part of our societies. It is continuously changing the way we perform our daily tasks and activities, influencing diverse sectors like business, arts, law, manufacturing, economics, and healthcare. Education is no exception to this radical change, forcing us to consider it from different perspectives and disciplines. Therefore, we propose to identify the impact of AI on education from two viewpoints: AI as a tool and AI as content. With this state-of-the-art analysis, we will explore how the EU AI Act addresses this phenomenon. Finally, we will provide recommendations on how the public and private sectors can address AI in education, with a particular focus on algorithmic audits. This entire endeavour will be guided by the principles of ethical AI governance.

Keywords: artificial intelligence, EU AI Act, Human Rights, education, algorithmic audits, algorithmic bias, regulation

Introduction: Artificial intelligence in education

Nowadays, artificial intelligence has become an essential part of our societies. It is continuously reshaping the way we approach daily tasks and activities, impacting diverse sectors such as industry, arts, law, manufacturing, economy, and health, among others. Education is also part of this radical change, compelling us to study it from different perspectives and disciplines due to its importance in our lives. Undoubtedly, education has the power to improve our quality of life, close gaps, and bring progress to our communities, to name a few benefits. High educational standards yield both individual and collective benefits. Artificial intelligence is also having a radical impact on education, from formal to informal education as well as from preschool to university and all levels of training. Considering education importance and AI advantages, we cannot ignore the 'elephant in the room' and must 'pick up the ball'.

First, to gain a comprehensive understanding, we must analyse the current state of AI in education. This analysis will help us identify its pros and cons, its challenges, and its risks. We propose exploring the impact of AI in education from two key perspectives: AI as a tool for learning and AI as educational content itself.

With this information in mind, we will discuss the international agenda in AI and education, focusing on the EU AI Act as the most relevant AI regulatory framework in the world (we will explain why we hold this view).

Finally, we will discuss the risks and challenges of AI in education and provide recommendations on how the public and private sectors should address them.

The use of AI in education

As we mentioned earlier, AI in education can be divided into two major categories: AI as a tool and AI as content. Let's examine each of them.

AI as a teaching tool

The deployment of artificial intelligence tools has also reached the field of education. We can find several examples addressing different needs. The most common are systems that help teachers design educational strategies, identify students' weaknesses and propose activities for improvement, provide evaluation tools, assist with homework, improve learning for students with brain disorders, and create more immersive and engaging activities, among others.

One of the most prominent cases is China, where facial recognition cameras are integrated into the classroom to monitor and evaluate students. Students there may also be required to wear headbands equipped with sensors. This technology continuously collects data, which is sent to parents and teachers and processed by an algorithm that makes suggestions to improve the learning process. This technology can also identify emotions, such as when a student loses concentration, has trouble with an exercise, or is bored. We will mention some examples.

Brainly is a knowledge-sharing community where hundreds of millions of students collaborate to solve the toughest homework problems. It values the knowledge that is already in the minds of many students to help those in need. Another case is Cognii, a virtual learning assistant that engages students in a chatbot-style learning conversation, prompting them to construct answers, providing instant formative assessment, and tutoring them with personalized hints and tips. Along the same lines, there is Apolo Kids, a tool that supports children and parents in their education by complementing traditional schooling and helping to strengthen and develop the skills needed for the future.

On the other hand, to help people with brain disorders such as depression and epilepsy, there is Neuroelectrics, which restores brain networks using novel neurocircuit therapeutics to overcome the limitations of current therapies.

Another innovative example is Alinia. This tool helps enterprises control and guide Gen AI applications based on their policies and preferences. Lastly, we can mention Change Dyslexia, a platform that improves reading and writing skills through fun games. It offers 42,000 games customized according to 24 cognitive skills, targeting both cognitive weaknesses and strengths.

Another point to analyse is the debate around the incorporation of GenAI in the education process. This can be viewed from two different perspectives: for teachers to teach (designing pedagogical strategies, creating activities, etc.) and for students to learn and complete tasks. The concern about AI, like ChatGPT, doing all school or university homework is real, and the truth is that in the future, students will use even more sophisticated technologies in their jobs. We must prepare students for the future, not for the past.

AI as educational content

Firstly, we need to answer a common question: Should AI be part of the curricula? Absolutely, yes. Now, you might ask: why? We will answer this with an example. A small town in the Extremadura region, in the south of Spain, called Almendralejo, became famous, but not for something to be proud of. A group of teenagers used generative AI to create nude photos of their female classmates. The Provincial Prosecutor's Office for minors in Badajoz implicated 26 minors (21 of whom were imputable because they were over 14 years old according to Spanish law 5/2000) as alleged culprits, and 21 teenage girls were identified as victims.

This despicable practice is known as 'fake porn' or 'deepfake pornography' (similar to deepfake news), which refers to 'deep learning' (DL). DL is a subset of machine learning (the most common AI model) that uses multi-layered neural networks (called deep neural networks). Generative AI (GenAI), such as DALL-E 2 by OpenAI, Stable Diffusion, or Mid-journey, is the technology behind the creation of new data (text, video, images, voice, etc.) and is a subset of deep learning. There are differences among them: they use different technical architectures; DL is often used for discriminative tasks (like classifying images or predicting outcomes based on a set of inputs), while GenAI aims to generate new content that follows the patterns it has learned from its training data; DL tends to find specific answers, whereas GenAI generates new data (Reidand & Jing, 2023), etc.

That technology is not new, but today it has become more sophisticated. Years ago, it was very easy to detect that the content was fake, but after the launch of ChatGPT, it has become democratized, meaning that anyone can use it. The ubiquity of artificial intelligence in society compels us to be aware of its risks, especially considering that it is intensifying and widening social gaps. Vulnerable, marginalized, and underrepresented groups are the first to suffer from AI misuse. Regarding fake porn, most of the systems used to create nude images encourage users to try it with images of women. If you search 'Naked photos with AI' on Google, the first result is AInude.ai, which says 'Undress any girl photo or image to AI nudes NOW!'. These systems are more accurate with women because there is more data available, allowing the AI to learn more effectively about female bodies.

Another major problem is algorithmic bias, which refers, from a social sciences perspective to the discrimination and unequal treatment by AI outputs. Digital platforms, including social media, are central to this issue. Social media is managed by algorithms that determine what we see, what we can say, and what we consume. They subtly influence what we buy, whom we date, and even how we vote (e.g. the Cambridge Analytica case). Moreover, beauty filters are a prime tool for reinforcing stereotypes (Danesi, 2021). These filters often standardize faces according to a Caucasian ideal, perpetuating racial biases against Black people (Riccio et al., 2024). One notable instance was Twitter's (Chowdhury, 2021) – now X's – saliency algorithm, which cropped images, often eliminating Black individuals (Danesi, 2022). The consequence: social media content often lacks diversity, promoting a homogeneous society with narrow and harmful beauty standards where slim, sculpted bodies, white skin, upturned noses, and prominent cheekbones dominate.

A study by the American Psychological Association found that teens are spending nearly 5 hours daily on social media, and 41 % of teens with the highest social media use rate their overall mental health as poor or very poor (DeAngelis, 2024). The same association indicates that brain development from ages 10–13 (the outset of puberty) until approximately the mid-twenties is linked with hypersensitivity to social feedback and stimuli. This means that youth are particularly engaged in behaviours seeking personalized feedback, praise, or attention from peers. Key highlights include AI-recommended content can have a profound impact and be challenging to avoid within this age range; likes and follower counts activate neural regions associated with repetitive behaviours, potentially exerting greater influence on youth attitudes and behaviour compared to adults; and the use of youth data for tailored ad content (McCabe et al., 2024).

Considering the risks associated with AI, especially its profound impact on minors, how can we neglect teaching ethical AI use? Cases like Almendralejo point out that the first step is education, rather than exclusively relying on legislation, prohibition, and punishment. Children now learn to use cell phones before they can even speak, and algorithms heavily influence their thinking, communication, and worldview. Once again, we cannot ignore the elephant in the room.

In the final part of this chapter, we will discuss essential topics that must be included in the curricula.

The international context and ethical considerations in AI governance

The context described above is being addressed by some international legislation and documents. The transversal pillar of AI development should be the 'Ethics Governance of AI' (EGAI). EGAI is an essential and mandatory guide for the development of artificial intelligence. AI governance involves the ethical embedding, adaptation, assessment, and building of AI, and it should be implemented throughout the entire life-cycle of the technology, including the stages of research and development, design and manufacturing, experimental promotion, and deployment and application. Regarding role configuration, multiple stakeholders should assume different roles, including providing ethical factual information, expertise, and analysis, as well as expressing ethical emotions or providing ethical regulation tools under different governance strategies. This implies that the Ethics Governance of AI is a transversal, multi-sectoral, transdisciplinary, and global effort that applies from beginning to end and involves all actors. Another significant aspect is the continuous evaluation of the plan to readapt it if required. The exponential and permanent growth of AI requires constant review of risks, challenges, and objectives (Danesi & Torres, 2024).

This approach has to be followed by the quintuple-helix model of innovation, which includes university-industry-government relations (triple helix), media-based and culture-based public and civil society (fourth helix), and natural environments of society (quintuple helix). Although the triple helix model already includes education, the complex social fabric necessitates a move to the quintuple helix. It emphasizes the essential socioecological transition of society and the economy in the twenty-first century, making it ecologically sensitive. Therefore, the natural environments of society and the economy should also be seen as drivers for knowledge production and innovation, thus defining opportunities for the knowledge economy. The European Commission in 2009 identified the socioecological transition as a major challenge for the future (Carayannis et al., 2012).

Several groups have called for regulation or at least a specific action plan regarding AI in education. The European Commission published the Ethical Guidelines on the Use of Artificial Intelligence (AI) and Data in Teaching and Learning for Teachers, which is part of the Digital Education Action Plan (2021–2027). The AI Act also includes important insights that will be presented below.

UNESCO has made significant contributions in the field including the 'Recommendation on the Ethics of Artificial Intelligence', the 'Beijing Consensus on Artificial Intelligence in Education', the 'Guidance for Generative AI in Education and Research', several reports such as 'Harnessing the Era of Artificial Intelligence in Higher Education: A Primer for Higher Education Stakeholders', 'Artificial Intelligence in

Education: Challenges and Opportunities for Sustainable Development, Computational Thinking', 'Artificial Intelligence and Education in Latin America', 'State of the Education Report for India, 2022: Artificial Intelligence in Education'. 'Here, There and Everywhere, and Education in the Age of Artificial Intelligence', among others.

As part of the World Economic Forum Annual Meeting, the organization published seven principles to consider when creating guidance to ensure the responsible and effective use of AI in education: (1) Purpose: Explicitly connect the use of AI to educational goals. (2) Compliance: Affirm adherence to existing policies. (3) Knowledge: Promote AI literacy. (4) Balance: Realize the benefits of AI and address the risks. (5) Integrity: Advance academic integrity. (6) Agency: Maintain human decision-making. (7) Evaluation: Continuously assess the impact of AI. This last point is essential because AI can incorporate biases throughout its entire life cycle, so systems must be audited periodically.

Countries are also addressing this topic. The UK Government issued a policy paper on generative artificial intelligence (AI) in education, outlining the Department for Education's (DfE) position on using generative AI, including large language models (LLMs) like ChatGPT or Google Bard, in the education sector. This statement was informed by the government's white paper on a pro-innovation approach to AI regulation. The document explains what generative AI is, its opportunities for the education sector, its limits, and how to protect data, pupils, and staff. It also includes information about formal assessments, mentioning the guidance 'AI Use in Assessments: Protecting the Integrity of Qualifications'.

The paper highlights the need for the education sector to prepare students for changing workplaces and to teach them how to use emerging technologies safely and appropriately.

In turn, Colombia's Government delivered the 'Roadmap in Artificial Intelligence', which includes a section on 'Education, Research, and Innovation'. This section aims to create educational and talent programmes in AI, facilitating access to and understanding of this technology at the community level, training professionals and students, and stimulating research in academic institutions.

There are also other meaningful documents addressing AI in education, such as the Model AI Law for Latin America and the Caribbean by the Parlamento Latinoamericano y Caribeño, and 'The Future of Artificial Intelligence in Education in Latin America' by ProFuturo and OEI.

Regulating AI in education: The EU AI Act

Why is the EU AI Act so important?

The EU AI Act is known as the first comprehensive regulation of artificial intelligence. Its importance is due to various factors. This is not rushed legislation; the EU has been working on it for years. Of course, it can have many aspects that could be improved or included (e.g. civil liability rules apart from the Directive on adapting non-contractual civil liability rules to artificial intelligence – the AI Liability Directive – or the adaptation of the Product Liability Directive), but the extensive work and deep analysis of the matter are evident.

Take, for example, the European Parliament resolution of 16 February 2017, with recommendations to the Commission on Civil Law Rules on Robotics; the Opinion of the European Economic and Social Committee on 'Artificial intelligence – The consequences of artificial intelligence on the (digital) single market, production, consumption, employment, and society'; and the three legislative initiatives regarding the Ethics framework for AI, Liability for AI causing damage, and Intellectual property rights approved on 20 October 2020.

Second, the AI Act will be mandatory for the 27 member states of the European Union, representing a market of 447 million consumers. This law will likely cause 'The Brussels Effect', which refers to the globalization of EU rules (e.g. GDPR). It is argued that the EU dominates the world through the involuntary externalization of regulations by creating a common regulatory framework. This is one of its main strengths, and as a result, the EU influences global affairs more than the US with its military power or China with its overseas projects (Bradford, 2019).

Third, the AI Act is comprehensive legislation about AI, dealing with multiple areas. Additionally, it employs a legislative technique based on prevention. Another important aspect of the act is its risk-based approach, which defines four levels of risk for AI systems: (1) Unacceptable risk, (2) High risk, (3) Limited risk, and (4) Minimal or no risk. Let's examine its impact on education.

The impact of the EU AI Act on education

The AI Act states that 'the deployment of AI systems in education is important to promote high-quality digital education and training and to allow all learners and teachers to acquire and share the necessary digital skills and competences, including media literacy, and critical thinking, to take an active part in the economy, society, and in democratic processes' (recital number 56). However, it is also aware of the risks that AI systems assume, so it contains detailed rules related to some of these risks.

The first one is article number 4, which regulates 'AI literacy'. Providers and deployers of AI systems are forced to take measures to 'ensure, to their best extent, a sufficient level of AI literacy of their staff and other persons dealing with the operation and use of AI systems on their behalf, taking into account their technical knowledge, experience, education and training and the context the AI systems are to be used in, and considering the persons or groups of persons on whom the AI systems are to be used'.

We consider this article very valuable because, as we examine this topic, people using or working with AI need to be aware of its risks, especially those deploying it in critical areas. This training should include topics related to data privacy, consumer rights, algorithmic bias, risk management systems, and the ethical governance of AI, among others.

The Act also establishes that AI systems which can infer the emotions of a natural person are prohibited in the areas of the workplace and educational institutions, except where the AI system is intended for medical or safety reasons.

AI emotion recognition, also known as affective computing, is a subfield of computer vision, which enables computers to identify and understand objects and people in images and videos. For example, computer vision is widely used in autonomous vehicles to interpret the environment and make decisions to 'move' the car. These vehicles have multiple cameras that collect images (e.g. whether a pedestrian is crossing the street, the colour of the traffic light, or the traffic signal signs), which are processed by an algorithm to decide what actions to take (move forward, accelerate, brake). Facial Emotion Recognition (FER) is a subfield of emotion AI that focuses on detecting and interpreting emotions from facial expressions. It is frequently used to create more human-like interactions with users due to its capability to understand people's feelings and moods.

Algorithmic bias and other risks are inherent in affective computing systems. Studies show that these systems are less accurate at predicting facial emotions in Black people (Rhue, 2018), and there are several difficulties in interpreting emotions across different cultures; for instance, a smile does not mean the same thing in Germany, Argentina, and Japan (Purdy et al., 2019). Using these kinds of systems in education or the workplace can lead to restricted access to education and employment, resulting in violations of Human Rights.

Regarding high-risk systems (art. 6), which can be used but only after meeting numerous requirements, several of these are listed in Annex III under the title 'Education and Vocational Training'. These include: (a) AI systems intended to be used to determine access or admission to educational and vocational training institutions at all levels, or to assign individuals to such institutions; (b) AI systems intended to evaluate learning outcomes, including those used to guide the learning process of individuals in educational and vocational training institutions at all levels; (c) AI systems intended to assess the appropriate level of education an individual will receive or be able to access within educational and vocational training institutions; and (d) AI systems intended to monitor and detect prohibited behaviour of students during tests within educational and vocational training institutions.

The argument for including these systems can be found in recital number 56, which highlights the potential dangers concerned by certain educational AI systems. Some of these systems are used for determining access or admission, assigning individuals to educational and vocational training institutions or programmes at all levels, evaluating learning outcomes, and assessing the appropriate level of education for individuals, considerably impacting the education and training opportunities available to them. Additionally, they are used for monitoring and detecting prohibited behaviour during tests, which can strongly impact a person's educational and professional trajectory, hence affecting their ability to secure a livelihood. Improperly designed and used, these systems can be highly intrusive and may violate the rights to education and training, as well as the rights against discrimination and the perpetuation of historical discrimination patterns (e.g. against women, certain age groups, persons with disabilities, or individuals of specific racial, ethnic, or sexual orientation backgrounds).

All these systems must comply with: (a) risk management system (a continuous iterative process planned and run throughout the entire lifecycle of a high-risk AI system, requiring regular systematic review and updating); (b) Data and data governance (techniques involving the training of AI models with data shall be developed on the basis of training, validation and testing data sets); (c) Technical documentation (drawn up before that system is placed on the market or put into service and shall be kept up-to-date meet the quality criteria); (d) Record-keeping (automatic recording of events 'logs' over their lifetime); (e) Transparency and provision of information to deployers; (f) Human oversight; (g) Accuracy, robustness and cybersecurity; among others (art. 8 et seq).

In addition, AI systems mentioned above must undergo an assessment of their impact on fundamental rights that the use of such systems may produce, as stipulated in Article 27. This obligation falls on the deployers and includes (a) a description of the processes by which the high-risk AI system will be used, in agreement with its intended purpose; (b) a specification of the duration and frequency of use for each high-risk AI system; and (c) identification of the categories of individuals and groups likely to be affected by its use within the specific context.

We firmly support the testing of high-risk algorithms, especially in sensitive areas such as education, as an effective measure to prevent bias.

Recommendations for ensuring ethical governance of AI in education: Auditing high-risk algorithms

The use of AI in education can bring about significant benefits but also involves substantial risks. Consequently, the first step is awareness, particularly in raising awareness about these potential dangers. To contribute valuable insights to this field, we will outline challenges and provide recommendations for both the private and public sectors to achieve ethical governance of AI in education systems.

Risks and challenges

AI risks are associated with algorithmic bias and AI hallucinations. Algorithmic bias was explained in the section 'AI as educational content', while AI hallucinations involve AI generating plausible yet imaginary facts (University of Oxford, 2024). Effective technical tools, such as Amazon Bedrock, act as 'guardrails' to prevent hallucinations. Researchers are also developing new methods, such as entropy-based uncertainty estimators for large language models (LLMs), to detect arbitrary and incorrect generations known as confabulations. Farquhar et al. (2024) recently suggested a method that assesses uncertainty at the semantic level rather than specific word sequences. By recognizing prompts likely to produce confabulations, their approach strengthens user awareness of when caution is necessary with LLMs and expands possibilities for their use despite reliability concerns.

Both algorithmic biases and hallucinations can lead to catastrophic scenarios in education. Algorithmic bias can produce discriminatory outcomes that result, for example, in excluding certain groups from educational opportunities, thus exacerbating social inequalities. On the other hand, hallucinations can trigger unreal predictions, possibly teaching incorrect information or providing erroneous advice to educators that may not be suitable for students.

Another important concern applies to the legal framework, particularly in the privacy field. According to the study 'The Impact of AI on Education in Spain', conducted by Empantallados.com and GAD3, a majority of surveyed families (83 %) and teachers (90 %) express concerns about privacy policies and the use of personal data by AI tools. In contrast, only half of the minors interviewed (47 %) share these worries. There is an urgent need for a specific privacy framework in education. Information about minors' health conditions or cognitive issues may affect their future access to employment, credit opportunities, or insurance policies.

Another major challenge is preserving and protecting culture and traditions. The widespread adoption of artificial intelligence systems globally, without adaptation to the unique identities of each country, region, city, and even smaller communities, risks vanishing certain dialects, cultures, and traditions. This issue is constituted by a lack of data and foreign-made AI developments. To confront this, some systems offer users the ability to choose from different Spanish accents. For instance, PartyRock provides a platform where users can create AI-generated applications in a playground environment powered by Amazon Bedrock, promoting learning about generative AI.

Transhumanism presents numerous challenges, illustrated by companies like Elon Musk's Neuralink, which support integrating AI chips into our brains, might result in dystopian scenarios. While using technology to aid individuals with certain pathologies is globally accepted, the prospect of augmented humans raises significant ethical questions. Cyborgs introduce two major dilemmas: first, the potential for increased inequality, as not everyone will have equal access to bodily incorporation of technologies; second, the future of educational spaces. Will we separate learning environments between augmented and non-augmented students? Naturally, the entrance exams must be differentiated.

Recommendations and 'call to action'

Taking into account the new paradigms described throughout this text, we propose the following recommendations to address the challenges and risks of the arrival of AI from an educational perspective:

First and foremost, we need to integrate AI both as a tool and as a subject into education. This implies various aspects, including capacity building for all actors involved in education, particularly teachers and policymakers. We have the primary responsibility to thoroughly understand these new technologies, adapt our teaching methods, and create engaging content to ensure students' safety in using technology (as exemplified by the case of Almendralejo). One of the primary obstacles to achieving this goal is the lengthy and bureaucratic processes involved in modifying curricula that do not keep pace with the rapid evolution of societies today.

Therefore, teachers, who are in the classrooms every day, have immense power and responsibility to transcend outdated educational content. We need to act immediately. Ethical governance of AI is crucial. This includes teaching the value of privacy, emphasizing the importance of fact-checking (mandatory double-checking), discussing the impact of fake content such as porn fakes on teenagers, promoting healthy social media use, and more (Rothwell, 2023). Another essential aspect is integrating content related to hard sciences, for instance, programming and understanding how to communicate with computers (prompt engineers). Scientific research demonstrates the benefits of teaching computational (Ruiz et al., 2024) thinking (Su & Yang, 2023) and artificial intelligence (Kit Ng et al., 2023) in early childhood education. Moreover, General AI (GenAI) deserves a dedicated chapter: exploring (Jiahong, 2023a&b) its potential as an ally, understanding its risks, and promoting creativity in its use.

We propose integrating content into both formal and informal education at all stages of learning, from kindergarten through university, with a particular focus on technical careers. The emphasis should be on teaching students how to think critically rather than memorizing content that may become outdated tomorrow. The key is to enable the ability to 'learn how to learn' independently.

Secondly, Ethics Governance of Artificial Intelligence (EGAI) must be a cornerstone of public policy and included in the agendas of both the public and private sectors. In addition to the aspects mentioned earlier, it requires a strategic focus on mitigating inequalities, for example, ensuring equitable access to technology, equipping people with the skills demanded by the current and future labour markets, and developing tools to prevent algorithmic bias and hallucinations. Following mandates outlined in the AI Act and initiatives like the Spanish Artificial Intelligence Supervision Agency (AESIA), high-risk AI systems must go through regular audits.

In conclusion, it is the first time in history where students often have more knowledge about certain phenomena than their teachers (Prothero, 2023). Astonishingly, only 1 in 10 educators feel adequately equipped with the fundamental knowledge of artificial intelligence to teach or effectively integrate it into their work (EdWeek Research Center, 2023). How can this be allowed?

References

Bradford, A. (2019). The Brussels effect: How the European Union rules the world. *Oxford Academic.* https://doi.org/10.1093/oso/9780190088 583.001.0001

Carayannis, E. G., Barth, T. D., & Campbell, D. F (2012). The Quintuple Helix innovation model: Global warming as a challenge and driver for innovation. *Journal of Innovation and Entrepreneurship, 1,* 2. https://doi.org/10.1186/2192-5372-1-2

Chowdhury, R. (2021, 19 May, Wednesday). *Sharing learnings about our image cropping algorithm.* Twitter blog. https://blog.x.com/engineering/en_us/topics/insights/2021/sharing-learnings-about-our-image-cropping-algorithm

Danesi, C. (2021). The impact of artificial intelligence on women's rights: A legal point of view. In K. Miller & K. Wendt (Ed.), *The Fourth Industrial Revolution and its impact on ethics. Sustainable finance.* Springer. https://doi.org/10.1007/978-3-030-57020-0_20

Danesi, C. (2022). *Struggling against algorithmic bias: Civil liability and other legal remedies.* Cacucci Editore.

Danesi, C., & Torres Jarrín, M. (2024). 'Artificial intelligence & foreign affairs: Reflections and general overview on AI, human rights, ethics and global governance. In *Artificial intelligence & foreign affairs: AI, human rights, ethics and global governance.* Peter Lang.

De Angelis, T. (2024). Teens are spending nearly 5 hours daily on social media. Here are the mental health outcomes. Forty-one percent of teens with the highest social media use rate their overall mental health as poor or very poor. *American Physiological Association, 55*(3). Accessed 04 July 2024, from https://www.apa.org/monitor/2024/04/teen-social-use-mental-health#:~:text=4.8%20hours,of%20their%20social%20media%20time

EdWeek Research Center, 2023, "Teachers Desperately Need AI Training. How Many Are Getting It?", available 17/12/24 https://www.edweek.org/technology/teachers-desperately-need-ai-training-how-many-are-getting-it/2024/03.

Farquhar, S., Kossen, J., & Kuhn, L. (2024). Detecting hallucinations in large language models using semantic entropy. *Nature, 630,* 625–630. https://doi.org/10.1038/s41586-024-07421-0

Jiahong, S. (2023a). A systematic review of integrating computational thinking in early childhood education. *Science Direct.*

Jiahong, S. (2023b). Artificial intelligence (AI) literacy in early childhood education: The challenges and opportunities. *Science Direct.*

Kenneth, R. N., & Liu, J. (2023). *A brief introduction to GenAI.* MIDAS – University of Michigan.

McCabe, A., & Prinstein, M (2024). Potential risks of content, features, and functions: The science of how social media affects youth. *American Physiological Association.*

Prothero, A. (2023, July 14). What educators know about artificial intelligence, in 3 charts. *Education Week.*

Purdy, M., Zealley, J., & Maseli, O. (2019). The risks of using AI to interpret human emotions. *Harvard Business Review.*

Rhue, L. (2018). Racial influence on automated perceptions of emotions. *SSRN.* https://ssrn.com/abstract=3281765; http://dx.doi.org/10.2139/ssrn.3281765

Riccio, P., Colin, J., Ogolla, S., & Oliver, N. (2024). Mirror, mirror on the wall, who is the whitest of all? Racial biases in social media beauty filters. *Social Media + Society, 10*(2). https://doi.org/10.1177/2056305124 1239295

Rothwell, J. (2023). *How parenting and self-control mediate the link between social media use and mental health.* Institute for Family Studies. https:// ifstudies.org/ifs-admin/resources/briefs/ifs-gallup-parentingsocialmedi ascreentime-october2023-1.pdf

Ruiz, M., Blanco, F., & Ferrero, M. (2024). Which learning techniques supported by cognitive research do students use at secondary school? Prevalence and associations with students. *Cognitive Research: Principles and Implications.* https://doi.org/10.1186/s41235-024-00567-5

Su, J., Kit Ng, D., Chu, S., (2023) "Artificial Intelligence (AI) Literacy in Early Childhood Education: The Challenges and Opportunities", Science Direct, Computers and Education: Artificial Intelligence, Volume 4, 2023, 100124.

Su, J. and Yang, W. (2023) Unlocking the Power of ChatGPT: A Framework for Applying Generative AI in Education, Sage Journals.

University of Oxford. (2024). *Major research into 'hallucinating' generative models advances reliability of artificial intelligence.*

Chapter 3

The evolution of research practices in the digital era: Between old demands and new challenges

Montserrat Alom Bartrolí

Abstract: In an era characterized by the growing use of digital tools within university settings, researchers in the social sciences and humanities are confronted with both old demands that have not faded out and new expectations that are not always convergent. In most cases, information and communication technology tools are affecting the way research is being devised and conducted to respond to such diverse demands. This chapter intends to provide a critical overview of the evolution of research practices nowadays, by presenting a selection of the most salient trends that are often being impacted by the digital. We will conclude by advocating for the need for responsible international collaborations and human-centred research training to address emerging ethical challenges and concerns.

Keywords: research practices, research trends, research collaboration, research ethics, digital impact, AI tools, SSH, knowledge production, research training, universities

We certainly live in an era that is characterized by the growing use of digital tools in the higher education and research fields. Although talking about research practices in the digital era doesn't necessarily mean that a digital component is interacting with them, in most cases information and communication technology (ICT) tools are somehow affecting the way research is being devised and conducted. Without the pretension of being exhaustive, this chapter thus seeks to provide a critical overview of the evolution of research practices nowadays, that is, in the digital era by presenting a selection of the most salient trends that are indeed being impacted by the digital.

And we will do so by focusing on social sciences and humanities research, which is confronted with both old issues and new challenges that respond either to longstanding expectations that have evolved over time or to newly born demands coming from more recent political and socio-economic actors' needs. We will take stock of some of the tensions between which researchers are caught up as a result of changes in the profession and the context in which research is practised, but also of the maintenance of old concerns that have not been resolved. Throughout the chapter, we will see that such research practices may be driven (or not) by responsible, more open, inclusive and/or ethical considerations.

As the reader will notice, we do not automatically advocate for the use or inclusion of digital devices in social sciences and humanities research nor indiscriminately criticize such a use. Having said that, we move away from the common belief that 'technology is neither good nor bad, it's what you do with it that makes a difference'. We rather align our-selves with Winner's (2002) book, *The Whale and the Reactor: A Search for Limits in an Age of High Technology*, whose main theory shows that technology may already be biased from the start if thorough reflection is lacking at the design phase. It is our belief that reflection on both the benefits and the limits offered by the digital component must be present throughout the entire research process to effectively put ICT tools at the service of the human and not the other way around.

Introduction: A desire for more human-centred research practices in the digital age?

In recent years society's expectations regarding research have increased and become manifold: the knowledge produced is expected to be useful, research processes should be transparent and democratic, the funds invested must be accounted for and the impact of research shall be evaluated, just to name a few. Likewise, research is called upon to be more responsible and committed across the world with a view to contrib-uting to major social challenges and, *in fine*, to the common good.

Researchers alongside their home institutions, both in Northern and Southern countries, are obliged to take into account this growing number of demands, which come from a multiplicity of fronts: research funding agencies, international philanthropic foundations, national and interna-tional organizations, government, the business sector, non-governmental organizations (NGOs) and other civil society groups. These demands, which may be converging, but in some cases are conflicting, seem to be quite desirable from a human-centred perspective as they put the spotlight on essential values and principles such as transparency, democracy, well-being and so on.

At the same time, the 'science in society' paradigm, which has been translated into different ways by adopting slightly different expressions (e.g. 'science for society', 'science with society'), has changed boundaries among actors while redefining their roles: 'science and technology are now governed at an increasing number of sites, involving ever more diverse sets of actors in more disparate ways. This leads to complex and new forms of distribution of power and constant struggle over the directions to take. These arrangements are neither stable nor is it always clear how the governance efforts relate to each other' (Felt et al., 2013, p. 6). As a result of this growing number of actors and science-production settings, practices and efforts to coordinate them are scattered, while old logics coexist with recent ones, generating both renewed opportunities and lasting tensions.

Within this context, ICT tools have paved their way over the past decades and ended up by imposing themselves globally in a myriad of forms. Many processes and approaches seem almost inconceivable without resorting to their products.

The publications system: Between mainstream science and alternative circuits

We will start by referring to the dominant logics that drive research since the very beginning of the creation of the research system and which, therefore, keep conveying issues of power in its implementation (Vessuri, 2015). We point out here the widely known publication race best defined by the 'publish or perish' motto, which emanates from a system that rewards and classifies researchers according to their h-index, that is, the number of articles published in highly ranked journals and the number of citations. This system, which has been proved to be biased, lays on a restricted set of scientific criteria that contribute to perpetuating hegemonic relations since it only benefits a few 'big players' in the research field (Felt et al., 2013; Hicks et al., 2015). Although the composition of the group of 'big players' has evolved over the past years due to the emergence of a multipolar world (including countries such as China, Brazil or South Africa), the majority of institutions and researchers remain excluded from this core group (Barré, 2010; UNESCO, 2016).

To counter the so-called mainstream science that relies on such infrastructure and mode of functioning, over the years local, national and regional publication circuits, often favouring publications in local languages, have emerged in non-hegemonic countries, mostly pioneered by the Latin American region (Beigel, 2013, 2021c; Beigel & Salatino, 2015, 2015; Losego & Arvanitis, 2008). Indeed, following the creation of a Latin American regional circuit of recognition in the 40s, the regionalization movement gained momentum thanks to the foundation of intergovernmental organizations like the Economic Commission for Latin America and the Caribbean (CEPAL in Spanish) and regional research networks like the Latin American Council on Social Sciences (CLACSO). The Latin American regional circuit of publications, which started to develop in the 70s, presented itself as an alternative to those built and governed by hegemonic countries while being at the avant-garde of the open access movement. From then on, Latin America started to build its own information and indexing systems, to train librarians, to develop regional networks and publishing databases (e.g. LatinIndex, Biblat), while enacting open access laws (for instance, Argentina in 2013, Mexico in 2014). Today, 95 % of the around 7,000 journals indexed in Latin American online scientific libraries like Scielo or Redalyc are diamond open access, which means that neither the author nor the reader pays; and only 2 % of these journals belong to well-known big publishers (Beigel, 2021b, 2021a).[1] Alternative publication circuits by non-Western countries have maintained the old dilemma that opposes local positioning to international presence (Hanafi, 2011; Kreimer, 2013). However, this dual way of tackling the issue has also evolved, first with the emergence of 'global research' intended to address global issues and, second, thanks to studies showing that, for a researcher, being locally grounded and internationally recognized are not necessarily incompatible (Arvanitis & Alom Bartrolí, 2020).

---

[1]   Figures come from Fernanda Beigel's lecture at the Global Research Institute of Paris (GRIP) Colloquium 'The other globalisation', Paris, France, 25 November 2021.

The open access movement has widely spread across the world well beyond countries defying the *status quo*. The impetus provided by the European Union is very meaningful in this regard as it involves the active promotion of open science, in particular by making it mandatory for EU-funds beneficiaries to publish open access and to manage research data in a responsible manner in line with the FAIR principles. International reference organizations like the United Nations Educational Scientific and Cultural Organisation (UNESCO) have also got on board by developing their own initiatives such as the UNESCO Global Open Science Partnership that is meant to gather all the stakeholders involved in open science advancement around the world.[2]

Moreover, open access is being implemented by well-established publishing houses (like Elsevier or Springer) that have embraced this way of communicating scientific results by turning it into a for-profit/commercially based option (golden open access being quite pricy). Aside from the modality in which open access is offered (either free of charge or paying), it benefits from the creation of a whole system of actors, networks and infrastructures (in particular current research information systems or CRIS) based on information technology advances.

Traditional university rankings versus alternative evaluation methods

The role of digital resources in relation to publications seems to be twofold: on the one hand, it has contributed to the creation of the above-mentioned alternative circuits and, on the other, it has also given way to alternative, sometimes complementary, modes of evaluating and classifying researchers and their institutions around the world. Indeed, the development of altmetrics allows for measuring the attention that a given piece of research receives on the net. And an increasingly number of assessment systems have emerged these past years, like the U-multirank from the European Union, which is geared towards embracing more dimensions than those traditionally taken into account (like international orientation or regional engagement),[3] or the Newman Assessment

[2]   See the UNESCO website: https://en.unesco.org/science-sustainable-future/open-science/partnership

[3]   U-Multirank website: https://www.umultirank.org/university-rankings/2021-2022/

system by the International Federation of Catholic Universities (IFCU), which relies on artificial intelligence (AI) and, far from publication-related data, evaluates universities in accordance with their socially responsible policies and practices (Alom Bartrolí, 2021; Alom & Mabille, 2020).[4]

Despite these alternative proposals, the race to publishing keeps going on: in countries like Brazil or in institutions like business schools, the pressure is on for researchers to publish ever more articles in A-ranked journals, setting aside any other considerations inherent to the research job or to psychological well-being, not to mention reconciling work and family life. The Leiden Manifesto released by scientometricians, social scientists and research administrators testifies to this (Hicks et al., 2015, p. 430): 'we have watched with increasing alarm the pervasive misap-plication of indicators to the evaluation of scientific performance. (...) Across the world, universities have become obsessed with their position in global rankings (such as the Shanghai Ranking and Times Higher Education's list), even when such lists are based on what are, in our view, inaccurate data and arbitrary indicators'; in a few words, 'the problem is that evaluation is now led by the data rather than by judgement' (Hicks et al., 2015, p. 429). In this regard, proposals have been made to broaden out the range of aspects ('inputs') that are being considered for the eval-uation in order to come out with more diverse 'outputs', that is, results that take into account plural perspectives (Rafols & Stirling, 2021). Another example is provided by the Declaration on Research Assess-ment (DORA), released in 2012 in San Francisco, United States, which also warns us about the excesses generated by the current dynamics by recognizing the need to improve the evaluation of researchers and their scholarly work.

Due to this pressure towards publishing, the multiple require-ments to fulfil when carrying out research projects, and the evolu-tion of the teacher's profession, the polarization between professors that basically conduct teaching (becoming like mentors that are well-equipped in the use of digital technologies) and those that devote almost exclusively to research has been exacerbated. And this trend leads us to the sinews of war as put forward by Hubert and Louvel (2012), namely, funds allocation to keep on carrying out research.

---

[4]   Newman evaluation website: www.rsu-fiuc.org

Indeed, during the past years research funding has experienced a major shift with the increase and, lastly, overwhelming predominance of project-based funding at the expense of core funding, which was the traditional mode of financing higher education institutions and research centres. This shift has been accompanied by the irruption of management practices issued from the new public management, in particular from the business sector (Pollitt et al., 2007). The new requests in terms of transparency and accountability, but also the short-term horizons related to project frameworks that have become the new normal tend to generate tensions between financial resources and workload, but also between resources in a larger sense (human or technical) and skills necessary to accomplish research endeavours that can generate impact and, equally important, comply with deadlines (Hubert & Louvel, 2012).

Promoting responsible research practices

As shown by Latour (1995), research is grounded on written materials that are shared and validated by peers. Recognition by peers is no doubt an essential feature of the researcher's job. However, the time and efforts devoted to drafting books and articles to get scientific recognition may be difficult to combine with the numerous requirements that have been added to research during the past years. Tensions may well arise between the efforts to get one's research recognized by peers (and its own institution) and the development of responsible research practices.

Indeed, many voices call for research to produce knowledge that may contribute to responding to major social challenges in the twenty-first century, sometimes out of the questioning of the value of science, sometimes out of major concerns spreading across all actors and sectors (Augustin et al., 2014; Bonneuil & Joly, 2013; Georghiou, 2015). A wide variety of initiatives have emerged to build bridges between science and society in a spirit of joint responsibility and willingness to work for the common good (like Fab labs or science shops). One of the most well-known initiatives is the science policy framework conceived by the European Commission under the acronym RRI (Responsible Research and Innovation). The *Rome Declaration on Responsible Research and Innovation* defines RRI as 'the ongoing process of aligning research and innovation to the values, needs and expectations of society' (Council of the European Union, 2014, p. 1). RRI gathers five key dimensions deemed essential to conduct responsible research practices: ethics, societal engagement, gender equality, open access/science and science education.[5] Research thus may be responsible *internally* by guaranteeing integrity, developing an ethical reflection about goals and impacts, paying attention to gender balance, caring for human resources' working conditions... Research may also be responsible *externally* by targeting vulnerable groups within society, responding to major societal challenges, designing and budgeting evaluation schemes that, alongside scientific impact, also consider socio-economic impact, just to name a few. The five dimensions defined by RRI are associated with a series of values regarded as central to our societies, namely diversity and inclusiveness, anticipation and reflexivity, openness and transparency, and responsiveness and adaptation.

In line with this approach, the European Commission has also developed the HR Excellence in Research Award (HRS4R), that is, a label that recognizes institutions' efforts to align their human resources policies with 40 principles as defined by a dedicated Charter & Code.[6] Indeed, one aspect that deserves urgent attention is human resources management, which is far from being humanistic in many institutions around the world. In this regard, universities should commit to ensuring a human-centred work environment by including in their scientific policy a wider range of aspects for the evaluation and reward of researchers, their projects and their production, but also by establishing working conditions that allow for developing a career in research without having to renounce family life.

The Commission's framework has the merit of having brought together a series of key dimensions under a single umbrella for the first time. RRI's impact is obvious on other organization's understanding of research policies like the GUNI network (GUNI, 2022). Alongside RRI, several innovative initiatives have been promoted both within and outside the European Union, some of which rely on ICT infrastructure, like crowdsourcing research projects that fall within the framework of the so-called citizen science.

---

[5]   RRI website: https://www.rri-practice.eu/about-rri-practice/what-is-rri/
[6]   HRS4R website: https://euraxess.ec.europa.eu/jobs/hrs4r

The case of the decolonization of science: A power-balanced approach to science?

The decolonization of science is quite a recent trend in the line of research responsibility, which, besides being the subject to heated debate, is gaining momentum in Europe and Africa, but also in North America and Latin America. Although many voices have advocated for including non-Western vision and perspectives in research since long (in particular, authors in the field of social studies of science and technology in the South), often referring to other forms of knowledge like indigenous knowledge, the movement as such has taken shape in the past few years with the view to uncovering how racial, colonial, political and/or hierarchical considerations inform research and practice (Kervran et al., 2017). By questioning Western vision's hegemonic predominance in addressing and apprehending research issues, scholars adhering to this movement overtly put forward the importance of equity-driven approaches to research that allow for interrogating power dynamics (Adendorff et al., 2022). This approach questions the lenses through which researchers examine their topics due to cultural and intellectual discourses and theories generally relying on the myth of the Western superiority, which dates back to colonial times. If critical review allowing for leaving behind the baggage of colonialism is no doubt most welcomed, we should be aware that such a process entails various types of risks like nationalistic approaches that produce and circulate inaccurate or unrealistic knowledge, a rejection of various forms of modern science or even deeper distrust in science (Abdoulaye Barro, 2010).

Defining national/regional and disciplinary digital strategies

The European Commission also promotes the idea that higher education and research digitalization will lead towards more inclusive and accessible societies. Even though some elements related to the digital domain are already present in the RRI framework, the Commission developed a specific digital strategy to gain digital sovereignty and set standards to be followed by the greatest number of citizens as part of its 2019–2024 priorities.[7] Such a vision is also endorsed by organizations

---

[7] Information available on: https://ec.europa.eu/info/strategy/priorities-2019-2024/europe-fit-digital-age_en

like GUNI, which dedicates two chapters of its last report to the notion of 'a digital-human future' linked to 'more inclusive and accessible universities' (GUNI, 2022).

Institutions in other regions of the world are also implementing their own digital strategies, like the Digital Research Alliance of Canada, who is funded by the Canadian government to transform the way in which research practices, data and results are being organized, managed, stored and used in the country.[8] The issue of digitalization is also bringing together efforts in Latin American countries with, for instance, the regional observatory focused on digital development created by CEPAL to identify and monitor progress of indicators related to the digital transformation across sectors.[9]

In the African continent various projects, often supported by foreign organizations, are being implemented to improve research infrastructure's scope and quality such as the Francophone University Agency (AUF)'s PRICNAC project, funded by the European Union, which aims at strengthening research, innovation and digital culture in eight countries from Central Africa (Cameroon, Congo, Gabon, Equatorial Guinea, Central African Republic, Sao Tome and Principe, Democratic Republic of Congo and Chad),[10] or the 'Mapping research infrastructure' project run by the Association of African Universities (AAU) and funded by the Canadian International Development Research Centre (IDRC) to enhance the resilience of science systems in Sub-Saharan Africa.[11]

The case of digital humanities: A new lease on life for the humanities?

The exponential growth of digital humanities has widely contributed to putting humanities to the forefront. Such an achievement would not have been possible without the design and implementation of specific digital research infrastructures (RIs), which may take a large variety of forms like repositories, comprehensive databases of analytical data and

---

[8]   Alliance website: https://alliancecan.ca/en

[9]   Regional observatory website: https://www.cepal.org/es/proyectos/observatorio-regional-desarrollo-digital

[10] AUF website: https://www.auf.org/

[11] Information available on: https://aau.org/mapping-research-infrastructure-to-enhance-the-resilience-of-science-systems-in-sub-saharan-africa/

metadata, digitized collections, virtual access to museums or galleries, facilities for research on diverse stimuli (audio, speech, textual, visual, etc.), facilities to perform restoration of cultural heritage objects and digital libraries/archives (ESF, 2011). Digital RIs offer researchers 'new and productive ways to explore old questions and develop new ones', while securing the preservation of valuable or endangered materials thanks to digitization processes. Indeed, it is argued that making 'our cultural heritage accessible in digital form' as well as associating it with other resources 'opens a new frontier for Humanities research for addressing "grand challenges" in the Humanities themselves and at the interface with other research domains' (ESF, 2011, p. 2).

Various coalitions have been created during the past years to advocate for the value of humanities. With the advent of digital RIs matching specific needs of the humanities community, these coalitions tend to promote the benefits of digital humanities at a large scale by offering resources, expert advice, training and advocacy support to their members. One of the most active is the National Humanities Alliance, which was founded in 1981 in the United States and gathers over 200 member organizations nationwide (National Humanities Alliance, 2022; NHA, 2013). In the European continent, the Digital Research Infrastructure for the Arts and Humanities (DARIAH), which was established as a European Research Infrastructure Consortium (ERIC) in 2014, is made up of 20 members, one observer and several cooperating partners in six non-member countries to enhance and support digitally enabled research and teaching across the arts and humanities across Europe.[12] The Alliance of Digital Humanities Organizations (ADHO) has even a larger scope since it brings together institutions from around the world with a view to promoting and supporting digital research and teaching across all humanities disciplines.

The creation of coalitions is helpful as 'digital infrastructures are developing rapidly but unevenly, and there is an urgent need for coordination, standardization and sharing of experience to prevent unnecessary duplication and the atomisation of good initiatives' (ESF, 2011, p. 2). Yet, many alliances assume that digitally based resources are automatically beneficial to advance the humanities cause, but seem to lack thorough reflection about negative consequences associated with digital

---

[12] Dariah website: https://www.dariah.eu/about/dariah-in-nutshell/

RIs use, like the exclusion of large groups within society from internet access, IT equipment, necessary funds or skills (Plouy, 2020). Unlike what people tend to think, the digital divide is not only a major concern in many Southern countries but also in Western nations like the United States, where it affects for the most part individuals from low-income backgrounds (Butterfield et al., 2020). Thus, without denying the enormous impetus that digital technology has given to the humanities, strategies should be devised to anticipate or, at least, mitigate the adverse effects that may result from the massive use of these new technologies in the disciplines concerned.

Researchers' presence on the net and use of ICT tools on the rise

The traditional presence and links developed face-to-face in project conferences have been accompanied by a numeric presence on the net, which can take many forms: registering for an ORCID identifying code, creating its own blog, feeding platforms dedicated to sharing work with peers (e.g. ResearchGate, Academia), circulating its work through open access sites, displaying bibliographical references on commercial websites (e.g. publishers' site, for-profit sites like Amazon), building websites devoted to specific projects, being present on online networks (e.g. LinkedIn, Tweeter).

Besides the concerns that such a growing presence raises in terms of cyber risks related to intellectual property and personal data privacy, it must be acknowledged that a growing number of plugins and software solutions (often open source), some of which were designed by researchers themselves (e.g. Extractify), are effectively supporting research methodology requirements in terms of facilitating data collection, coding, analysis and so on. Likewise, evolution in the digital age lays on the ability to better exploit information and sources of information that are increasingly comprehensive and complex, that is, big data. The digital revolution involved switching from an industrial society to a service society based on large amounts of data that fuel the economy (Cointot & Eychenne, 2014). The potential of big data has given rise to the development of cutting-edge IT equipment, often costly, new jobs and types of services provided, but the limitations associated with it have led to heated debates and other options such as 'small data' analysis.

Undoubtedly, the digital component is omnipresent in many social science disciplines like in marketing as shown by the Marketing Science Institute (MSI) 2020–2022 research priorities, which mention for instance research and development on omnichannel promotion and distribution, and the customer-technology interface in martech research. The MSI invests in better understanding what challenges and opportunities new technologies like automation/robotics, 5G, voice activation or virtual/augmented reality are creating for the discipline. Indeed, 'technology offers customers an array of new ways to interact with firms, fundamentally altering the purchase experience and raising concerns about data privacy' (MSI, 2020, p. 5). This means that technological innovations are not only being used by researchers to conduct their research but are also strongly affecting the topics they are studying nowadays.

Finally, following the exponential development of technological software, devices and platforms, often AI-aided or cloud-based, Edtechs are becoming increasingly present in higher education mainly by partnering or offering their services to learning institutions (Mellul, 2021). By promoting emerging technologies such as augmented reality, virtual reality or gamification, they are clearly defying traditional forms of approaching the learning experience within higher education settings. However, their areas of action remain limited to teaching and learning, they rarely include academic research.

AI research applications: Concerns and call for reflection

The use of AI in research is rapidly expanding in different sectors and sciences (e.g. educational sciences, neurosciences, marketing, and future studies), giving rise to undeniable benefits both for researchers' practices and the research process as such. While some researchers have started using ChatGPT to explore potential research topics, to find out data for their studies in a quick manner or to generate graphs and images, just to name a few, AI continues to raise suspicion about data privacy, property rights and preciseness as black-boxed systems out of the reach of non-experts; and also about ethical and human-related considerations regarding the values conveyed, the place and role of the human being. Let us mention, for instance, the controversial use of ChatGPT as a co-author in collective papers or for data treatment and analysis purposes in various disciplines. And, if the recent case of the machine-learning system that outperformed a human team of researchers in its calculations caught everyone's attention, we should keep in mind that even the most sophisticated systems have been crafted by the human being (Callaway, 2020). Indeed, the most important aspect in this debate is the view one can find behind AI development. As pointed out by F. De Lara López from Pontificia Universidad Católica de Chile, Chile, '(…) there is a widespread operation of reduction of the human being to a positivistic point of view. (…) There is a computer-based vision of the mind and the human being. So, of course, in this sense computers can be better than human beings for these operations (…). But other dimensions should be taken into account when talking about being human: the values, the projects, the ideas on how to live, the political dreams, justice… and these are all dimensions that we cannot reduce to a computational understanding of the human being' (presentation at the First academic workshop of the NHNAI project, Lyon Catholic University, Lyon, France, 10–11 March 2022).

From a historical perspective, as early as the Second World War similar questions were raised about what was feasible and what was desirable, in other words, about the potentialities of technological advance and the limits to establish to avoid downsides; it was also the time of the 'end of innocence' as researchers' responsibility started to be pointed out. Today technology-based innovations continue to be ahead of any kind of ethical or moral consideration since the rhythms each one follows are not reported to be the same. This means that reflection about their positive and negative consequences always tends to come in the second place, once innovations are already out there. The Baconian equation between knowledge and power no longer works in the same way (Salomon, 2006); we certainly can do much more than we know (Salomon-Bayet, 2004).

In this regard, the need to anticipate risks (ethical, physical, social, economic, etc.) appears as an essential element of any research programme making use of technologies like AI. The aim to anticipate, transform and control societal futures through science and technology has caught increasing attention from analysts as well as research centres, some of which have massively invested in building anticipatory methods. The latter rely on the view that we may and should shape our future (understood as a technoscientific future) by making the right choices. Social sciences in particular are playing a crucial role in discussing the process that may lead to such developments and the actors that should be associated with the same (Felt et al., 2013).

Concerns raised by AI misconception or misuse have given way to specific responses from intergovernmental organizations like the European Commissions' proposal for an ethical regulation of AI (Torres Jarrín, 2021), as well as from international coalitions like the 'Global partnership on artificial intelligence (GPAI)', which gathers 25 international partners to ensure the responsible development and use of AI by supporting cutting-edge multidisciplinary research and applied activities on trustworthy AI-related priorities.[13] Another coalition like the Association of Pacific Rim Universities (APRU) has identified the digital economy as one of its key areas of work; in partnership with United Nations ESCAP and Google.org, the association mobilizes intellectual resources of universities in the Asia-Pacific to support AI for social good.[14] Likewise, the NHNAI project, which is coordinated by Lyon Catholic University under the aegis of IFCU, seeks to gain understanding about what it means to be human at the time of neurosciences and AI with a view to providing relevant stakeholders in various regions of the world with an ethical compass to frame action regarding educational, health and governance-related issues.[15] Some individual research centres have also endorsed this cause by developing frameworks for the ethical regulation of technology like the Markkula Framework for Ethical Decision-Making or the Ethics in Technology Practice Tool, both of them designed by the Markkula Center for Applied Ethics at Santa Clara University, United States.[16]

Conclusion: A need for responsible international collaborations and human-centred research training

Taking into account the current configuration of the research world and the pervasiveness of the digital in researchers' practices, international collaborations seem to be essential to meet various of the challenges

---

[13] GPAI website: https://www.gpai.ai/

[14] APRU website: https://www.apru.org/our-work/pacific-rim-challenges/digital-economy/

[15] NHNAI project website: www.nhnai.org

[16] Markkula Center for Applied Ethics website: https://www.scu.edu/ethics/

posed while counteracting the logics of competitiveness that continue to dominate the field, and lead to a paradox that requires from researchers and their institutions to be competitive and cooperative at the same time (Pestre, 2003).

International cooperation is rising year after year as witnessed by the increasing number of joint research projects at the international level, but also by the foundation of numerous alliances of universities, which often include diverse stakeholders (Gazni et al., 2012). Following the COVID-19 outbreak, cooperation has proven its immense benefits for society at large, in particular after researchers across the world united their efforts in an unprecedented way to share knowledge about the virus. After the Young European Research Universities Network (YERUN): 'Research strengths are currently scattered among countries and institutions. Centralizing all efforts and research capacity is not an easy task, but it becomes crucial for increasing and speeding up research collaborations. That is the case with COVID-19 research that has witnessed the creation of specific platforms in which all available research outputs are put together. That should be extended to other research disciplines and areas' (YERUN, 2020, p. 41). In spite of the raise of ICT-based research infrastructure available in the form of repositories, platforms and so on, sharing research data still remains quite a touchy issue today. No doubt, the financial and political logics underlying many organizations' and governments' research policies also contribute to knowledge fragmentation in a research landscape where contending forces continue to be the norm.

Among the future short- and long-term challenges that have been predicted to affect international research collaborations are public funding availability and partnership composition. As a result of the COVID-19 crisis, reduced public funding for research collaboration may worsen existing inequalities and partnerships composition may vary due to a changing geopolitical context as already witnessed by the debates that mainly go on in Europe and the United States about whether excluding or not Chinese or Russian researchers from joint research programmes (GUNI, 2022). In any case, scientific collaborations, in particular those including low-income countries, should always be guided by openness, solidarity and mutual enrichment. Research funding bodies, in turn, should promote policies that rely on co-construction efforts with the beneficiaries and that respond more closely to local needs.

Last but not least, researchers, who may be both designers and users of digital technologies, have the responsibility to critically analyse: on the one hand, the short- but also long-term implications of the innovations they are about to build at various levels and, on the other hand, the impacts that the choice of a specific ICT infrastructure may have on their work and on the individuals concerned by the latter. Universities together with other actors, either at the national or supranational level, should set standards that ensure: first, the formulation of guidelines that are being adhered to by the largest number of stakeholders with a view to coordinating initiatives and thus preventing fragmentation; and, second, the inclusion of such critical elements in science education addressed to all students regardless of the disciplines in which they are involved. It appears thus strongly advisable to include training modules on the challenges posed by research today in the curricula to equip future researchers with the knowledge and skills needed to work in favour of the common good. Although some universities have made the effort to add some courses on scientific integrity (e.g. French institutions), most modules tend to limit themselves to dissertation writing and similar practical topics, whereas future researchers should be urgently trained to approach research in a critically human-centred manner.

References

Abdoulaye Barro, A. (2010). Coopération scientifique et débat sur les 'sciences sociales africaines' au CODESRIA. *Cahiers de la recherche sur l'éducation et les savoirs, 9*, 53–72. http://cres.revues.org/362

Adendorff, H., Blackie, M. A. L., Fataar, A., Maluleka, P., & Hlatshwayo, M. N. (Eds.). (2022). *Decolonising knowledge and knowers. Struggles for university transformation in South Africa*. Routledge.

Alom Bartrolí, M. (2021). The university social responsibility framework by the International Federation of Catholic Universities: A case of 'intelligent' co-creation. In L. Tauginienė & R. Pučetaitė (Eds.), *Managing social responsibility in universities: Organisational responses to sustainability* (pp. 7–26). Palgrave Macmillan.

Alom, M., & Mabille, F. (2020). *A reference framework for assessing university social responsibility: From theory to practice*. CIRAD-IFCU.

Arvanitis, R., & Alom Bartrolí, M. (2020). Le financement de la recherche dans les pays non-hégémoniques: Coopération internationale et compétence nationale. *L'éducation en débats: analyse comparée, 10*(2), 304–320. https://doi.org/10.51186/journals/ed.2020.10-2.e353

Augustin, M., Baudrin, M., Dauguet, B., Di Manno, S., van Engelen, B., Mari Maliepaard, E., Raimbault, B., Ribberink, N., Seibel, L., & Waltzing, A. (2014). *Assessing the value of science: Reflections on science 2013–2014* (p. 60). Radboud Honours Academy.

Barré, R. (2010). Pour une géopolitique de la recherche. *Géoéconomie, 2*(53), 13–31.

Beigel, F. (2013). Centros y periferias en la circulación internacional del conocimiento. *Nueva Sociedad, 245,* 110–123.

Beigel, F. (2021a). A multi-scale perspective for assessing publishing circuits in non-hegemonic countries. *Tapuya: Latin American Science, Technology and Society, 4*(1). https://doi.org/10.1080/25729861.2020.1845923

Beigel, F. (2021b). *Las revistas nacionales y su valoración en los procesos de evaluación* (Herramientas para promover nuevas políticas evaluativas Tool 3; Hacia la transformación de los sistemas de evaluación en América latina y el Caribe, p. 29). CLACSO-FOLEC.

Beigel, F. (2021c). *Promoting bibliodiversity and defending multilingualism* (Tools to promote new evaluation policies Tool 2; Toward the transformation of evaluation systems in Latin America and the Caribbean, p. 21). CLACSO-FOLEC.

Beigel, F., & Salatino, M. (2015). Circuitos segmentados de consagración académica: Las revistas de ciencias sociales y humanas en la Argentina. *Información, cultura y sociedad, 32,* 11–36.

Bonneuil, C., & Joly, P.-B. (2013). *Sciences, techniques et société.* La Découverte.

Butterfield, R., MItchell, V., & Mulinge, A. (2020). *Disrupt the digital divide. Improving access for all K-12 students* (p. 25) [Policy brief]. Code Nation. https://drive.google.com/file/d/1j7TJeirBQoR8-LaX3weGpt21w dD3U35l/view

Callaway, E. (2020). 'It will change everything': AI makes gigantic leap in solving protein structures. *Nature, 588,* 203–204. https://doi.org/10.1038/d41586-020-03348-4

Cointot, J.-C., & Eychenne, Y. (2014). *La révolution Big Data.* Dunod.

Council of the European Union. (2014). *Rome declaration on Responsible Research and Innovation* (p. 2). https://digital-strategy.ec.europa.eu/en/library/rome-declaration-responsible-research-and-innovation-europe

ESF. (2011). *Research infrastructures in the digital humanities* (Science Policy Briefing N° 42; p. 43).

Felt, U., Barben, D., Irwin, A., Joly, P.-B., Rip, A., Stirling, A., & Stöckelová, T. (2013). *Science in society: Caring for our futures in turbulent times* (Science Policy Briefing; p. 36).

Gazni, A., Sugimoto, C. R., & Didegah, F. (2012). Mapping world scientific collaboration: Authors, institutions, and countries. *Journal of the American Society for Information Science and Technology, 63*(2), 323–335.

Georghiou, L. (2015). *Value of research* (p. 15). Commission européenne.

GUNI. (2022). *New visions for higher education towards 2030* (Special issue N° 8; Higher education in the world). https://www.guninetwork.org/files/guni_heiw_8_complete_-_new_visions_for_higher_education_towards 2030.pdf

Hanafi, S. (2011). University systems in the Arab East: Publish globally and perish locally vs. Publish locally and perish globally. *Current Sociology, 59*(3), 291–309.

Hicks, D., Wouters, P., Waltman, L., De Rijcke, S., & Rafols, I. (2015). Bibliometrics: The Leiden manifesto for research metrics. *Nature, 520*, 429–431. https://doi.org/10.1038/520429a

Hubert, M., & Louvel, S. (2012). Le financement sur projet: Quelles conséquences sur le travail des chercheurs ? *Mouvements, 3*(71), 13–24.

Kervran, D. D., Kleiche-Dray, M., & Quet, M. (2017). Les STS ont-elles un Sud? *Revue d'anthropologie des connaissances, 11*(3), 423–454.

Kreimer, P. (2013). Internacionalización y tensiones para un uso social de la ciencia latinoamericana. In O. Restrepo Forero (Ed.), *Ensamblando estados* (pp. 437–452). Universidad nacional de Colombia.

Langdon, W. (2002). *La baleine et le réacteur: À la recherche de limites au temps de la haute technologie.* Descartes & Cie.

Latour, B. (1995). *Le métier de chercheur: Regard d'un anthropologue.* INRA.

Losego, P., & Arvanitis, R. (2008). La science dans les pays non hégémoniques. *Revue d'anthropologie des connaissances, 2*(3), 334–342.

Mellul, C. (2021). *The fourth industrial revolution in higher education and work: An assessment.* IFCU.

MSI. (2020). *Research priorities 2020–2022* (p. 10). https://www.msi.org/wp-content/uploads/2020/06/MSI_RP20-22.pdf

National Humanities Alliance. (2022). *Humanities policy priorities. FY 2023* (p. 8).

ation. Insights from research assessment. In P. Dahler-Larsen (Ed.), *A research agenda for evaluation* (pp. 165–193). Edward Elgar.

Salomon, J.-J. (2006). *Les scientifiques entre savoir et pouvoir*. Editions Albin Michel.

Salomon-Bayet, C. (2004). Variations sur le temps. *Bulletin de la société française de philosophie, 1*, 28.

Torres Jarrín, M. (2021). La UE & la gobernanza ética de la inteligencia artificial: Inteligencia artificial & diplomacia. *Cuadernos salmantinos de filosofía, 48*, 213–234.

UNESCO. (2016). *UNESCO Science report: Towards 2030* (p. 795).

Vessuri, H. (2015). Global social science discourse: A Southern perspective on the world. *Current Sociology Monograph, 63*(2), 297–313.

YERUN. (2020). *The world of higher education after COVID-19. How COVID-19 has affected young universities* (p. 46). https://yerun.eu/wp-content/uploads/2020/07/YERUN-Covid-VFinal-OnlineSpread.pdf

Chapter 4

Making sense of digital technologies in Eastern Africa's universities: Lessons from Covid-19 and peace studies

GEORGE MUTALEMWA

Abstract: The onslaught of Covid-19 has demystified the digital divide in higher education in Africa and across the globe. This chapter analyses the opportunities and challenges informing the use of digital technology (DT) in select Eastern African universities during Covid-19 and provides post-pandemic recommendations. The chapter argues that despite the north-south development divide, there exists a digital divide among and between universities in the so-called global South. Informed by the university revitalization theory (URT), the chapter contends that the differences between universities globally and in Eastern Africa should be minimized through prioritization of DT and international collaboration rather than competition.

Keywords: digital technology, university, Eastern Africa, internationalization, URT, information and communication technology, development

Introduction

Digital technology (DT) has revolutionized the twenty-first century in levels unprecedented across the world (Vargo et al., 2020). However, the digital revolution has not been universally experienced. Whereas countries in the northern hemisphere have had a comparative advantage on the use of DT, the countries in the southern hemisphere have lagged behind. Although the southern hemisphere has certain common characteristics, differences in individual countries need to be appraised. These differences also exist within and between individual countries and *ipso facto* among individual universities in those countries. This chapter builds on the use of DT among selected universities in East Africa during Covid-19 to analyse the digital divide.

DT refer to electronic tools, systems, devices and resources that generate, store or process data that enable virtual learning and conferencing (Victoria Government, 2022). Notable among DT are mobile phones, social media, and multimedia. The word 'digital' comes from Latin – digitus, finger – and refers to one of the oldest tools for counting. When information is stored, transmitted or forwarded in digital format, it is converted into numbers – at the most basic machine-level as 'zeroes and ones'. The term represents technology that relies on the use of microprocessors; hence, computers and applications that are dependent on computers such as the Internet, as well as other devices such as video cameras, and mobile devices such as phones and personal-digital assistants (PDAs) (IGI Global, 2022).

Informed by the university revitalization theory (URT) (Mutalemwa, 2019), SDG 4 on skills for a digital world, target 4.4 by 2030 (UN, 2022) and African Agenda 2063, target 1.2 on technology (African Union Commission, 2015), this chapter argues that while the digital divide has been apparent since the beginning of the digital revolution, the onslaught of the Covid-19 global pandemic has made the digital disparities even more pronounced. E-learning has become a new normal. Covid-19 has made virtual learning a reality but not in all universities smacking of social inequality and hence a need to close the digital divide. This is because while students with access to e-learning can pursue their studies those without the access can hardly continue with their studies during the pandemic unless and until the in-person student-lecturer interactive environment is in place, whose presence is often unpredictable during a global pandemic.

Advantages of e-learning and teaching

There is a myriad of advantages in e-learning (Croasdaile, 2009; Salmons & Wilson, 2008). These include avoiding unnecessary gatherings and learning in the comfort of one's room provided the learning environment is conducive. While students might be spared the hustle of regular transport challenges and reduce travel costs and subsequent stress, they may encounter the lack of electricity and/ or Internet access in their homes thus making learning from home complicated. In addition, students can take advantage of online resources while learning to be more independent.

Students learn time management skills because e-learning is strict with time, structured, highly systematized and catalysed by modern DT artificial intelligence (AI). E-learning complements lectures *in situ* with the opportunities of learning from very qualified staff from around the world. This is supported with free online lectures and tutorials available on the Internet and without strict cost implications. This complementarity may lead to international benchmarking and quality assurance thus making students academically strong.

The above-mentioned advantages may apply to academic staff as well. E-teaching would reduce, for instance, the time for marking assignments and examinations especially where students usually submit them handwritten. This would then create space for the academic staff to carry out other core functions such as innovating, doing research, publishing, attending or organizing conferences and seminars or webinars as well as providing public service, where African universities play a low key in international rankings amidst north-south imbalances as analysed by Marincola and Kariuki (2020).

Disadvantages of e-learning and teaching

Despite the advantages above mentioned, e-learning and teaching have some disadvantages. The disadvantages have been exacerbated by Covid-19 to such an extent that the pandemic has wiped out 20 years of education gains globally (UN, 2022). Probably the most noticeable one is the lack of interaction between and amongst students themselves, students and lecturers, between and among the lecturers themselves.

The face-to-face interaction is essential not only due to the personal academic encounters and experience but also for the extracurricular socialization (Beckett et al., 2009) where students learn social skills through in-person and interpersonal encounters. In addition, staff experience anxiety by using video conferencing as they feel monitored and controlled by their employers (Okabe-Miyamoto et al., 2021).

E-learning through student dialogues in Eastern Africa

In this unique collaborative online project, the Catholic University of Eastern Africa (CUEA), the Catholic University of South Sudan (CUoSS), the Catholic Peacebuilding Network (CPN) and the

Association of Catholic Universities and Higher Institutes of Africa and Madagascar (ACUHIAM) set out plans for a series of virtual dialogues among Justice and Peace students in universities across Eastern Africa to engage in conversation about the ways in which the global Covid-19 pandemic had impacted everyday lives, political contexts, educational experiences, religious practices, and regional and local peace and justice dynamics and efforts (CPN, 2021).

The focus on peace has been a priority of ACUHIAM since its establishment in 1989 with a Resolution that 'All ACUHIAM members to have a Peace Department and by extension a Department of Interreligious Studies to advance peace studies in Africa' (ACUHIAM General Assembly, 20–22 June 2022, Resolution 1). The students in the dialogues, except those from St. Augustine University of Tanzania (SAUT) came from peace and peace-related institutes. SAUT has not established a peace studies department.

The Eastern Africa Student Dialogues on Justice and Peace series aimed to connect Justice and Peace students across the region and build transnational justice and peace learning networks, as well as document the impact of Covid-19 on everyday life, higher learning and knowledge production processes in Eastern Africa. (CPN, 2021)

Background to the student dialogues

On 11 March 2020, the World Health Organization (WHO, 2020) announced the Covid-19 outbreak as a global health crisis. Around the same time, countries in the Eastern Africa region confirmed first infections and organized epidemic response efforts in the form of prevention and containment measures ranging from lockdowns and curfews, internal mobility restrictions, border closures and restrictions on cross-border movement. Included were school and university closures, bans on in-person social and religious gatherings, and the reorganization of markets and food systems (CPN, 2021).

Healthcare infrastructures in the region were largely unprepared for a large-scale health crisis and experienced limited critical care capacity or intensive care units and problems of structural underfunding and understaffing affecting biomedical interventions. Peoples across the region of East Africa, including students and faculty, had to adapt their social and behavioural practices, impacting family and public life. Covid-19 overlapped with and aggravated existing governing, economic, health, climate, food and housing crises in the region.

Although in the beginning of the pandemic, Covid-19 was often characterized as 'the great equalizer' because it seemingly did not differentiate between borders, ethnicities, disability status, age, or gender, the coronavirus pandemic magnified global learning inequalities and exposed regional differences. Some universities in Eastern Africa were able to shift from in-person to online and distance learning. Other universities closed indefinitely. Regional differences are driven by existing technological infrastructures and internet accessibility; varying government approaches and interventions; and available funding and resources. Within individual countries, the coronavirus pandemic also exposed intersectional inequalities. The global pandemic interacts with existing hierarchies and is producing novel disparities in higher learning and knowledge production and transmission.

Student dialogues themes and questions

The Eastern Africa Student Dialogues aimed at generating knowledge about regional and national Covid response efforts and how they impacted university education. The Dialogues also aimed at allowing students to document their experiences and understandings in their own voices. The Dialogues revolved around five broad, but interlinked themes: everyday living realities, political context, educational experiences and aspirations, religious practices, and regional and local peace and justice dynamics and efforts.

On everyday living realities, the dialogues posed a number of questions, namely: How did Covid-19 impact student livelihoods, everyday lives and family processes? What were social beliefs and behaviours around Covid-19 and how these impacted social experiences? What were the unique fears, hopes and expectations connected to the Covid-19 pandemic and how did these interact with existing fears, hopes and expectations? What was the mental health impact of Covid-19 and how did this interact with existing psycho-social stresses?

On the political context, the dialogues interrogated: How has Covid-19 impacted political and governance dynamics and practices? How Covid-19 influenced civil rights and freedom of speech? What public space existed to critique government interventions? How were the public health rules instrumentalized for political ends?

In relation to educational experiences and aspirations, the dialogues sought to find out: What was the impact of Covid-19 on learning experiences and practices? How Covid-19 reshaped university access? How Covid-19 informed educational aspirations? What inequalities were brought to bear? What did the universities do about these challenges? As far as religious practices were concerned, the dialogues discussed how the closure of churches and mosques impacted student religious experiences and worship practices.

Lastly, the dialogues analysed regional and local peace and justice dynamics and efforts through questions such as: What matters of justice did students see in their various countries and what were implications? Did Covid-19 create or worsen causes of conflict? What impact did Covid-19 have on multi-level peace processes and peace work?

Student dialogues process

A concept note was shared with select universities to ascertain interest to participate in a semester online project. Online editorial committees were set up in each participating institute. Editorial committees were made up of selected faculty and students and each editorial committee was headed by a faculty mentor who functioned as the main person of contact. Editorial committees were organized differently on the basis of university regulations for in-person gatherings and internet accessibility.

A communication mechanism was established between editorial committees of participating universities. Editorial committees met virtually to prepare for the Dialogues series. Bi-monthly dialogues around the five main themes, namely lived realities, political context, educational experiences, religious practices, justice and peace dynamics and efforts were held using Zoom – taking into account differences in internet accessibility across the participating universities.

Each dialogue was moderated by a faculty member of one of the participating universities. Dialogues were recorded and live-streamed and made available on a newly opened Facebook page and through other social media platforms and/or national radio stations. Dialogues built on each other and in between recorded dialogues students were invited to bring up issues relevant to them to redirect the process. Insights from the series of dialogues were meant to be combined in a special edition of the *Journal of Social Encounters.*

Dialogues participating universities

The participating universities included the Catholic University of Eastern Africa (CUEA), Centre for Social Justice and Ethics (Kenya) and Hekima College, Institute of Peace Studies and International Relations (Kenya): University of Hargeisa, Institute for Peace and Conflict Studies (Somaliland). South Sudan: Catholic University of South Sudan, Institute for Justice and Peace Studies (South Sudan) and University of Bahri, Centre of Peace and Development Studies (South Sudan); St. Augustine University of Tanzania (Tanzania) and Uganda Martyrs University, Centre for Ethics and Development Studies (Uganda).

The student dialogues were relevant, timely and innovative. The relevance stemmed from the content, namely peace and justice. Timeliness was significant because of the ongoing pandemic while taking advantage of the opportunities availed by DT. The dialogues were also unique in bringing international cooperation among institutions in Eastern Africa and between them and their western collaborative partners, hence setting a precedent and reference point to reckon with.

Webinars on peace studies for sustainable development in Africa

The dialogues amplified the need to offer a series of global webinars on Peace Studies for Sustainable Development in Africa. The idea which came from the Resolution of the General Assembly of the Association of Catholic Universities and Higher Institutes of Africa and Madagascar (ACUHIAM) was implemented by the ACUHIAM Secretariat at St. Augustine University of Tanzania (SAUT) in collaboration with the University of Vechta, Germany; UNESCO Chair, Nanjing University, China; George Mason University, Fairfax, Virginia, USA; The Association of Catholic Universities and Higher Institutes of Africa and Madagascar, Mwanza, Tanzania; The St. Augustine University of Tanzania, Mwanza, Tanzania; Universidad de Congreso, Mendoza, Argentina; Catholic Peacebuilding Network; International Federation of Catholic Universities and the International Peace Research Association (Spiegel et al., 2022).

The ongoing global peace webinar participants come from all continents. The webinars have been running for 90 minutes every Wednesday for about a year since October 2021. Participation showed that academics and students from Africa could take part in the online seminars alongside their participants from all over the world. Some of the challenges such as the use of unfamiliar platforms such as the use of the BigBlueButton (BBB) or Zoom were overcome with time for regular participants.

Inability to afford reliable Internet was also manifest as it kept some people away, made them participate on an irregular basis or produce background noise which interfered with the flow of presentations because of joining a webinar through shared laptops and mobile phones, sometimes in crowded areas. This was also partly due to lack of knowledge or experience on how online meetings work. Online meetings need a certain level of maturity, experience and ability to respect and listen to others rather than distract or obstruct the flow of presentations and discussions. Hence DT literacy should combine technical know-how and interpersonal communication skills.

The ongoing Global Peace webinars indicate that digital technology is capable of bringing about quality education by leveraging on transcontinental learning and teaching experience from any expert in any academic field from anywhere in the world and at any scheduled time. It should be reiterated that although virtual meetings and e-learning have been going on pre-Covid-19, the pandemic has given DT a new impetus, making both Covid-19 and DT new normal. While e-learning should not replace face-to-face learning, the two should complement each other.

Opportunities and limits

Based on the research conducted by the author on the universities discussed here, all universities in Eastern Africa have access to the Internet and as such e-learning is possible to a certain extent. The data is based on field research as well as online interviews. Findings show that individual students have access to private internet providers and as such they can study online, if factors such as income and technology remain constant. All universities have an IT service where staff and students can get technical support if and when needed. However, Internet connection is usually weak which makes its use limited. This is often compounded by lack of reliable power supply. Although students have access to private internet providers, lack of stable financial situation makes it hard for them to buy internet bundles needed to study online.

Financial obligations also force universities to employ fewer IT staff than needed. Such staff are often underqualified and at times do other university duties besides the technical tasks they are employed to perform. They also experience unreliable Internet connection and the intermittent power supply. This goes hand in hand with lack of video conferencing, teleconferencing equipment and supporting infrastructure for the same. Power cuts also distract the staff and make them lose concentration and sometimes fail to retrieve data saved on their desktop computers, losing files and wasting time.

A youthful African population with prospects of attaining higher education qualifications in African universities and abroad is an opportunity to invest in their education using the best technology available. Typical undergraduate students in Eastern Africa aged between 20 and 23 were born and grew up at the height of information and communication technology (ICT) where the challenge is not lack of data but its management. As such current university students are better placed to use DT than their older counterparts, for example, those who graduated 25 years ago.

> When we first came to university, there was no mobile phone on campus. We were taught to use typewriters and later we began learning using computers, Microsoft word, MS DOS. (Interview 7.6.2022)

Creating an enabling DT learning environment

Creating an enabling learning environment through DT is a sine qua non in this globalizing era. However, there is a tendency of getting used to the status quo. It is easy to claim that power cuts and the lack of stable Internet connection are inevitable occurrences in the so-called developing countries of the global south and that there is not much that can be done to reverse the trend. This is related to the other hurdle, namely complacency with the minimum. Complacency means that there are no higher targets, values or aspirations for change, improvement or development: Complacency may be equated with self-underdevelopment. That is where a radical change in attitude becomes a categorical imperative (Kant, 1785). Otherwise, change may be hard to operationalize.

The unreliable power supply could be minimized through the use of alternative energy. Solar power in countries that enjoy 12 hours of sunlight almost daily in East Africa is a resource to reckon with. Hydro-electric power in African countries that have more rainwater that countries in Europe should be better positioned to provide needed electricity to avoid frequent power outages. It may be noted that Tanzania, for example, has more rainwater than Germany but hydroelectric dams in Tanzania suffer shortage of water every year. Rather than complaining about blackouts, students should be socialized to save water and trained to harvest it. This would be necessary to protect the environment and mitigate the negative effects of climate change.

Universities can collaborate with private internet providers, particularly mobile phone companies to subsidize prices of Internet bundles and thus supply wi-fi and mobile data in higher education institutions. Halotel and TIGO mobile phone companies have offered subsidized rates for students in designated areas. This is an offer that can be extended to supporting strong bandwidths and e-learning across universities. Here, negotiations between and among universities, private mobile phone companies and governments should be arranged to capitalize on the public-private partnership and corporate social responsibility.

The lack of essential equipment for online learning such as video conferencing is not impossible to address provided there is a commitment to it, which is referred to here as a political will. This commitment should be reflected in university DT policy and strategic plans. There is no possibility of establishing DT without planning and investment in it. Universities might not be self-sufficient in the acquisition and use of technical equipment. However, they may turn to collaborators with capacity in DT and work on joint programmes. This is one of the advantages of international networking as advanced by the URT (Mutalemwa, 2018).

Limited technical know-how can equally be addressed through capacity building. This would entail empowering IT staff and training new ones on a regular basis while providing an enabling environment for employment and staff retention and further development. Investing in people will definitely pay dividends as a return on investment is as predictable as it is necessary.

E-learning at St. Augustine University of Tanzania

St. Augustine University of Tanzania (SAUT) is a private higher learning institution owned by the Tanzania Episcopal Conference (TEC). It received a certificate of registration from the Higher Education Accreditation Council on 1 August 1997 and commenced with a bachelor's degree programme in Mass Communication in 1998 with first graduates in 2001. As the university gears up to celebrate its Silver Jubilee in 2023, it is worth assessing its achievement in the use of DT with reference to the Covid-19 pandemic. SAUT is a member institution of, inter alia, the Association of Catholic Universities and Higher Institutes of Africa and Madagascar (ACUHIAM) and the International Federation of Catholic Universities (IFCU) (SAUT Website, 2022).

The opportunities and limits earlier alluded to equally apply to SAUT in terms of availability of young people who go to university amidst DT challenges. SAUT, with a student population of 15,000 on the Main Campus in Mwanza, (SAUT, 2022) on the Southern shores of Lake Victoria, deserve a corresponding capacity in DT, which is currently far from being sufficient. This insufficiency was made even more apparent during the pandemic.

When universities were closed due to the pandemic by the order of the fifth phase government under the late President John Joseph Pombe Magufuli, students stayed idle for three months as there was no teaching going on. This situation was not unique to SAUT but applied to other universities in Tanzania. The reason why the time was wasted was lack of DT to provide e-teaching and e-learning. If history had to repeat itself now, the same scenario would be experienced due to lack of risk management and disaster preparedness.

SAUT owns video conferencing but with the capacity to provide e-learning. However, it is suitable for small a group of people, say around 20 at once and underutilized. For a population of 15,000 students this technology is inadequate. The university has solar panels which only supply electricity to the Archbishop Mario A. Mgulunde Learning Resource Centre, the university library. The solar power works as a backup when there is a power cut by TANESCO (Tanzania Electricity Supply Company), the state electricity supply company. The other source of power is a generator which provides electricity to a few buildings, particularly two buildings, namely the administration block and the academic block. This means the rest of the offices and lecture rooms go without electricity while the generator is running in those other places. The same applies to the wi-fi. Wi-fi is accessible at the administration and academic blocks only and usually with a low bandwidth.

> Have you seen the video conferencing at Bugando [Catholic University of Health and Allied Sciencesin Mwanza, Tanzania]. That's what we need. It can help hundreds of students at the same time. (Interview 17 June 2022)

The lack of stable and strong Internet connection necessitates the use of personal Internet cables among some academic staff as well as the purchase of personal internet bundles from mobile phone companies among academic and administrative staff as well as students. Not all staff can afford the cost of Internet cables. The cost is even exorbitant for students and therefore an intervention is necessary.

While grappling with the fundamental challenges of inadequate power supply, lack of adequate computers and intermittent Internet access, students, and to a lesser extent, staff members lack basic technological skills which fuel the digital divide. There are students at SAUT who cannot type or write an email because they have not learnt how to do so. Therefore, asking them to send an assignment as an email attachment becomes an insurmountable task. Hence, students need to acquire and develop skills in ICT.

The lack of typing skills makes students pay local kiosks and stationery shop owners off campus to type students' assignments and research papers. This adds to a financial burden for the students whose socio-economic strength is usually low. For the academics who cannot mark assignments on the computer, make students print out the assignments, which increases the amount of paper used including the additional costs of buying printing papers. For the students who depend on parents who are low-income earners, this becomes a double burden as they experience the digital divide amongst themselves based on income inequality in contradistinction with students coming from well-off families as explained by a student:

> We spend a lot of money on our assignments and some of us do not have our own computers. We ask our friends, but they are also using the computers. What can we do? We pay at kiosks in Nyamalango. (Interview 26 June 2022)

Lecturers also have their own challenges: 'Imagine you are supervising 40 students who are writing their BA thesis, and each one is coming to you several times with their thesis for marking and comments. Each time you make comments on their page, they need to return a new corrected page, and this becomes almost an endless exercise. A lot of paper is wasted. Using computers would save us a lot of paper' (Interview 10 June 2022). The same applies to IT staff:

> We can develop a software to set up the examination timetable, but the university administration does not allow us to so. They say there's no money. (Interview 27 June 2022)

The language barrier compromises the quality of e-learning. With the medium of instruction in Tanzania being English, students surf the Internet with sources written in that language, which is not the language of daily communication and discussion, which is Swahili. To understand a scientific paper written in English, students must have an adequate command of the language. This applies to online tutorials and lectures which are also in English. This problem is graver for Tanzanians who did not go to good English medium schools. In this increasingly globalizing world (Liu & Spiegel, 2015), the mastery of globalizing languages is a *sine qua non*.

E-learning at the Catholic University of Eastern Africa

The Catholic University of Eastern Africa (CUEA) in Nairobi is owned by the Association of Member Episcopal Conferences of Eastern Africa (AMECEA). It was established in 1984 (CUEA Website, 2022). The university, like SAUT, is a member institution of the Association of Catholic Universities and Higher Institutes of Africa and Madagascar (ACUHIAM) and the International Federation of Catholic Universities (IFCU) among other partner organizations both private and public.

Contrary to Tanzania which closed universities for three months due to Covid-19 and responded in its own unorthodox manner to the pandemic (Patterson, 2022), Kenya closed universities for one year and followed the rubrics of the World Health Organizations (WHO) on how to protect oneself and others. Students at CUEA did not have access to e-learning which literally meant they lost the entire academic year. AMECEA countries include Eritrea, Ethiopia, Kenya, Malawi, Sudan/South Sudan, Uganda and Zambia. AMECEA has the potency to launch a digital revolution if it makes DT a priority. Again, the political will is at stake here.

E-learning at Tangaza College

Tangaza College is a constituent college of the Catholic University of Eastern Africa (CUEA) also based in Nairobi. It was established in 1986 (Tangaza, 2022). Whereas, e-learning was not possible at CUEA, it was possible at its constituent college, Tangaza College. Tangaza is an internationally interreligious institution with staff and students coming from over 50 countries and numerous religious congregations and orders from all continents (Tangaza, 2022). This international collegiality might have helped to put in place the infrastucture for e-learning. This is a model not only to be admired but also to be replicated particularly in Africa. This international cooperation is at the heart of the people's organizations development theory PODT (Mutalemwa, 2015) upon which the university revitalization theory (URT) (Mutalemwa, 2018) is modelled. A single university working independently of others and without establishing academically strong international networks is parochial.

> Yes, Tangaza continued with online classes, CUEA couldn't coz it had challenges putting things in order. But later it managed, though very few departments. Tangaza college can't be compared to CUEA one. (Interview 3 May 2022)

The Catholic University of South Sudan

The Catholic University of South Sudan is a university located in South Sudan. CUofSS consists of two campuses; one in the capital of Juba, while the other is located in the city of Wau. The university is fairly new as it was established and operating since 2008. It was instrumental in organizing the student dialogues through effective collaboration between the staff and students who often used shared computers during the online dialogues.

Uganda Martyrs University

Uganda Martyrs University (UMU) is a faith-based private University owned by the Episcopal Conference of the Catholic Bishops of Uganda. UMU acknowledges the late Archbishop Kiwanuka as the Father of Catholic higher education in Uganda. When he first conceived the idea in the 1940s, circumstances did not allow establishing a university at that time.

However, this proposal was renewed during the 1980s and was endorsed by the Uganda Episcopal Conference in 1989. Uganda Martyrs University was officially launched in 1993 by His Excellency Yoweri Kaguta Museveni President of the Republic of Uganda. It received its civil Charter on 2nd April 2005.

University of Hargeisa

The University of Hargeisa started operation in the year 2000, It is the largest and leading chartered public university in the Republic of Somaliland and the largest University in Somaliland as a whole. It is the leading higher education institution and is committed to providing a wide range of undergraduate and postgraduate degree courses. It is the goal of the university to give all graduates the skills needed for success in their future careers and to contribute to wider processes of educational and professional development in Somaliland. It was the only public university which took part in the student dialogues.

URT application on digital technology

The University Revitalization Theory (URT) (Mutalemwa, 2018) is a relevant theory for the application on the development of DT. The theory is built on the premiss that confronted with a development issue, individuals seek for a solution through organizing and networking which brings about the solution they seek (Mutalemwa, 2015, 2018). URT is a four-stage process which continues in a spiral, namely needs assessment, process institutionalization, internationalization and transformation.

In the context of the challenges surrounding DT, the need for relevant technology is felt, assessed and identified at an individual or micro level. In this chapter, it is contended that while the DT need is a common phenomenon in the universities of the southern hemisphere, the onslaught of pandemics such as Covid-19, makes the need even more acute. The use of DT is related to the acquisition or provision of quality education as the goal and the availability of finances to acquire DT as a means to the end.

Needs assessment is an important first step but the problem identified cannot be solved at an individual level. They require institutional support. This brings them to the second step or meso level which is process institutionalization or the organizing step. This means that the need which was identified by individuals becomes the need of the institution. It becomes an agenda of the academic committee, administration, management board and senate. It gets into strategic plans and calls for implementation at the institutional level.

Process institutionalization is an important part. Indeed, it is necessary but not sufficient. This is because while the institution, particularly in Eastern Africa, owns the process and makes DT a priority, it may not have the capacity and capability to own the necessary DT to offer virtual courses. This limitation is related to lack of equipment, financial power and digital skills to run online programmes. The situation becomes intractable for private universities whose sole income comes from tuition fees and usually from low-income parents.

The lack of capacity within institutions dictates the shift from inward-looking solutions and claims of self-reliance and autonomy, which are usually parochial to global partnerships for sustainable development. The URT refers to this third step or macro level as internationalization, which means that individual institutions seek cooperation with other institutions to collaborate in addressing the need identified and assessed in step one, namely lack of or low DT capacity and capability. Internationalization means that institutions graduate from being local and myopic to embrace international standards of science, technology, innovation and service. The main means of internationalization is networking at the transnational and transcontinental levels. This is essential for collaborative research, exchange programmes, capacity building and DT literacy at all three levels, that is, micro, meso and macro as well as the combination of all levels in the fourth level, namely transformation.

In the final analysis, internationalization would lead to change or transformation, where individuals and institutions would build a strong network to address the need, in this case lack of DT competences as identified in step one, discussed in step two, worked upon in step three and realized in step four. This change or development would positively affect individuals and institutions as direct beneficiaries and eventually bring about the improvement in societal conditions, which is the essence of sustainable development based on quality education.

According to the URT, change or transformation is not the last step in itself because the theory eschews the linear model of development in a dynamic world. The theory argues that after transformation in a particular need, other needs might emerge. For example, new DT might be manufactured, artificial intelligence might become more sophisticated or mind-boggling viruses might challenge science and technology and tilt towards metaphysical interventions. Each one and all these mean that individuals, institutions and networks have to grapple with them and hence the process proceeds in a spiral by doing a needs assessment, process institutionalization, internationalization and transformation.

Conclusion

Covid-19 caught Eastern Africa universities unawares as it need all over the world. The difference is that for the universities which were digitally competent, the online teaching and learning became a viable alternative to face-to-face methods. Moreover, the response to Covid-19 across Eastern African universities was not uniform due the differences in the availability and therefore application of DT, which explained the digital divide between and among the universities in the southern hemisphere.

The student dialogues in Eastern Africa and the global webinars on peace studies for sustainable development in Africa indicated that the use of DT was possible and desirable, but students needed support in accessing the Internet and learning how to use online platforms such as Zoom. This could be done if there was a 'political will' to make e-learning a priority for all universities. This political will should be supported by students' commitment to acquire digital technology skills as a modern basic need.

The political will should be able to address the perennial question of income poverty which results in the inability to afford Internet bundles as well as sporadic power supply. The public-private-partnership model should make e-learning possible as a way through which governments and private sectors collaborate to solve societal challenges, notably the provision of quality education.

Risk management and disaster preparedness show that universities should have the relevant DT well in advance to avoid lack of e-teaching and e-learning as it happened for many universities during the Covid-19 pandemic in Eastern Africa. This paper proposes a pre-pandemic hybrid curriculum model where learning goes on virtually and in-person each semester almost simultaneously in a post-pandemic milieu to anticipate any eventualities or scenarios in the capricious viral mutations.

Building on the premiss that individuals such as students, staff and parents play a central role in problem identification and needs assessment, they play a better role when backed by an institution, namely a university. The institution, in turn, formalizes the need and seeks a solution through regional and transnational cooperation. This would lead to transformation, in this case capitalizing on digital technology as explained by the university revitalization theory.

References

ACUHIAM General Assembly Proceedings. 2017. Resolution 1 (20–22 June 2022), Nairobi, Kenya.

African Union Commission. (2015). *African Agenda 2063*.

AMECEA. (2022). AMECEA members. https://amecea.org/tanzania-tanzania-begins-preparations-for-hosting-the-amecea-plenary-2022/

Beckett, M., Borman, G., & Capizzano, J. (2009). *Structuring out-of-school time to improve academic achievement* (NCEE 2009-012). National Center for Education Evaluation and Regional Assistance (NCEE), Institute of Education Sciences (IES), US Department of Education (US ED).

CPN. (2021a). *Student dialogues*. https://web.facebook.com/Student-Dialogues-on-Justice-and-Peace-102993205029716/

CPN. (2021b). *Student Dialogues*. https://web.facebook.com/watch/live/?ref=watch_permalink&v=274435090888484

Croasdaile, S. (2009). Inter-organisational E-collaboration in education. In *Handbook of research on electronic collaboration and organizational synergy*. IGI Global. https://doi.org/10.4018/978-1-60566-106-3.ch002

CUEA. (2022). *CUEA facts*. https://www.cuea.edu/

IGI Global. (2022). *Digital technology*. In *Handbook of research on electronic collaboration and organizational synergy*. https://www.igi-global.com/dictionary/digital-technology/7723

Kant, I. (1785). *Categorical imperatives*. https://www.britannica.com/topic/categorical-imperative

Liu, C., & Spiegel, E. (2015). *Peacebuilding in a globalized world: An illustrated introduction to peace studies.* People's Publishing House.

Marincola, E., & Kariuki, T. (2020). *Quality research.* https://www.researchgate.net/publication/345196537_Quality_Research_in_Africa_and_Why_It_Is_Important/citation/download

Mutalemwa, G. (2015). *People's organisations in Tanzania: Strengths, challenges and implications for development.* University of Vechta.

Mutalemwa, G. (2018). African academic diaspora and the revitalisation of African universities. *Journal of Sociology and Development, 2*(1), 150–174.

Mutalemwa, G. (2019). Community-based organisations in Tanzania and development theory generation. *Journal of Sociology and Development, 3*(1), 93–122.

Okabe-Miyamoto, K., Durnell, E., Howell, R. T., & Zizi, M. (2021). Negative video conferencing meetings during COVID-19 undermined worker subjective productivity. *Human Behaviour and Emerging Technologies, 3*(5), 1067–1083. https://doi.org/10.1002/hbe2.317

Patterson, A. (2022). *The Tanzanian State response to COVID-19: Why low capacity, discursive legitimacy, and twilight authority matter* (UNU Working Paper 2022/34). UNU-WIDER.

Salmons, J., & Wilson, L. (2008). *Handbook of research on electronic collaboration and organisational synergy.* IGI Global. https://doi.org/10.4018/978-1-60566-106-3

SAUT. (2022). St. Augustine University of Tanzania. https://saut.ac.tz/pages/background.php

Spiegel, E., Mutalemwa, G., Cheng, L., & Kurtz, L. (Eds.). (2022). *Peace studies for sustainable peace in Africa: Conflicts and peace oriented conflict resolution.* Springer.

Tangaza. (2022). Tangaza University College. https://www.somo.co.ke/about-tangaza-university-college-sm1-32

UN. (2022). SDGs Department of Economic and Social Affairs. https://sdgs.un.org/goals/goal4

Vargo, D., Zhu, L., Benwell, B., & Yan, Z. (2020). Digital Technology use during COVID-19 pandemic special issue on COVID-19. *Human Behaviour with Emerging Technologies, 3*(1) 13–24. https://doi.org/10.1002/hbe2.242

Victoria Government. (2022). *Teaching resources.* https://www.educat
ion.vic.gov.au/school/teachers/teachingresources/digital/Pages/virt
ual.aspx

WHO. (2020). *COVID-19.* https://www.who.int/europe/emergencies/sit
uations/covid-19

Chapter 5

University governance in the Fourth Industrial Revolution

Mayte Gómez Marcos

Abstract: The Fourth Industrial Revolution has automated work and thus created an increasingly flexible and uncertain job market. Multiple exponential technologies such as artificial intelligence, biotechnologies or nanomaterials are producing changes at a fast pace. Workers must train in digital and human competencies for jobs that are still unknown and must continue to do so throughout their lives.

This new paradigm is leading to transformations in the field of training, and universities will have to reinvent themselves and offer a quick response if they do not want to be left behind. Reconfiguring their governance is therefore more necessary than ever, adapting it to the Fourth Industrial Revolution. This chapter presents a new university governance model 4.0 that allows universities to redesign their structures and governance to take on new leadership roles in the digital era.

Keywords: university, higher education, university governance, university system

Introduction

Higher education has evolved slowly over time, and developed in different political and cultural contexts. Contrary to popular belief that universities have barely varied their meaning and way of doing things for centuries, reality reveals a slow yet constant process of transformation responding to the needs of each era (Unceta, 2011).

The arrival of the Fourth Industrial Revolution in the early 2000s is an unprecedented disruptive innovation. This revolution is characterized by integrating multiple exponential technologies such as artificial intelligence, big data, algorithms, biotechnologies and nanomaterials. The fusion of these technologies and their interaction across physical, digital and biological domains will have profound consequences (Schwab, 2016; Schwab & Davis, 2018) and will change how we live, work and relate with others. The Future of Jobs Report 2020 (World Economic Forum, 2020) states that 85 million jobs will disappear in 2025, creating 97 million new jobs in their place. Data analysts and scientists, experts in artificial intelligence, specialists in culture or digital product developers will be some of the new jobs in demand by the market. Others that we may not even be able to imagine yet. But what we can be sure of is that this new scenario will bring about a profound change in society and require universities to reinvent themselves.

Students must be prepared for jobs that today do not exist and to do this, they must acquire technical skills and cross-cutting competencies. They must also do so throughout their lives to reinvent themselves as the changes occur. This will force universities to create interdisciplinary curriculums focusing on the development of hard and soft skills, redirect their curricular content to foster flexibility, promote ethical and sustainable education to facilitate appropriate use of technology and design hybrid training independent of space and time. Research and the transfer of knowledge must also be managed under the umbrella of digitalization, globalization and innovation. Moreover, these changes will take place in a new, more competitive scenario as leading technology companies are emerging, willing to become providers of knowledge and to compete for the training of the workers of tomorrow.

Universities must be quick to react if they do not want to fall behind; knowledge will not stop because they take time to adapt. Nowadays, many universities still have an excessively rigid, bureaucratic, traditional governance structure with no clear leadership or strategic thinking. But the time has come to reconfigure this structure as they will otherwise be incapable of providing the proactive response that society demands.

The university governance 4.0 presented in this chapter aims to adapt internal university management and culture to a future marked by complexity and uncertainty. A new, agile, flexible and efficient model based on eight main elements: organizational culture, leadership, strategic planning and management, heterarchical structure, digital literacy, comprehensive literacy, attracting and retaining talent and internationalization.

A chapter that aims to reflect on the future of universities in the digital era. More specifically, it reviews the main changes arising in the Fourth Industrial Revolution, analyses different governance theories and presents a new university governance 4.0 model adapted to the new demands of the Fourth Industrial Revolution.

Universities in the Fourth Industrial Revolution

Rapid progress in science and technology at the beginning of the twenty-first century generates a series of phenomena with no precedent in the history of humanity. The integration of multiple exponential technologies such as artificial intelligence, the internet of things, 3D printing, nanotechnology or biotechnology give rise to the so-called Fourth Industrial Revolution. The fusion of these technologies and their interaction across physical, digital and biological domains will have profound consequences for all agents in a globalized world (Schwab, 2016; Schwab & Davis, 2018) and will change how we live, work and relate with others. This revolution was accelerated by the Covid-19 pandemic that forced society to rethink and give a greater role to digitalization and process automation (Ordóñez-Matamoros et al., 2021).

The concept of the Fourth Industrial Revolution was coined in 2016 by Klaus Schwab, founder of the World Economic Forum. He sustains that it is not simply a revolution prolonged by its predecessor, rather it is a transformation different from anything that humankind has experienced ever before due to its speed, scope and impact. Social, cultural, institutional, economic, political and environmental structures will transform at great speed (Schwab, 2016) and that will redefine employment.

The World Economic Forum identifies four specific technology developments of the Fourth Industrial Revolution that will be decisive for the growth of businesses and job markets: ubiquitous high-speed mobile internet, artificial intelligence, big data and cloud technology (World Economic Forum, 2018). Three types of jobs for the future job market are also differentiated: stable jobs maintained over time (managers, human resource specialists, sales and marketing professionals, university professors); redundant jobs condemned to disappear (accountants, cashiers, lawyers, bank tellers); and new jobs created in the future thanks to the advancement of technology (data analysts and scientists, experts in artificial intelligence and machine learning, innovation professionals, specialists in culture). The Future of Jobs Report 2020 (World Economic Forum, 2020) states that 85 million jobs will disappear in 2025, creating 97 million new jobs in their place. These new profiles will require new skills, which will force universities to adapt their curriculums.

In the Fourth Industrial Revolution, the acquisition of competencies will no longer be limited to the university years; workers must continue to train throughout their careers to adapt to ongoing changes. A flexible academic offer and the breakdown of degrees into new, smaller, accredited educational formats will be key aspects to provide the skills needed for the job market (Rodríguez-Abitia & Bribiesca-Correa, 2021). Universities will therefore have an opportunity to stand out with lifelong learning. According to Blessinger (2015), to achieve this they must create flexible structures to satisfy the lifelong learning needs of all segments of society. The creation of smart curriculums will be increasingly necessary, described as a curriculum that designs the structure of degrees and curricular itineraries based on computerization, where students associate their learning with job market demands (Vladimir, 2020).

This evolution of the job market requires a review of degrees to analyse whether they respond to the training required of people, citizens and professionals in this millennium to be able to address a future marked by uncertainty and complexity (Ruíz-Corbella & López-Gómez, 2019). We are facing a new scenario that understands universities as a community capable of training excellent professionals – high level of training, capacity to innovate and internationalization – guided at the same time by an ethic of responsibility focused on achieving professional, ethical and social results (Teichler, 2015; Zgaga, 2014). As proposed by Barnett (2017), an ecological university is prioritized that addresses at least seven ecosystems: knowledge, the economy, social institutions, learning, individual persons, culture and the natural environment. Along the same lines, Schwab (2016) also points out that training must be geared towards different types of intelligence: contextual, elevating the mind to understand and apply knowledge; emotional, where relationships with others integrate thought and feeling; inspired, with a sense of purpose and passion for the common good; and physical, with the guarantee of health and well-being to be able to make and transform the world. Aoun (2017) also argues that universities should promote curricular content that includes exponential learning and integrates technology, data literacy and human literacy. Exponential learning broadens capacities and increases the speed of learning to develop free individuals who can address continuous challenges and create new realities.

Changes in training caused by the Fourth Industrial Revolution are leading some technology companies to want to enter the field of education and compete with universities. Tech giant Google has created the Grow with Google initiative offering different Career Certificates, training courses lasting three to six months, granting them the same value as a university degree. These certificates also provide access to job vacancies at the company or 50 other companies, including Walmart, Intel or Bank of America, which have created a consortium with Google. In addition to Google, Amazon also offers training itineraries to complement regulated higher education through its AWS Academy.

It is still early to assess whether professionals with studies accredited by Google or Amazon will be more in demand than others with a university education. These qualifications may only be attractive in the short term as they train for specific positions that could cease to be relevant over the years but, at the moment, these new knowledge providers are responding to the market trend of demanding knowledge, skills and competencies rather than a specific qualification.

Another notable trend is hybrid training in science and humanities. The use of exponential technologies is leading us to build a society in which risk and ethical dilemmas are continuously present. So, in order to keep technology at the service of society, profiles must be promoted that provide a vision for both the design of technology solutions and their use.

Unlike the previous industrial revolutions, the characteristic speed of the Fourth Industrial Revolution will require a more proactive response from universities at all levels; they must make decisions and take on new leadership roles. This will mean redesigning governance structures and models to increase their strategic capacities and quickly adapt to the environment (Bruner, 2011) and university governance will become a key factor for their survival in the digital era.

Background of university governance

The origin of the university as an institution with its specific organization, rights, privileges and duties lies in professor-student associations that arose and obtained legal recognition in the early thirteenth century

(Phelan, 1960). University organizations increased their functions of the years to respond to society's demands (Corson, 1971; Buss, 1975), becoming so convoluted that they start to require appropriate forms of governance. It could therefore be said that university governance has been present, tacitly or explicitly, from the very origins of these institutions. However, as their complexity increases, how procedures, structures, processes and regulations for decision-making are analysed gains greater importance.

Universities initially operate as small groups of students and professors organized to discover truth in the arts and sciences (Desy, 1960). They have a sense of community and decisions are taken jointly and gregariously (Ganga-Contreras et al., 2017). Their growth and diversification lead to different agents coexisting in the institution: academic community, administrative authorities, union and/or trade organizations and students. A separation between academics and authorities thus begins to emerge, causing conflicts in governance (Acosta-silva et al., 2021) and forcing the creation of participation spaces for decision-making. As Baldridge (1973) points out, the larger the university, the more freedom academics have in their work and the harder it becomes to manage the institution.

In the 1960s and 1970s, universities were searching for operability to enable them to reflect the interests of their different stakeholders. Internal organization must attend to the different social agents and foster cooperation among them (Ganga-Contreras et al., 2018). Without explicitly mentioning the word governance, Faulkner (1958) analyses which elements must be addressed: purposes of the institution; formulation and deliberation of objectives; curricular frameworks; the role of students; the role of administrative staff; and the role of faculty executives. Yoder (1962) also believes that participatory management spaces must be built to resolve conflicts between the different parties based on four pillars: engagement, communication, student administration and faculty missions. According to Ikenberry (1971), six elements must be considered in the governance system: decrease in autonomy; increase in regulatory frameworks; recognition of the conflict and how it is managed; decentralization; challenges associated with professionalization; and loss of the myth of professors.

In addition to greater participation in decision-making, university regulations grow to protect the rights of professors and students. Increasingly participatory management and the rise in internal regulations make governance more complex and different interpretations begin to emerge. Despite this, the concept is still in a process of consolidation (Ganga-Contreras et al., 2014) and no definition is universally accepted by the scientific community at present (Acosta-Silva et al., 2021).

Towards university governance 4.0

The transformation of universities in the Fourth Industrial Revolution is a reason for concern and also a unique opportunity for growth. The emergence of giants like Google or Amazon, ready to become the new providers of knowledge, will convert higher education into a highly competitive market. If leading universities need strategic thinking to maintain their position, more modest institutions must ask themselves important questions if they want to survive (Rodríguez-Espinar, 2018). Opening up to change is a prerequisite for the transformation (Rodríguez-Abitia & Bribiesca-Correa, 2021); but this change will only be possible with agile and flexible governance. Analysing how universities organize their academic, financial and administrative aspects is therefore imperative; in the same way, it is essential to understand how each unit relates with other entities involved in the decision-making process (Valdes-Montecino & Ganga-Contreras, 2021).

Schmal and Cabrales (2018) state that governance is associated with a process that guides the behaviour of an organization not only in terms of division of work and distribution of authority, but the values that will drive it to achieve its objectives. This is how institutions organize their governance, their management and relationships to ensure their objectives (Brunner, 2011). According to Valdez-Montecino and Ganga-Contreras (2021), it can be understood as a series of actions, processes, internal and external actions by university authorities and their highest collegiate bodies, which interact through their organization with the form of governing, developing and executing the mission objectives based on their decisions.

Salmi (2019) argues that favourable university governance must foster strategic planning and management, innovation and efficient decision-making. Innovation must be twofold: on one hand, new forms of institutional governance and management of scientific and academic resources; this could impact teaching career definition, access to positions and mobility. On the other hand, it involves teaching and research in new spaces for interdisciplinary exchange beyond the traditional chair structure (Pérez-Centeno et al., 2017).

Fernández-Lamarra and Pérez-Centeno (2020) propose four axes for university governance: the long-term as a horizon and vision for building the future; democratization and social development as goals to ensure relevance; planning as a tool for participation, generating consensus to ensure its viability; and innovation and real transformation as criteria to ensure change and continuous improvement.

Universities need a new governance model that encompasses management, efficiency and effectiveness guidelines with objectives for teaching and student training, research and transfer, etc., without losing sight of social objectives (Amarante et al., 2017). A new, decentralized, strategic and entrepreneurial system in line with its mission and consistent with the system of values, principles and priorities established in the culture of each organization (De Vicenzi, 2020).

The university governance 4.0 model presented in this chapter aims to be more than a definition and respond to the deficiencies of current management. Excessive bureaucracy, overlapping functions, lack of meritocracy, rigid governance structures, concentration of power in a single person or position, misalignment or lack of collaborative work are still common in the management of many universities. Governing a university means reflecting, shaping, building, adjusting and harmonizing; moving away from inertia, routine, custom and authoritarianism. Complex scenarios such as the Fourth Industrial Revolution require agile, flexible and efficient governance. Appropriate strategic planning and optimization of resources and processes will allow universities to focus on their true raison d'être: teaching, research, transfer of knowledge and social responsibility.

University governance 4.0 should be made up of the following elements:

• Organizational culture

A system of beliefs and values consistent with the institution's objectives and purposes must be defined. Fostering this culture is the starting point for changing the governance model. This culture gains greater importance in the case of universities as organizations that should be at the service of society. Their employees must share a common project, and know what the academic institution expects of them and where the strategy is headed.

Different actions can stimulate the organizational culture, such as developing core values to promote teams that understand, share, follow and incorporate them in their work; fostering transparency by sharing information with the university community as a whole; promoting recognition and reward; stimulating autonomy; increasing job flexibility; and promoting team atmospheres to direct them towards specific objectives.

• Leadership

Leadership plays a pivotal role as it becomes a catalyst for driving internal processes and orienting the university community towards its mission.

The chancellor is the main leader of the university and, therefore, must have specific training for their work to have a positive impact on institutional performance. Those responsible for strategy must also have leadership qualities to be able to direct their teams towards specific objectives. The main characteristics required of university leaders are integrity, commitment, coherence, long-term vision and continuous interaction with members of the organization.

• Strategic planning and management

A suitable, flexible strategic planning and management process allows universities to promote important developments. The identification of priority development and planning areas based on quality criteria and generating consensus are fundamental.

Depending on its mission, each university must thoroughly analyse the environment and attempt to discover threats and opportunities based on the organization's strengths and weaknesses. Analysis of past and current performance must be part of future planning with measurable medium-term objectives. Developments must then be monitored and assessed to detect emerging issues that could affect the strategy.

• Heterarchical structure

The structure of each institution must be configured according to its mission and strategy. Universities are loosely coupled institutions with two types of bureaucracy that must interact to achieve shared goals: academic and administrative. This interaction requires a structure that facilitates joint participation in decision-making and intense collaboration for an effective interconnection between people working in different areas.

It must be a heterarchical rather than hierarchical structure that enables academic community employees to perform roles with cross-cutting duties and hierarchies, reduces bureaucracy and focuses on results. A university structure made up of different elements interacting in a network is proposed with human resources at the centre as they are the university's greatest asset. These resources must be aligned with the mission and strategy through a shared culture. Internationalization should also permeate throughout the institution; it must not be viewed as a separate activity. Six additional elements are also configured: strategic staff comprised of the chancellor, vice-chancellors and leaders of the main lines set in the strategic plan; a technostructure that includes processes to support administrative processes; teaching, based on faculties and governance boards; research, with research groups; transfer, managing research outcomes and partnerships with businesses; and social responsibility, deployed in units created for aspects such as sustainability, volunteering, gender equality or social inclusion.

This heterarchical structure will facilitate the creation of multidisciplinary working groups oriented towards fulfilling certain actions of the strategic plan that combine different knowledge, functions, levels and organizational, geographic and cultural lines.

- Digital literacy

Digital literacy is defined as training the university community to properly use digital tools and facilities to manage, integrate, assess, analysis and synthesize digital resources and build new knowledge.

The arrival of artificial intelligence means that all processes can be digitalized and, to achieve this, the university community needs training to acquire new forms of working. Change must take place in all processes: student recruitment, access and admissions, alumni management, student prediction and monitoring, digital career offices, teaching, research and transfer.

- Comprehensive literacy

Soft skill training is another requirement for university personnel. The goal is not only to attract well-qualified employees but also to enable them to work as a team to benefit the organization.

If soft skills are increasingly necessary for future workers, they are also vital for all members of the university organization. The academic community needs training in competencies such as learning to learn, global thinking, teamwork, intercultural skills, innovation, critical reasoning and entrepreneurial spirit.

• Attracting and retaining talent

Talent – students, teaching and research staff and administration and services staff – has a relevant position as a strategic element at national and international level. Universities need a plan to attract and retain talent if they want to become leaders of knowledge and quickly adapt to the requirements of the Fourth Industrial Revolution.

Criteria for selecting and promoting university personnel must be well defined and internationally comparable. Quality agencies must therefore apply unified standards to attract talent worldwide.

• Internationalization

Borders should not limit spaces for exchanging teaching, research and management. Internationalization is a multidimensional process that should permeate throughout the institution; it must not be viewed as a separate activity and be integrated in the institutional culture.

Encouraging internationalization means creating a planned change that encompasses cooperation, mobility, personal and programme recognition, accreditation, research, transfer, employability and cooperation.

This governance 4.0 will equip universities with the necessary structure to train citizens in digital and human competencies while also promoting research to explore and resolve problems that arise in an innovative way; and finally, to lead the transfer of knowledge to productive fields, social responsibility to intensify social cohesion, culture and public values in the digital era. If business and institutional governance is changing to adapt to the Fourth Industrial Revolution, universities must also change their culture and internal organization to fulfil the expectations of society.

Conclusions

Universities have always given a slow but constant response to the social, political and economic needs of society, but the arrival of the Fourth Industrial Revolution appears to be changing the scenario faster than ever.

The university of the future must prepare students for jobs that do not yet exist and promote lifelong education, independent of time and space. New learning strategies must develop competencies so that students can learn to learn and adapt to any change. Curricular content must be refocused to foster flexibility, and interdisciplinary curriculums will be created to develop professional and personal skills. The academic community must also be connected to a wealth of knowledge that provides lifelong training. Universities will also be key in applying technologies in an ethical and sustainable manner.

This change will only be possible with an agile, flexible and efficient organizational structure. Rigid governance structures, concentrating authority in individuals with no specific leadership training and excessive bureaucracy will no longer be possible. Institutional, academic, curricular and administrative management structures will be reconfigured.

A new challenge based on university governance. Innovation and change will be the conceptual foundations for future management. Organizational culture, leadership, strategic planning and management, heterarchical structure, digital literacy, comprehensive literacy, attracting and retaining talent and internationalization will be the elements of the new university governance 4.0, which seeks to adapt to the new demands of the Fourth Industrial Revolution.

According to Ortega y Gasset, the university must be at the service of people, of the community and, especially, at the service of the culture of each era. It is relatively easy to predict that technological disruption and digital transformation will cause a rapid and profound change in society. The exact impact of this change and whether universities will be capable of adapting remain a mystery. But if they are not capable of achieving the reconfiguration and literacy of their own governance, they will hardly be able to lead the training of the future. The transformation must also stem from the academic community itself because, as pointed out by Clark Kerr several decades ago, the agents who are part of the institution are the best suited to comprehend it.

References

Acosta-Silva, A., Ganga-Contreras, F., & Rama-Vitale, C. (2021). Gobernanza universitaria: enfoques y alcances conceptuales. *Revista Iberoamericana de Educación Superior, 33*(12), 3–17. https://doi. org/10.22201/iisue.20072872e.2021.33.854

Amarante, J. M., Crubellate, J. M., & Meyer Junior, V. (2017). Estrategiasem Universidade: uma analise comparativa sob a perspectiva institucional. *Revista Gestão Universitária na América Latina–Gual, 10*(1), 190–212. https://doi.org/10.5007/1983-4535.2017v10n1p190.

Aoun, J. E. (2017). *Robot proof: Higher Education in the age of artificial intelligence.* MIT Press.

Baldridge, V. (1973). Research: College cize and professional freedom. *Change, 5*(4), 11–63.

Barnett, R. (2017). *The ecological university: A feasible utopia.* Routledge.

Blessinger, P. (2015, 11 September). Why global higher Education must be democratised. *University World News,* 318. https://www.universityworldn ews.com/post.php?story=2015090815175230

Brunner, J. (2011). Gobernanza universitaria: dinámicas y tendencias. *Revista de Educación, 355,* 137–159.

Buss, A. (1975). Systems theory, generation theory, and the university: Some predictions. *Higher Education, 4*(4), 429–445.

Corson, J. (1971). The modernization of the university: The impact of function on governance. *The Journal of Higher Education, 42*(6), 430–441

Desy, J. (1960). La universidad y el estado. In *Congreso de Pax Romana, misión de la universidad* (pp. 99–119). Ciudad y Espíritu.

De Vicenzi, R. (2020). Gobernanza 4.0. en la Educación Superior. In F. Ganga-Contreras, E. González Gil, O. L. Ostos Ortiz, & L. A. Hernández Merchán (Eds.), *Gobernanza Universitaria. Experiencias e investigaciones en Lationamérica.* USTA.

Faulkner, D. (1958). The formulation of institutional objectives. *The Journal of Higher Education, 29*(8), 425–469.

Fernandez-Lamarra, N., & Pérez-Centeno, C. (2020). La Reforma Universitaria en Argentina y en América Latina: principios, trascendencia y futuro. In *Cien años de Reforma Universitaria. Las principales apelaciones a la Universidad* (T.I). Ediciones Coneau.

Ganga-Contreras, F., Abello, J., & Quiroz, J. (2014). Gobernanza universitaria: una mirada histórica y conceptual. In F. Ganga, J. Abello, & J. Quiroz (Eds.), *Gobernanza universitaria: aproximaciones teóricas y empíricas* (pp. 11–20). Universidad de Los Lagos.

Ganga-Contreras, F., Pérez-Martínez, A., & Mansilla, J. (2018). Paradigmas emergentes en la gobernanza universitaria: una aproximación teórica. *Utopía y Praxis Latinoamericana, 23*(83).

Ganga-Contreras, F., Quiroz, J., & Fossatti, P. (2017). Análisis sincrónico de la gobernanza universitaria: una mirada teórica a los años sesenta y setenta. *Educaçao e Pesquisa, 43*(2), 553–568. https://doi.org/10.1590/S1517-9702201608135289

Ikenberry, S. (1971). Reestructuring College and university organization and governance: An introduction. *The Journal of Higher Education, 42*(6), 421–429. https://doi.org/10.2307/1979072

Ordóñez-Matamoros, G., Centeno, J. P., & Orozco-Castro, L. (2021). Las ciencias sociales y humanidades en la cuarta revolución industrial. Retos y Oportunidades. In J. C. Henao & M. A. Pinzón-Camargo (Eds.), *Disrupción tecnológica, transformación digital y sociedad. ¿Cuarta revolución industrial? Contribuciones tecnosociales para la transformación social*. Universidad Externado de Colombia.

Phelan, G. (1960). Orígenes y evolución histórica de la universidad. In *Congreso de pax romana, misión de la universidad*. Ciudad y Espíritu.

Perez Centeno, C., Claverie, J., & Afonso, V. (2017). *Las profesiones académicas en Argentina. Perspectivas a partir de la homologación del Convenio Colectivo para los Docentes de las Instituciones Universitarias*. VIII Encuentro Nacional y V Latinoamericano: La Universidad como objeto de investigación. 'La Reforma Universitaria entre dos siglos'. Celebrada el 3, 4 y 5 mayo. Universidad Nacional del Litoral.

Ruiz-Corbella, M., & López-Gómez, E. (2019). The role of the university in 21st century: Understand its origin in order to project its future. *Revista de la Educación Superior, 48*(189), 1–19.

Rodríguez-Abitia, G., & Bribiesca-Correa, G. (2021). Assessing digital transformation in universities. *Future Internet, 13*(2), 52. https://doi.org/10.3390/fi13020052

Rodríguez-Espinar, S. (2018). La Universidad: una visión desde 'fuera' orientada al futuro. *Revista de Investigación Educativa, 36*(1), 15–38. https://doi.org/10.6018/rie.36.1.309041

Salmi, J. (2019). *El desafío de crear universidades de rango mundial*. Banco Mundial.

Schmal, R., & Cabrales, F. (2018). El desafío de la gobernanza universitaria: El caso chileno. *Ensaio: Avaliação e Políticas Públicas em Educação, 26*(100), 822–848. https://doi.org/10.1590/s0104-40362018002601309

Schwab, K. (2016). *The Fourth Industrial Revolution*. World Economic Forum.

Schwab, K., & Davis, N. (2018). *Shaping the future of the fourth industrial revolution*. Currency.

Teichler, U. (2015). Changing perspectives: The professional relevance of Higher Education on the way towards the highly-educated society. *European Journal of Education, 50*(4), 461–477.

Unceta Satrústegui, A. (2011). La educación superior en tránsito: ¿Es Bolonia la ruta idónea para la innovación? *Arbor, 187*(752), 1119–1131. https://doi.org/10.3989/arbor.2011.752n6008

Valdés-Montecinos, M., & Ganga- Contreras, F. (2021). Gobernanza universitaria: Aproximaciones teóricas de los grupos de interés en Instituciones de Educación Superior. *Revista de Ciencias Sociales, 27*(3), 441–459.

Vladimir Carbajal-Amaya, R. (2020). University of the future and forth industrial revolution. Towards an innovative university. Prospective analysis. *Revista Electrónica Calidad en la Educación Superior, 11*(2), 15–26. http://dx.doi.org/10.22458/caes.v11i2.3321

World Economic Forum. (2018). *The future of jobs report*. Centre for the New Economy and Society. https://www.weforum.org/reports/the-future-of-jobs-report-2018

World Economic Forum. (2020). *The future of jobs report*. https://www3.weforum.org/docs/WEF_Future_of_Jobs_2020.pdf

Yoder, D. (1962). The faculty role in university governance: A faculty member's perception the diagnosis and treatment of organizational pip. *The Journal of the Academy of Management, 5*(3), 222–229. https://doi.org/10.2307/254474

Zgaga, P. (2014). The role of higher education centres in research and policy: A case from a European periphery. *Studies in Higher Education, 39*(8), 1393–1404.

Chapter 6

University education in the era of generative artificial intelligence

CLAUDIA CHIAVARINO, ALESSIO ROCCHI,
ROBERTO SANTORO, AND CLAUDIO TARDITI

Abstract: Since the release of ChatGPT in November 2022, there has been increasing interest in the possible uses (and misuses) of generative artificial intelligence (AI) in education. Benefits of generative AI include personalized assessment, interactive learning, and tutoring with tailored ongoing feedback. However, there are also inherent limitations, such as biases, generation of wrong information, and privacy issues. As the field is rapidly evolving, it is essential to comprehend the readiness of universities in facing the opportunities and the challenges posed by these tools. This chapter aims to explore the potential benefits and drawbacks of generative AI in promoting teaching and learning in universities, and to identify the digital and pedagogical competences required to safely and constructively implement it in university education contexts.

Keywords: generative AI, university education, teacher-student relationship, collaborative learning, AI tools, knowledge, information, meaning

Introduction

Today, most of humanity lives in an Artificial Intelligence-mediated world. Over the past 10 years there has been an unprecedented growth of technology and AI capabilities which is affecting all areas of society, challenging university education to maintain its relevance (Bearman & Ajjawi, 2023). In particular, since November 2022, when U.S. company OpenAI released ChatGPT (which stands for Chat Generative Pre-trained Transformer) into the public domain, the world's attention has been focused on generative artificial intelligence.

Generative AI uses neural network to create new and original content learning from massive amounts of trained data (Aydın & Karaarslan, 2023). In particular, GPT is a language model that adopts supervised and reinforcement learning techniques to acquire the patterns and structures of language and produce human-like content in response to users' requests. ChatGPT is designed to excel in applications such as chatbots, virtual assistants, language translation, and text generation (OpenAI, 2022). Within the university context, ChatGPT can be successfully applied across diverse disciplines, from STEM (science, technology, engineering and mathematics) subjects to humanities and social sciences.

While the potentialities of generative AI tools in tertiary education are being widely experimented, the debate is flourishing on their limits and dangers, leaving institutions uncertain about how to approach AI-based innovations. The current literature highlights the ambivalence whereby universities are relinquishing their control over advanced education while the Internet emerges as the predominant infrastructure for accessing and exchanging knowledge and information on a global scale, serving as both a repository and a platform for knowledge dissemination. As the field is rapidly evolving, it is essential to foster universities' readiness in facing the opportunities and challenges posed by these tools, shifting the focus from procedural knowledge (How to do it) to understanding the underlying rationale (Why we are doing it). Consequently, a greater emphasis on issues related to ethical considerations, collaborative practices, cultural diversity and the environmental impact of actions is strongly needed (Moscardini et al., 2022).

In the present chapter, we propose a contribution to further sketch the potential benefits and drawbacks of generative AI in relation to the future of university education. First, we will review some of the recent literature on the relationship between students and teachers in AI-driven universities. Second, the potential role of AI in fostering collaborative learning processes will be analysed. Subsequently, some of the tools that are most commonly used for knowledge access and processing in academic contexts will be examined, discussing potential advantages and downsides. Finally, drawing on information theories, we propose a reflection on the relationship between information, entropy and meaning in human and artificial intelligence.

The teacher-student relationship in AI-based education

In educational settings, generative AI can assist 24/7 teachers and students by providing personalized tutoring and learning support, by tailoring ongoing feedback during formative assessment activities, and by allowing rapid and automated assessment and evaluation. AI may also support teachers in predicting students' outcomes and potentially preventing dropouts, as well as in curriculum design and lectures preparation and delivery, ensuring improved accessibility and inclusion (Bahroun et al., 2023).

As the transformative influence of AI in education continues to unfold, concerns have been raised regarding its impact on education quality. In particular, researchers discuss the long-term impacts of AI on educational systems and highlight the risk of 'removing people' from the teaching-learning process, weakening the role of interpersonal connection between teachers and students (Barros et al., 2023). In other words: by unleashing new pedagogical possibilities, generative AI challenges traditional teaching methodologies and encourages universities to revisit the teacher-student relationship.

At its heart, teaching is a human interaction, where the quality of student-teacher bonds is crucial for fostering a supportive and collaborative environment. Teachers' communication has a dual emotional impact on students: they not only transmit their own connection to the subjects they teach (e.g. curiosity, passion), but also play a pastoral and nurturing role (e.g. empathy, care) (Moore & Kuol, 2007). These emotionally charged interactions are fundamental to cognitive functions like attention, memory, and decision-making, influencing how the individual will adjust her/his social conduct in future relational settings. From an educator's perspective, the challenge becomes the following: how can AI-based education help develop students as competent and skilled individuals, equipping them to fully participate in social, cultural, and economic life?

Al-Mughairi and Bhaskar (2024) adopted an interpretative phenomenological approach to identify a number of factors that encourage and inhibit teachers to adopt generative AI tools. Among the motivating factors they found: desire to explore innovative education technologies; possibility to customize teaching and learning processes; potential to save time through automatized procedures; recognition of the value of generative AI for technical and professional development. On the other hand, inhibiting factors included: concerns of the reliability and accuracy of the information provided by the AI; reduction in collaboration and reliance on colleagues; worries about privacy and data security; challenges related to the lack of institutional support through guidelines and policies; risk of overreliance and dependence on AI tools.

Grájeda and colleagues (2024) provided a complementary investigation on university students' perceptions on the impact of AI tools use on learning and teaching. Their results show an overall positive impact of AI tools on student academic experiences, in particular in enhancing comprehension, creativity, and productivity. However, they also underline the role of AI proficiency among both students and teachers, as well as the importance that AI may be viewed as a pedagogical evolution and not merely as a technological shift.

In order to address this challenge, teachers must keep in mind – in all stages of AI tools use and application – that the purpose of technology in higher education is not limited to simply transmitting information, monitoring or evaluating. Instead, its fundamental objective is to enrich thinking capacity and enrich the educational process (Popenici & Kerr, 2017).

As suggested by the 2024 Science for Policy report by the Joint Research Centre (JRC) on 'Unpacking the impact of digital technologies in Education', instead of focusing on learning outcomes, the impact of new technologies should be explored in relation to their potential to enable the creation of rich and inclusive learning environments (Giannoutsou et al., 2024). To this end, several self-reflection tools for digital capacity development have been developed: for instance, SELFIE (which stands for 'Self-reflection on Effective Learning by Fostering the use of Innovative Educational technologies', European Commission, 2020) follows a pedagogical perspective based on the DigCompOrg framework (Kampylis et al., 2015) to enable educational organizations to engage in collective reflection on how they have integrated digital technologies in their practice.

This calls for a reconsideration of university teachers' role and pedagogical models, in order to preserve the purpose and core values of tertiary education and maintain a balance between educational mission and technological innovation. It is suggested that teachers shift their role from traditional instructors to mentors and facilitators, fostering environments where students see value in attending classes and engaging with teachers and peers (Barros et al., 2023). Opportunities for meaningful discussions and emotional support, which are crucial for holistic learning experiences and to develop curiosity and critical thinking, should remain at the core of the teaching process, ensuring a harmonious integration of AI tools because emphasis is placed on the process and not (solely) on the outcome.

The use of generative AI for collaborative learning

Collaborative learning, where students work together to achieve common learning goals, would seem to be a privileged approach to place knowledge and learning in this new overall landscape. It facilitates collaborative exploration and comprehension of concepts, leading to deeper insights beyond conventional instructional approaches. It emphasizes the significance of social engagement and collective effort in the learning process. This approach cultivates competencies like effective communication, analytical reasoning and creative problem-solving (Mena-Guacas et al., 2023).

The use of generative AI for collaborative learning is a recent phenomenon: it seems to offer several advantages for teachers and students (Tan et al., 2022). One of the main contributions is the ability to stimulate creativity and innovation (Benvenuti et al., 2023). Through the generation of original content, generative AI can inspire students to explore new ideas and approaches, encouraging diversity of thinking and experimentation. Generative AI-powered tools can generate learning materials tailored to cooperative activities and offer instantaneous feedback and clarification to students as they engage in cooperative learning tasks. For example, if a student poses a question or expresses confusion about a concept, an AI-powered chatbot can provide immediate responses, explanations, or additional examples to help clarify the topic and support the student's understanding. This real-time assistance ensures that students receive timely support to address their learning needs and maintain momentum in their collaborative work. Or even, an AI-powered tutoring system can break down a complex problem into smaller, more manageable steps and provide step-by-step guidance to help students progress toward a solution collaboratively.

A second crucial aspect is the ability of generative AI to facilitate collaboration and knowledge sharing among students. AI algorithms can assist in forming heterogeneous groups based on students' skills, interests, or learning styles. By optimizing group composition, AI can promote effective collaboration and maximize learning outcomes. Then, through digital platforms that integrate AI tools, students can work together to create projects, documents or presentations, with the assistance of technology in information processing and synthesis. AI-powered assessment tools can automatically evaluate students' contributions to collaborative activities, such as group discussions or project work and provide detailed feedback based on predefined criteria or learning objectives. By providing feedback on both individual and group performance, AI-powered tools can help students reflect on their collaborative skills and identify areas for improvement, fostering a culture of continuous learning and development within cooperative learning teams. AI algorithms can also dynamically adjust group composition based on real-time feedback and performance data.

Generative AI can support learning customization by adapting teaching materials to students' specific needs (Hartley et al., 2024). Using machine-learning algorithms, AI can analyse students' progress and suggest relevant content and activities appropriate to their level of competence and learning preferences. AI systems can understand individual students' strengths, weaknesses, and learning styles, enabling the generation of learning materials that are highly relevant and engaging: some students may prefer visual learning, while others may excel with auditory or kinaesthetic learning approaches. AI algorithms can analyse students' interactions with learning materials, such as their response times, preferences for multimedia content and performance on different types of activities, to tailor the presentation and delivery of educational content accordingly. Additionally, AI-generated content can be translated into multiple languages, making educational materials more accessible to diverse student populations. So, AI-powered tools can enhance the accessibility and diversity of learning resources in cooperative learning environments by creating a wide range of multimedia content, including text, images, videos, and interactive simulations, to accommodate different learning preferences and abilities.

By leveraging the power of AI, educators can create learning environments that facilitate meaningful peer-to-peer interactions, foster collaboration and teamwork and empower students to excel in collaborative learning environments. Nonetheless, although there are manifold advantages of AI in education, it is imperative to proceed with caution when integrating it and carefully weigh the ethical considerations

(Gallent-Torres et al., 2023). Additionally, it is crucial to guarantee that AI systems are crafted to enhance and assist human educators and students rather than supplant them. This implies the necessity to ask profound inquiries regarding one's identity, the concept of self, the essence of knowledge, and the acquisition thereof (Lodge et al., 2023).

AI tools for knowledge access and processing

We therefore turn to discuss some still unresolved issues of the most commonly used tools based on generative AI which, in today's academic contexts, aim at facilitating and accelerating access and processing of scientific knowledge.

The first problem relates to the training datasets of generative AIs, which, combined with probabilistic algorithms, strongly condition and guide their production. While a huge amount of data is necessary to obtain satisfactory results, the necessary selection of sources can lead to inaccurate, erroneous, misleading or even dangerous answers from the chatbot. In fact, the large language models that underpin these systems seem almost by their very nature to be constantly exposed to human and machine biases, right from the composition and training of the datasets. To give just a few examples: the lack of transparency and non-neutrality in the selection of sources and the labelling of data by human operators; the inevitable reduction in the resolution of the information generated by the machine in order to be able to interpret these huge amounts of data and make them usable, through automatic categorization and the stratified identification of correlations by successive approximations. Such procedures of cumulative information functionalization lead to the loss of the differences and anomalies present in the data sets, anomalies which in certain cases may even have a heuristic value, acting as an antidote to the risk of single thinking.

A second problem, partly related to the previous one, is the phenomenon that has been inaccurately described as 'hallucination', whereby these tools sometimes invent information or produce answers that are even convincingly written but completely unfounded, or in other cases end up generating illegal, offensive or discriminatory content. The correction of such hallucinations, given the prohibitive cost of retraining the models, is often entrusted to a phantom and underpaid workforce, whose task is to label any errors made by the generative AIs, training them with a kind of negative reinforcement to drastically reduce the likelihood of such 'hallucinations' being repeated. Such labelling operations, while tactically solving some of the short-term problems that plague chatbots, may paradoxically become a further source of bias for the system due to the structural biases that characterize the human operators in charge of such actions and the cultural pressures to which they are voluntarily or involuntarily subjected.

An interesting attempt to overcome, or at least mitigate, the above problems has been made by Consensus, an application based on GPT-4 trained on over 210 million scientific papers and articles from Semantic Scholar. According to https://consensus.app/, the app was created with the aim of making expert knowledge accessible to all. The application is still in beta, but when queried it is already able to provide a mini review of the scientific literature related to the question asked. It has a clean and user-friendly interface and, on request, can also produce short reviews based on a selected number of scientific articles. It is also possible to ask questions in the form of yes/no answers, against which the app returns a graph expressing the degree of consensus of the scientific community on the topic. The developers seem to be aware of the limitations of these tools, as evidenced by several warnings on the site urging caution and verification of the results generated by the app. Nevertheless, the app is already being marketed with different subscription formulas, replicating the business model already present in other well-known generative AIs. Another application similar to Consensus, but with its own peculiarities, is Elicit (https://elicit.com/), which has a dataset of over 125 million scientific articles. In March 2024, it was enriched with new tabular functionalities, such as the possibility to compare and contrast documents, to summarize several documents according to a specific dimension (e.g. their methodology), to ask clarification questions on a single article or on discussion topics, and to critique an article.

These are promising tools to support scientific research and are constantly evolving, but there are still some unsettled issues, first and foremost that of a hegemonic risk in accessing knowledge. Given the enormous and growing number of documents available, we need more than ever to trust on reliable navigation maps to identify the most relevant ones, but the frequent opacity of the AI systems through which we access knowledge risks weakening the trust we can place in them. Moreover, a model based on probabilistically calculated consensus deeply challenges the epistemology of different knowledge. Rankings based on popularity and authority (based on the number of citations of a scientific article and the prestige of the journal in which it is published), or in any case based on other more or less explicit criteria, could lead to a kind of 'knowledge bubble', in which those who are more visible become more and more visible and receive more and more citations, thus increasing their own success and perhaps relegating to algorithmic oblivion studies that are of quality but not sufficiently visible to set trends. There is also a risk of homologation of knowledge if such tools are systematically used as the main source of research, which is encouraged by their extreme ease of use.

An even more advanced tool for scientific writing is Jenni (https://app.jenni.ai/), which is able to draft a scientific article very quickly from a sufficiently articulated prompt. The most obvious advantage of using this tool (which claims to already serve more than 12,000 researchers) is a considerable saving of time in the drafting of a text accompanied by pre-selected citations, but the doubt remains that, like other generative AIs, it may end up consolidating a functionalist drift of knowledge, according to the motto 'publish or perish', which has sometimes led some researchers to sacrifice the quality or originality of their scientific production on the altar of quantity and regularity of publication. It should also be noted that these co-authoring tools have a retroactive effect on the human author, at least partially altering his or her thinking and beliefs (Jakesch et al., 2023). The question also remains as to whether, in the long run, they do not end up weakening the structuring of critical-reflective thinking, which requires long periods of time that are certainly not aligned with the rhythms imposed by the now hegemonic imperative (even in many universities) of consumerist productivity.

A third and final tool we consider is Vectara (https://console.vectara.com/), which, unlike the previous ones, allows the generative AI to be trained on a set of documents chosen by the user and to implement an interface to query the chatbot on the chosen corpus of data. This aspect, although it requires additional technical work, could be interesting for universities in several ways, from the creation of document collections aimed at technical-administrative support for students, to the creation of specialized thematic databases for groups or research projects. Preliminary tests carried out by us on a limited dataset have shown a certain reliability of the tool, which correctly cites the sources it has consulted when responding to user queries.

Finally, it is worth pointing out another critical element common to all these instruments. Even without putting utopian or dystopian accents on the various generative AIs, it is worth stressing their profoundly retrotopic character: we are faced with autonomous agents that are surprising but basically only capable of summarizing, assembling and rewriting in a thousand different ways the knowledge already produced by humans, expressing a linguistic generativity that is infinite but incapable of real innovation. These unconscious nooscopes, which base their fortune on the extractivism of knowledge (Joler & Pasquinelli, 2020), require from the scientific community an additional critical reflection capable of unmasking their deformations and biases. These are not too dissimilar to those that also characterize human beings, but the mimetic play and supposed neutrality of machines may give them even more credit than we are used to giving our human fellows, These are not too dissimilar to those that also characterize human beings, but, through the mimetic game and the supposed neutrality of machines, they may even enjoy more credit than we are used to granting our fellow humans, although their actual creative contribution is decidedly low (Nguyen Thanh et al., 2023). We should also point out an epistemic leap made by these new tools: the digital academic databases (such as Google Scholar or the paid ones published by various editors) act as search engines between different papers and still allow the user to select the ones that interest him, albeit from a list ordered according to relevance criteria established by the algorithm; the generative AIs discussed here, on the other hand, propose texts with independently selected citations, deciding which others to omit without even listing them. The texts produced in this way may well have their own internal coherence and logical credibility, but at the same time we are faced with a further reduction of human agency and scientific responsibility.

Information, entropy, and meaning in human and artificial intelligence

As emphasized in the previous sections, the introduction of generative AI in education had an impressive impact on both teaching strategies and collaborative learning (Roll & Wylie, 2016). Nevertheless, it is worth noting that the enormous flow of information that the AI can process does not necessarily involve an equal generation of new meanings (Adriaans & van Benthem, 2008). Thus, what we feel as a lack of 'creativity' in AI with respect to our intelligence clearly demonstrates that our account of intelligence is far from being univocal (Mitchell, 2020). Overall, we suggest that the concept of intelligence should be defined by the capacity of a certain (human or artificial) system of handling – that is, combining, synthetizing, communicating, etc. – a certain amount of information.

Let us shortly discuss this view in order to demonstrate what is really at stake with AI's introduction in education. It seems uncontroversial that there are three main stances in the technical literature on information theories: a) knowledge, logic, what is conveyed in informative answers; b) probabilistic, theoretic information, measured quantitatively; c) algorithmic, code compression, measured quantitatively. Oversimplifying a bit, (a) is the world of epistemic logic and linguistic semantics, (b) that of Shannon's (1948) information theory, and (c) that of Kolmogorov's (1965) theory complexity, linked to the foundations of computation. Rather than being opposing domains, they offer three complementary perspectives of the same concept of information, like three clusters of themes and research styles.

However, provided that our contribution focuses on education, and once assumed that education is deeply intertwined to communication, here we mainly consider the stance b). Thus, in Shannon's view, information may be encoded in a *range of possibilities*: brief, the different ways the real situation might be. For instance, at the start of a card game, the range consists of the different possible deals of the cards. Numerically, this view reflects in the standard representation of information in bits being the (weighted) base-two logarithm of the size of the range. More dynamically, on this view, new information is that which reduces the current range. In other words, the more information becomes precise, the more its range of possibilities decreases. This is the standard logical sense of information in which a proposition P *updates* the current set of words W to (w in W/w makes P true). This notion is relative to a 'logical space' describing the options. It is also relative to agents, since the update happens to what they know about the world. According to this view, information always emerges as a restriction of the range of possibilities. In physical language, information results from the limitation of entropy, that is, on the choice of the sender to communicate a particular meaning oriented at a specific feedback.

As a matter of fact, the probabilistic account of information as a reduction of entropy requires a precise distinction between information and meaning. Indeed, whereas information reduces the infinite range of its possibilities in the shape of *data*, meaning results from a manifold of intentional acts (Searle, 1950). Therefore, meaning is always a process throughout which information becomes significant for one or more subjects. It is precisely along this process that, on the one hand, information acquires its educational relevance, although, on the other hand, it remains exposed to misunderstandings, manipulations, alterations, etc. Regardless of its logical consistence, information can be deeply significant for many people or totally meaningless: on closer inspection, the definition of intelligence we suggested above, as 'the capacity of a system of handling information' is to be specified as 'the capacity of a system of conferring meaning to information'.

According to this analysis, the distinction between information and meaning affects both human and artificial intelligence. In such a view, a wide transdisciplinary programme of research is needed about the complex structural features of meaning-attribution. Provided that only meaning-attribution produces feedback, only an archaeological approach to human and artificial intelligence is in a position to shed light on the future of AI in education. In other words, what is really at stake with AI is an in-depth comprehension of how both human mind and AI elaborate meaning from information. From this standpoint, the very popular opposition between natural and artificial intelligence should shift into a new framework where natural and artificial intelligence, both keeping their peculiarity, are deeply intertwined.

In this sense, Malabou (2019) developed a very insightful account of evolution of intelligence, where AI turns out to be a possible extension of human mind. Malabou's approach is based upon three metamorphoses: (a) the characterization of intelligence as a measurable entity that can be assessed with tests and is associated with IQ; (b) intelligence as epigeneticism; and, finally, (c) the age of intelligence becoming automatic once and for all as a result of removal of the rigid frontiers between nature and artifice. Far from reducing to a simple 'robotization', the increasingly refined simulation of 'natural' intelligence fosters a new approach to human intelligence, which would reveal the essential nature of its complicity with technological simulation. In Malabou's words,

> in this time of 'cognitive capitalism,' with the threat of a destruction of humanity as a result of the achievements of AI and the fragility of the notion of collective intelligence, it is not possible to embrace the upcoming

changes without developing new logics of resistance as we move from the second metamorphosis to the third. But this resistance must in no way negate the active exploration of the new configurations of meaning opened today by AI and its unprecedented alliance with biology, philosophy, and cybernetics. (2019, p. 16)

Conclusions

The integration of generative AI into university education presents a paradigm shift with significant implications. The potential of ChatGPT and similar technologies to revolutionize learning experiences through personalization and accessibility is immense. The integration of generative AI into collaborative learning environments has the potential to become a catalyst for innovation in knowledge acquisition. In particular, it may facilitate dynamic and interactive learning experiences that are responsive to the needs of each student, promoting an inclusive and supportive educational atmosphere.

However, the adoption of generative AI tools must be approached with caution, considering the pedagogical, ethical and practical challenges they pose. We have reviewed some still unresolved issues, related to the selection of sources to be included in the training sets, to the lack of transparency, to the management of distortions and biases. In addition, despite the capabilities of generative AI in processing vast amounts of information, it often lacks the ability to generate new meanings. Meaning-attribution is crucial for both human and artificial intelligence to confer significance to information. Therefore, regardless of the further development of these and other tools, human criticality, creativity and ethics, coupled with careful oversight and recurrent verification, remain and will remain fundamental elements for the advancement of science and humanity in the various and complementary fields of knowledge.

As university institutions move forward and recognize the potential of generative AI to revolutionize the way we learn, collaborate, and solve problems together, it is imperative that they also foster digital literacy and critical thinking skills among students and educators alike, ensuring that generative AI serves as a complement to, rather than a replacement for, the human element in education. More globally, universities should position themselves as a learning community which promotes a comprehensive reflection on meaning-attribution, as achieved both by humans and by AIs, preparing them for a future where AI is a ubiquitous part of life and work.

References

Adriaans, P., & van Benthem, J. (2008). *Philosophy of information*. Elsevier.

Al-Mughairi, H., & Bhaskar, P. (2024). Exploring the factors affecting the adoption AI techniques in higher education: Insights from teachers' perspectives on ChatGPT. *Journal of Research in Innovative Teaching & Learning*. https://doi.org/10.1108/JRIT-09-2023-0129

Aydin, Ö., & Karaarslan, E. (2023). Is ChatGPT leading generative AI? What is beyond expectations? *Academic Platform Journal of Engineering and Smart Systems, 11*(3), 118–134.

Bahroun, Z., Anane, C., Ahmed, V., & Zacca, A. (2023). Transforming education: A comprehensive review of generative artificial intelligence in educational settings through bibliometric and content analysis. *Sustainability, 15*(17), 12983.

Barros, A., Prasad, A., & Śliwa, M. (2023). Generative artificial intelligence and academia: Implication for research, teaching and service. *Management Learning, 54*(5), 597–604.

Bearman, M., & Ajjawi, R. (2023). Learning to work with the black box: Pedagogy for a world with artificial intelligence. *British Journal of Educational Technology, 54*(5), 1160–1173.

Benvenuti, M., Cangelosi, A., Weinberger, A., Mazzoni, E., Benassi, M., Barbaresi, M., & Orsoni, M. (2023). Artificial intelligence and human behavioral development: A perspective on new skills and competences acquisition for the educational context. *Computers in Human Behavior, 148*, 107903.

European Commission. (2020). SELFIE website. https://education.ec.europa.eu/selfie

Gallent Torres, C., Zapata-González, A., & Ortego-Hernando, J. L. (2023). The impact of Generative Artificial Intelligence in higher education: A focus on ethics and academic integrity. *RELIEVE, 29*(2), 1–19.

Giannoutsou, N., Ioannou, A., Timotheou, S., Miliou, O., Dimitriadis, Y., Cachia, R., Villagrá- Sobrino, S., & Martínez-Monéz, A. (2024). *Unpacking the impact of digital technologies in education*. Publications Office of the European Union.

Grájeda, A., Burgos, J., Córdova, P., & Sanjinés, A. (2024). Assessing student-perceived impact of using artificial intelligence tools: Construction of a synthetic index of application in higher education. *Cogent Education*, *11*(1), 2287917.

Hartley, K., Hayak, M., & Ko, U. H. (2024). Artificial intelligence supporting independent student learning: An evaluative case study of ChatGPT and learning to code. *Education Sciences*, *14*(2), 120.

Jakesch, M., Bhat, A., Buschek, D., Zalmanson, L., & Naaman, M. (2023). Co-writing with opinionated language models affects users' views. *Proceedings of the 2023 CHI Conference on Human Factors in Computing Systems, Hamburg, Germany*, pp. 1–15.

Joler, V., & Pasquinelli, M. (2020). *The nooscope manifested: Artificial intelligence as instrument of knowledge extractivism*. https://nooscope.ai/

Kampylis, P., Punie, Y., & Devine, J. (2015). *Promoting effective digital-age learning – A European framework for digitally-competent educational organizations* (No. JRC98209). Joint Research Centre (Seville site).

Kolmogorov, A. (1965) Three approaches to the quantitative definition of information. *Problems Inform. Transmission*, *1*(I), 17.

Lodge, J. M., de Barba, P., & Broadbent, J. (2023). Learning with generative artificial intelligence within a network of co-regulation. *Journal of University Teaching and Learning Practice*, *20*(7), 1–10.

Malabou, C. (2019). *Morphing intelligence. From IQ measurement to artificial brains*. Columbia University Press.

Mena-Guacas, A. F., Urueña Rodríguez, J. A., Santana Trujillo, D. M., Gómez-Galán, J., & López-Meneses, E. (2023). Collaborative learning and skill development for educational growth of artificial intelligence: A systematic review. *Contemporary Educational Technology*, *15*(3), ep428.

Mitchell, M. (2020). *Artificial intelligence. A guide for thinking humans*. Pelican.

Moore, S., & Kuol, N. (2007). Matters of the heart: Exploring the emotional dimensions of educational experience in recollected accounts of excellent teaching. *International Journal for Academic Development*, *12*(2), 87–98.

Moscardini, A. O., Strachan, R., & Vlasova, T. (2022). The role of universities in modern society. *Studies in Higher Education*, *47*(4), 812–830.

Nguyen Thanh, B., Vo, D. T. H., Nguyen Nhat, M., Pham, T. T. T., Thai Trung, H., & Ha Xuan, S. (2023). Race with the machines: Assessing the capability of generative AI in solving authentic assessments. *Australasian Journal of Educational Technology, 39*(5), 59–81.

OpenAI. (2022). *Chatgpt: Optimizing language models for dialogue.*

Roll, I., & Wylie, R. (2016). Evolution and revolution in artificial intelligence in education. *International Journal of Artificial Intelligence in Education, 26*(2), 582–599.

Tan, S. C., Lee, A. V. Y., & Lee, M. (2022). A systematic review of artificial intelligence techniques for collaborative learning over the past two decades. *Computers and Education: Artificial Intelligence, 3*, 100097.

Chapter 7

Higher Education Institutions in the digital age: Polyhedral reflections from the perspective of social responsibility

Francisco De Ferari Correa,
Fernando Vergara Henríquez, and
Pedro Pablo Achondo Moya

Abstract: In the digital age, universities have a social responsibility to adapt to the changing demands of their times and of scientific and theoretical paradigms and to prepare their academics and students for a dynamic working environment. This involves integrating educational technologies, fostering digital inclusion and promoting equity of access to education. In addition, institutions should cultivate digital ethics, cybersecurity and contribute to sustainable development through research and programmes that address contemporary challenges. University Social Responsibility (USR) involves not only academic education but also the positive impact on society and the promotion of ethical values in the digital age. The emerging questions regarding the human situation within these transformations must be addressed from ethical values that are applied in a social responsibility.

Keywords: Higher education institutions, Universities, University social responsibility, Educational technologies, Ethical values, Digital age

Introduction: The digital age as a challenge and deep transformation

This chapter seeks to present the challenges that the digital era poses to Higher Education Institutions (HEIs) and, at the same time, to present the theoretical-practical notion of University Social Responsibility (USR) as an ethical mechanism to combat the gaps, excesses and injustices that the digital era is radicalizing. We do so in a 'polyhedral' way, to quote Pope Francis and his ecclesiological image (EG 236), which assumes the difference and, at the same time, the horizontality of social relations. Thinking in the way of the polyhedron means balancing judgements, encouraging hope and embracing diversity; as well as understanding that different models of HEIs and notions of USR cooperate, collaborate and complement each other's contributions in this demanding and creative digital age.

The digital era can be understood instrumentally as the current period in human history characterized by the convergence of information and communication technologies (ICTs) and their integration into all aspects of personal existence, social, cultural and economic life. It began at the end of the twentieth century with the digital revolution, which marked the transition from analogue to digital technologies. Its main features are the widespread use of ICTs: digital technologies such as the Internet, computers, smartphones and social networks, which have become ubiquitous tools in everyday life. It also involves mass access to information, communication that defies distances and platforms for interaction and exchange between people all over the world. This has permeated the economy, culture, the world of work, politics, and citizen participation, as well as the way of conceiving education and life in general. The digital era also presents new challenges, such as digital and technological divides, fake news, cybersecurity, misinformation, lack of clarity in the use of personal and institutional data, artificial intelligence, cyber-violence, harassment, and scams; in short, presents the urgent need for new ethical and moral approaches and a greater democratization of the tools, their uses and decisions that concern everyone.

The Spanish philosopher Daniel Innerarity (2022), makes a stark and realistic diagnosis of the situation of the contemporary subject with respect to the knowledge and its rational capacity to construct knowledge in the face of the 'deregulation of the cognitive market' in a scenario of information and computer chaos, calling it a technopopulism that dissolves pluralism with the promise of solving all the human problems that it paradoxically causes only with more technology; our times are times of uncertainty where knowledge is no guarantee of trust, peace and coexistence, because 'the more we know collectively, the less self-sufficient we are individually'. We blindly trust the theories coming from science, but we radically distrust the other, an equation that only disorients and makes us 'oscillate between an excessive naivety and a lack of control of our critical capacities'. Paradoxically, our 'overburdened subjectivity' puts us in a 'situation of innocent minority (to use Kant's famous expression, *a sensu contrario*)'. The advance in knowledge, in the rational exercise of criticism, in the theoretical dimension of existence, today, 'makes us, at the same time, wiser and more ignorant' (2022, p. 13).

Meanwhile, Byung-Chul Han (2014a, 2014b, 2014c, 2018) has worked on the rationality that emerges under the digital era, its social consequences and various limitations and problems. For Han, the digital era, unlike the pre-digital era, which we could call industrial or analogue, no longer consists of a form of control over bodies, as Foucault (2007) demonstrated, but over the mind (Han, 2014c). New technologies, and, in particular, smartphones and social networks and, more recently, artificial intelligence, have led to a myriad of consequences, many of them unthinkable.

The mysterious allure that technologies provoke should come as no surprise. The possibilities are astonishing and well known. Everything is within reach of a click: an online course, information about any culture, the translation of a piece of writing, music from anywhere in the world, libraries, knowledge and whatever else one can imagine. The digital era is the era of radical availability and opens its doors to what was previously inaccessible to the majority, democratizing access, but deepening existential differences and precariousness. In this sense, it can be said that an unprecedented cultural democratization is taking place. Although this statement has nuances because access to the tools is not available to everyone, nor are the contents. Hence the suspicions of the philosopher Byung-Chul Han, who says that this dazzle is not at all naïve. Behind all this maelstrom of information, contacts and data circulation, there are specific people who have made decisions based on self-interested and guided by ends that are not always declared and that are found within a socio-economic and commercial system associated with profit, profit and discarding (Francisco, 2013). In this sense, the digital era is eminently economic rather than social.

Han's (2018, 2014a) analysis argues that the digital age has exacerbated a culture of spectacle and entertainment, on the one hand; and that under the prism of transparency, everything is published, commented on, shared, on the other hand. Transparency has led to the loss of mystery. Nothing remains in the shadows or undiscovered. Everything becomes evident. In the same way, and what is most problematic in terms of higher education, has to do with the speed, rapidity and instantaneity of digital information. This has led to the disappearance of narrative and exacerbated the volume of consumption. In other words, the digital age is a time when it is all about data, it is a numerical age. Data does not tell a story, there is no narrative, as Byung-Chul Han (2014c) would say. In this sense, Pope Francis touches on a key point in his Message XLIX[1] (2015) of the Day of Social Communications. Francis invites us to 'relearn how to narrate': *Narrating means that our lives are interwoven in a unitary plot, that the voices are multiple and that each one is irreplaceable.*

In the same vein, the Korean philosopher warns of the risk that *the networked, digitised subject is a panopticon of itself; an entrepreneur of itself that exploits itself* (2014c, p. 93). Han is critical of so-called Big Data – another name for the digital age – alluding to its lack of spirit, an additive mechanism devoid of imagination and creativity. In a world where the improbable, the unknown, the surprising, the singular, the event, the encounter do not happen; neither will history and therefore the future. Such a world is a world blind to the future. Hence the importance that not all of our world (or personal and interpersonal reality) is within this new digital forum.

On the other hand, the volume of information and data circulation has been generating an intoxicated society. This is manifested in the number of diseases that affect the human psyche, such as the diseases of the twenty-first century (Han, 2014b). This fact correlates in the social and university movement fighting for better mental health. The shrinking of time has hurried life and the way we communicate and relate to each other. That is why we are, Byung-Chul Han (2014b) says, a society of the tired. Lonely and tired we wander the digital universe, mentally exhausted and self-compelled to respond, post, show up, be present and be recognized.

A clear challenge for university work and higher education will be to leave time for reflection, for thinking, because it is an exercise that requires time, not instantaneity or speed. The speed of thought must not be replaced by the instantaneousness of data or algorithms, as this makes it impossible to understand reality between humans. Reflection, conversation, and slow and meditated reading are transformed into counter-cultural activities to the speed of the digital. To what extent does university social responsibility allow us to balance the digital maelstrom

---

[1]   http://w2.vatican.va/content/francesco/es/messages/communications.index.html

and make it possible for higher education institutions not to lose their reflective, humanist, social and liberating character?

The university in the digital era

The digital era and the interconnected society challenge higher education with the demand for new knowledge and the performance of new roles (Álvarez & Prieto, 2023). The accelerated digital transformations, the new information-communication technologies, artificial intelligence and the entire ecosystem of relationships that are being established have a global scope and there is no higher education institution that has not been challenged in this respect, opening up a world of possibilities and risks in which they must assume a proactive and leading role.

As Álvarez and Prieto (2023) state, the integration and incorporation of technological advances in higher education not only transforms teaching-learning methodologies, but also redefines the role and functions of HEIs in the digital society and has an impact on all the substantive functions of the institutions' being and work. In many of the institutions, the processes of student follow-up have been automated, digital competences have been incorporated into the graduate profiles of the degree programmes, data mechanisms have been developed for the characterization of students in order to take timely measures in the event of student dropout, etc. Platforms are contracted to keep students informed and to keep graduates and employers of study institutions loyal. Postgraduate and continuing education programmes delivered remotely via purpose-built educational platforms are increasingly common.

Despite the enormous possibilities for inclusion that new technologies and the digital age offer, they can widen gaps and exacerbate existing inequalities in society. Access to technology and the skills to use it is not homogenous across a city, country or region. The Covid-19 pandemic was a clear expression of this. A significant number of students not only did not have access to a good internet signal, but also to equipment that would allow them to continue their studies in a normal way. These facts deepened, to a large extent, the structural inequalities of our societies. This was recently expressed by the participants in the follow-up meeting to the III Regional Conference on Higher Education in Latin America and the Caribbean – CRES+5 – held in March 2024 in Brazil:

Faced with this (COVID), higher education institutions implemented training plans and strategies, mostly based on the use of Information and Communication Technologies (ICT), for which teachers and students were not prepared, or only had incipient experience, This, together with the existence of a digital divide, demotivation and disorientation, ended up creating more school dropouts, rejection of virtuality, and an isolated and individualistic training process, which added to the already present affective and psychological problems experienced by the onslaught of the pandemic. (Declaration CRES+5, 2024)

Communities that lack adequate technological infrastructure or the necessary digital skills are at risk of being further marginalized in an increasingly digitized education system (Álvarez & Prieto, 2023).

University Social Responsibility (USR) as a way of being-doing-inhabiting universities

Higher education has undergone rapid and significant changes in the way it understands itself as well as in the social and public role that the societies in which it is embedded assign to it. The diversity of social, political, cultural and economic processes external to the institutions not only permeate their way of doing or responding to society but, above all, their way of being a higher education institution. HEIs experience new demands within their institutional project, that is, all these changes require educational institutions to review and transform their institutional projects (Mission/Vision), adapting their substantive functions: teaching, research, outreach and university management, to the challenges external to them.

University Social Responsibility (USR) has been one of the ways in which HEIs have understood their place in society. Globally, although with special development in Latin America and the Caribbean, the concept of USR has been consolidated over the last 20 years (De la Cruz, 2013; Gaete, 2011; Larrán & Andrades, 2015; Martí & Martí-Vilar, 2013) as a way not only of doing HEIs but also of being and inhabiting them. The way in which each institution understands SR will vary according to its own model of understanding as well as its identity and institutional project. We briefly present four models:

(A) A way of putting certain values and principles into practice

The term USR is understood as the implementation of certain fundamental values and principles of institutional projects. This approach can
be seen very clearly in those institutions of Christian-Catholic inspiration, associating USR with the principles of the Church's social thought.
The iconic Proyecto Universidad Construye País developed in Chile
between 2001–2006 defined USR as a certain capacity of HEIs to 'disseminate and put into practice a set of principles and values' which it categorizes as values at the personal, social and university levels (UCP, 26).

(B) A way to contribute to the country's development and/or social transformation

A central aspect of the social responsibility of HEIs is their public
commitment or service to communities. This approach will reinforce the
idea that the concept of USR is a way of putting into practice in the territories and communities the transformative aspiration of university being
and doing.[2] This approach focuses on the ultimate purpose of university being-doing, which is to contribute to the social and environmental
development of the country, although it does not necessarily question
those structures that have generated and continue to generate injustices
(De la Cruz, 2013). This approach is related to the dimension of linking
with the environment or social projection of the work of HEIs and is
expressed very clearly in the growing commitment of HEIs to the 2030
Sustainable Development Goals.

(C) A way to measure and manage external and internal impacts

This approach to USR will focus on managing the external and internal impacts of its work in line with other global movements such as
Corporate Social Responsibility. This way of understanding USR has
had a lot of adherence with the influence of the World Bank and the
Inter-American Development Bank in education policies for more than
30 years in the region. Efforts are based on the generation of goals and

---

[2]   There are different emphases or approaches in this regard. Some will reinforce
'Public engagement' as a contribution to public policies; others emphasize specific
projects at the service of communities (Community outreach); and others will
emphasize the training of students in social responsibility or commitment through
the curriculum (Civic engagement; cf. Irarrázaval, 2020, pp. 296–323).

compliance indicators, as well as on accountability processes expressed in institutional reports and sustainability reports. This approach also guides HEIs to improve their governance and institutional management, supported by the advances produced by digitization and associated tools for quality assurance and continuous improvement.

(D) A way to dialogue with stakeholders

Finally, a fairly widespread approach to USR in recent years is the one that understands this concept as a model of management and participation of the different groups that interact in and with HEIs. The theory underlying this understanding of USR is the idea of stakeholders, which has been widely developed over the last 50 years (Gaete, 2011; Larraín & Andrades, 2015). This approach considers the various groups and individuals affected in one way or another by the existence and action of HEIs since they have legitimate expectations in relation to the functioning of institutions vis-à-vis society. For these reasons, institutions must reorganize their functioning to provide mechanisms for listening to and participation of stakeholders, that is, they must take into account the leadership, academic and management staff, students, graduates, community partners, public entities and the productive sector, etc.

USR in the digital era as an element of identity for Catholic HEIs

University Social Responsibility as a humanist agent of individual and collective formation and transformation for the common good, sustained by a relational anthropology, that is to say, a conception centred on the person with the other as its horizon, is presented as a central element in Christian-inspired HEIs.

Since its origins, the Catholic university has been committed to contributing to the development of society by training professionals who are involved in their environment and socially responsible in their life and work in the tradition of the Gospel. This commitment translates into concrete, comprehensive, sustainable, relevant and evaluable responses, both from teaching, research, links with the environment and management of the development needs demanded by the different communities that make up the environment with which the institution interacts. In this way Pope Francis (2024) urged the delegation of the

International Federation of Catholic Universities in the context of its anniversary:

> We must always ask ourselves: what is the purpose of our science? What is the transformative potential of the knowledge we produce? What and whom do we serve? Neutrality is an illusion. Therefore, a Catholic university has to make decisions, and these decisions must reflect the Gospel. It must take a stand and demonstrate it by its actions in a transparent way, 'getting its hands dirty' evangelically in the transformation of the world and in the service of the human person.

In line with the above, the RSU has to do with an institutional response to the needs of today's society in which it is inserted: teaching, research, liaison and internal management. These functions are animated by the search for the promotion of justice, solidarity and equity through the inclusive construction of responses to the challenges of education in the context of integral and sustainable human development. HEIs are called to '*build intergenerational and intercultural alliances in favour of the care of the common home, of a vision of integral ecology that gives an effective response to the cry of the earth and the cry of the poor*' (Pope Francis, 2024).

The USSR invites us to a socially responsible solidarity that is not only called for by circumstance or improvisation, but also echoing the message of Pope John XXIII, it encourages us by his example to be aware of the demands of the common good, making it clear that they derive from the social conditions of each era and are closely linked to respect for and promotion of the integral development of the human person. Hence the concern for the formation of spaces of organized solidarity, articulated and closely linked to fraternity and a new system of social relations based on the common good. The concept of the common good is the best antidote, both theoretical and practical, to the indolent and insolent individualism of a modernity that is too triumphant in its rationalization, personalization and fragmentation, exacerbated today by the digital age.

For the university, the function of agent of social change means developing a dynamic process, a relevant and influential space that contributes to the integral growth of the individual and of society in accordance with its specific historical circumstances. For more than a century, this social requirement has been aimed at understanding, interpreting, preserving, reinforcing, promoting and disseminating national and regional cultures. In its service to society, the university must respond to the major problems of our time. In this way, different concepts have been used to describe the social function of the university, the most used being: social extension, social projection, social service and today *university social responsibility*, which, with their differences at the structural level of impact and modalities of practical application as lines of action.

As an institution, the university is dynamic and constantly renewing itself and exists for itself and for others, that is to say, the community of all the men and women who make it up. In the same way that this complicity and its influence on the human being it shelters is not an accident, but consubstantial to it, the University-Society link is not alien or derived from an act of institutional voluntarism but is rather an act of coherence and consequence with the very nature of the university institution animated by the search for human fulfilment.

In this way, University Social Responsibility is not seen as just another institutional dimension or point of view that is added to other existing ones in a complementary way and poses a series of challenges, but as a place of training and promotion of new sensibilities as well as institutional reflection-action inserted in the society of which it is part, in the problems that in the latter erode the quality of life, well-being and human coexistence in order to establish compatibility and coherence between discourse, action, reflection and the institutional mission. In the digitalized society, education for justice and solidarity, for respectful and collaborative coexistence must be provided.

Contributions of Pope Francis regarding Catholic HEIs and social responsibility

Pope Francis has referred on several occasions and has dedicated quite a few of his writings to the role of the Catholic University in the present time and in the face of the throwaway and digitalized culture. Here we present some of his approaches as inputs/challenges for the necessary reflection. As was seen in the introduction, it should be stressed that the challenge is not only theoretical but also practical and substantial, that is, it will require maintaining the Mission as a Catholic university in spite of the ever-changing scenarios and in the face of the growing commercial threat, the socio-cultural transformations and the entry of new anthropological conceptions. The HEI's approach to the digital age and its challenges should not be limited to analysing information or internal processes enhanced by digitalization but should rather trigger a profound reflection and transformation of its role in present and future society.

The challenge is global, that is, it challenges each member of the university community and commits them according to their own responsibility and professional capacity, as well as to the cultural character of the institution itself, with a focus on the centrality of the dignity of the human person. This is what Pope Francis said (2020) on the occasion of the launch of the Global Education Pact:

> To place the person, their value, their dignity, at the centre of all formal and informal educational processes, in order to highlight their own specificity, their beauty, their uniqueness and, at the same time, their capacity to relate to others and to the reality that surrounds them, rejecting those lifestyles that favour the spread of a throwaway culture.

The challenge is neutrality or impartiality, the danger of which is to dissolve the identity contours with which the university has been drawn since its beginnings. Thus Pope Francis (2024) urged the delegation of the International Federation of Catholic Universities in the context of its anniversary:

> We must always ask ourselves: what is the purpose of our science? What is the transformative potential of the knowledge we produce? What and whom do we serve? Neutrality is an illusion. Therefore, a Catholic university has to make decisions, and these decisions must reflect the Gospel. It must take a stand and demonstrate it by its actions in a transparent way, 'getting its hands dirty' evangelically in the transformation of the world and in the service of the human person.

The challenge is a matter of identity: to refocus education and training with young people and the local and national environment it serves as the beginning and end; the real contribution of the university will have to do with the human training of integral professionals as well as the generation of knowledge and active links with society in a bidirectional and committed way, in a changing era of accelerated changes and constant crises. This was critically diagnosed by Pope Francis in the Encyclical Laudato Si' (2015):

> Education is confronted with so-called rapidisation, which imprisons existence in the vortex of technological and digital speed, continually shifting reference points. In this context, identity itself loses consistency and psychological structure disintegrates in the face of an incessant mutation that 'contrasts the natural slowness of biological evolution'. (Laudato Si', 18)

The RSU challenge is to give meaning to professional education and training in a kind of complement of humanization expressed in integrality, commitment, solidarity and transformation. As Pope Francis said on the 57th World Day of Peace:

> Education in the use of forms of artificial intelligence should focus primarily on promoting critical thinking. Users of all ages, but especially young people, need to develop a capacity for discernment in the use of data and content obtained from the web or produced by artificial intelligence systems (...) Schools, universities and scientific societies are called upon to help students and professionals to take ownership of the social and ethical aspects of the development and use of the technology.

The challenge is to oppose the enthronement of individualism, utility and power in favour of truth, community and service. The responsibility of every Catholic university must be respected for its complementary contribution to the humanization and dignification of professional training. Francis expresses it in this way on the LVII World Day of Peace on 1 January 2024, n.6:

> The most advanced technical applications should not be used to facilitate the violent resolution of conflicts, but to pave the roads to peace. On a more positive note, if artificial intelligence were used to promote integral human development, it could introduce important innovations in agriculture, education and culture, an improvement in the standard of living of entire nations and peoples, the growth of human fraternity and social friendship. Ultimately, the way we use it to include the least, that is, the weakest and neediest of our brothers and sisters, is the measure of our humanity.

Conclusions: Responsible perspectives for Catholic universities in the digital age

The digital era, as we have seen, offers Catholic universities new and unprecedented tools to amplify their impact on society, as digital platforms make it possible to disseminate knowledge and University Social Responsibility projects to a wider significant territory through social networks, blogs, e-learning platforms and webinars, thus extending their initiatives and cooperation to a global audience and scale. In addition, it is possible to mobilize the university community, the significant territory it serves and society in general in promoting participation in USR projects such as volunteering, collections or awareness-raising events that make visible the universities' mission and their service to the various territories. In light of the above, Catholic universities can establish networks and alliances with other institutions through digital platforms to work together on University Social Responsibility projects.

The digital era also demands greater transparency, without forgetting the risks expressed by Byung-Chul Han (2014b) and better accountability in university social responsibility activities through the publication of reports that include and highlight their social and environmental impact, as well as through the use of digital tools for the evaluation and monitoring of projects, which allows universities to measure the impact of their initiatives, actions and activities and make adjustments to improve their effectiveness, ensuring the quality of their processes. The latter always requires institutional support for its members so as not to fall into a sort of data and numerical culture in university work.

On the other hand, interaction with stakeholders through digital platforms allows universities to receive comments and suggestions from the university community and society in general about their activities, enabling feedback and dialogue with the society in which it is inserted.

Finally, it is important to think about this relationship between University Social Responsibility and the digital era in the field of education, especially the training of responsible digital citizens with digital skills and a social conscience, including digital literacy in the curriculum or educational project, which allows students to develop the necessary skills to navigate the digital world in a responsible and critical manner; promoting the responsible use of digital technologies, teaching the university community about the risks and challenges of the digital age, such as cybercrime, misinformation and cyberbullying according to the core discipline with strong ethical underpinnings.

In short, the digital era offers universities a great opportunity to strengthen their commitment to social responsibility. The key lies in using digital tools responsibly and creatively to generate a positive impact on society because university education with social and responsible temperament must respond to the major challenge posed by today's society marked by individualism and inequality, by uncertainty and fragmentation, by proposing an education for fraternity and active citizenship of a reflective nature and critical awareness where people are endowed with a concern for social issues and for the development of their community. This requires an education for the construction of a meaning that gives unity to human existence, as Pope Francis calls for in Evangelii Gaudium: '*no to an economy of exclusion and inequality [because with] exclusion the very root of belonging to the society in which one lives is affected*' (n. 53) from '*the denial of the primacy of the human being*' (n. 55). The university, beyond offering training, professionalization and culture, must offer meaning, hope and truth: meaning in the face of the meaninglessness of the paradoxical contemporary culture; hope in the face of the apparent triumph of evil; and truth that is achieved in a dialogical, sustainable and supportive community.

The 'digital streets', in the words of Pope Francis (2013), are waiting for the society to seek out the newly wounded; they are also waiting for the Good Samaritan to come by again. They wait for God's tenderness to touch those who wander aimlessly – and without time – in these bustling 'streets'. There, HEIs in general and Catholic universities in particular have a task.

References

Álvarez, M., & Prieto, P. (2023). Presentación del dossier temático: 'La educación superior en la era digital'. *Revista Educación Superior y Sociedad*, *35*(2), 28–45. https://doi.org/10.54674/ess.v35i2.879

Baeza, J. (2021). La idea de Universidad en el Papa Francisco. *VERITAS*, *48*, 225–249.

Beltrán-Llevador, J., Íñigo-Bajo, E., & Mata-Segreda, A. (2014). La responsabilidad social universitaria, el reto de su construcción permanente. *La Revista Iberoamericana de Educación Superior*, *V*(14), 3–18.

De la Cruz, C. (2013). Los sentidos de la responsabilidad desde el prisma de la justicia: ¿quién es responsable de las injusticias estructurales de nuestra sociedad? *Sal Terrae*, *101*, 663–676.

Foucault, M. (2007). *Nacimiento de la biopolítica*. FCE.

Gaete, R. (2011). *Responsabilidad social universitaria: una nueva mirada a la relación de la universidad con la sociedad desde la perspectiva de las partes interesadas. Un estudio de caso* [Tesis Doctoral, Universidad de Valladolid, España].

Han, B.-Ch. (2018). *Buen entretenimiento*. Herder.

Han, B.-Ch. (2014a). *En el enjambre*. Herder.

Han, B.-Ch. (2014b). *La société de la fatigue*. Belval.

Han, B.-Ch. (2014c). *Psicopolítica*. Herder.

Innerarity, D. (2022). *La sociedad del desconocimiento*. Galaxia.

Irarrázaval, I. (2020). La vinculación universitaria con el medio y los mecanismos de reconocimiento académico. *Calidad en la educación, 52*, 296–323.

Larrán, J. M., & Andrades-Peña, F. (2015). Análisis de la responsabilidad social universitaria desde diferentes enfoques teóricos. *Revista Iberoamericana de Educación Superior (RIES)*, *VI*(15), 91–107. https://www.redalyc.org/pdf/2991/299133728005.pdf

Pacto Educativo Global. Vademecum en español. https://www.educationglobalcompact.org/resources/Risorse/vademecum-espanol.pdf

Papa Francisco. (2013). *Mensaje para la XLVII Jornada Mundial de las Comunicaciones Sociales 2013*.

Papa Francisco. (2023). *Diálogo con los Rectores de las Universidades de América Latina*.

Papa Francisco. (2024). *Discurso a la delegación de la Federación Internacional de Universidades Católicas (FIUC) con motivo de su centenario*.

Papa Francisco. (2024). *Mensaje para la celebración de la 57 Jornada Mundial de la Paz: Inteligencia artificial y paz*.

Proyecto Universidad construye País. (2006). *Responsabilidad Social Universitaria: Una manera de ser universidad, Santiago*.

UNESCO. (2023). Dossier temático: 'La educación superior en la era digital'. *Revista educación superior y sociedad, 35*(2).

UNESCO-IESALC. (2024). *Declaración de la CRES+5*. https://www.iesalc.unesco.org/2024/04/17/43313/

UNESCO-IESALC. (2008). El movimiento de responsabilidad social de la universidad: una comprensión novedosa de la misión universitaria. *Nueva Época, 13*(2).

Varios Autores. (2022). *Resignificación de la Responsabilidad Social. A 20 años del proyecto Universidad Construye País, Ediciones Universitarias de Valparaíso, Chile*. https://euv.cl/wp-content/uploads/2022/11/resignificacionrs.pdf

Chapter 8

AI and physician-patient relationship: The role of university teaching hospitals in mitigating depersonalization of healthcare in Africa

EMMANUEL WABANHU

Abstract: This paper examines the potential advantages and ethical concerns associated with the integration of AI into the medical education curricula in the university teaching hospitals and medical centres within the African context. It particularly addresses the central question of in what ways can university teaching hospitals and medical centres help to effectively mitigate the depersonalization associated with the use AI in medical and health education as well as in healthcare systems in Africa. Definitely, if it is not carefully and responsibly integrated in healthcare, AI has the capacity to strip healthcare in Africa of its human touch and the Ubuntu aspect, which emphasizes interconnectedness, community, and humaneness. This situation necessitates therefore university teaching hospitals and medical centres in Africa to embrace the ethical obligation to find a middle ground between the ethically responsible integration of AI in healthcare and the moral obligation to maintain the conventional doctor-patient relationship in the digital era. Faculties of health sciences in all the university teaching hospitals in Africa must ensure that they teach and produce medical graduates who prioritize safeguarding the Ubuntu aspect of medicine, the human interactions and empathy training and ethical considerations to ensure that they clearly understand the traditional significance of physician-patient relationships.

Keywords: physician-patient relationship, Ubuntu-centred medice, healthcare depersonalization, African universities, community life, ethical and anthropocentric AI, biomedical ethical training, transdisciplinary approach, vitalogy, moral tradition of abundant life

Introduction

Artificial intelligence (AI) technology is among the numerous innovations that have emerged in the digital age. The ethical implications of its implementation in diverse domains persist and have been a source of concern in healthcare (doctor-patient relationship), education (exam integrity), politics (democracy credibility), security (privacy), economics (intellectual property patent rights), and security (privacy). Thus, numerous academic institutions such as university teaching hospitals and medical centres, governments, non-governmental organizations, and businesses are concerned about the known and unknown outcomes of implementing AI in those fields. Overall, they are collectively troubled by the ethical dilemma surrounding the potential position and function of humans in the digital age, marked by the widespread integration of artificial intelligence across several domains.

This paper critically highlights the potential advantages and ethical concerns associated with the integration of AI into the medical education curricula in the university teaching hospitals and medical centres within the African context. It particularly addresses the central question of in what ways can university teaching hospitals and medical centres help to effectively mitigate the depersonalization associated with the use AI in medical and health education as well as in healthcare systems in Africa. If it is not carefully and responsibly integrated in healthcare, AI has the capacity to strip healthcare in Africa of its human touch and *Ubuntu* aspect which emphasizes interconnectedness, community, and humaneness. This situation necessitates therefore university teaching hospitals and medical centres in Africa to embrace the ethical obligation to find a middle ground between the ethically responsible integration of AI in healthcare and the moral obligation to maintain the conventional doctor-patient relationship in the digital era. Faculties of health sciences in all the university teaching hospitals in Africa must ensure that they teach and produce medical graduates who prioritize safeguarding the *Ubuntu* aspect of medicine, the human interactions and empathy training and ethical considerations to ensure that they clearly understand the traditional significance of physician-patient relationships. These encounters should involve physicians engaging with patients as concrete persons with dignity and rights, rather than treating them solely as clinical cases.

This paper will proceed as follows: (1) it briefly presents the notion of artificial intelligence as an invention of the digital age; (2) it highlights the potential opportunities and challenges associated with the integration of AI in the university teaching hospitals and in healthcare systems in Africa; (3) it argues for the reaffirmation of the Catholic-inspired preferential option for the physician-patient relationship in an AI age; and finally (4), it suggests some ways in which the university teaching hospitals in Africa can contribute to reaffirming the traditional physician-patient encounter in view of mitigating the depersonalization through promoting the *Ubuntu*-centred healthcare in the digital age. The paper ends with a brief conclusion.

Artificial intelligence: An invention of the digital age

The most recent development in computer science that mimics human intelligence is known as artificial intelligence (AI). It is a computational computer system that is capable of imitating human brain activity and carrying out operations that typically call for human intelligence. The tasks of perception, reasoning, learning, and decision-making are a few examples of these tasks which can be simulated by AI. It is in this context of its tasks that the Pontifical Academy for Life has defined AI as 'the ability of a machine to reproduce human capabilities, such as reasoning, learning, and planning. AI systems can adapt their behaviour by analysing the effects of previous actions and working autonomously' (Pontifical Academy for Life, 2024). As a result, AI has permeated everyone's life due to its ability to simulate the human brain and perform what formally only humans can do. As stated by the Pontifical Academy for Life:

> AI chooses the online advertisements we view, selects the best candidates for a job interview, makes medical diagnoses, assesses our financial reliability if we apply for a mortgage, measures out water and pesticides in agriculture, guides us through traffic thanks to GPS systems, learns from machine translation, handles emergency calls, optimizes logistics and much, much more. From cybersecurity to public administration, AI is now pervasive. (Pontifical Academy for Life, 2024)

Nevertheless, while AI has the power to replicate human (brain) capacities, which results in the transformation of human individuals in our society, it has its own limitations. One of the drawbacks of AI is that intelligence and neurological consciousness are intrinsically biological properties, which the present AI systems lack. Because only humans have ontologically self-awareness, common sense, analogy, and ambiguity, machines cannot and will not be able to take over the place of human beings in the world, as some apocalyptic scientists suggest. The capabilities of the present computational models of intelligence, such as the Turing Test, machine learning, and neural networks, are also limited to intellectual comprehension, responsible creativity, ethical empathy, and moral judgement. They can only accept problems or data that are well-structured, evaluate them, look for patterns, and offer the best solution. Actually, their intention is to mimic the problem-solving methods of human thought and action. And this is only possible when they are organized and fed with data to enable efficient operation. By examining the results of earlier acts and acting independently, AI systems can then adjust their behaviour and ultimately act autonomously.

The existing AI is also limited to tackling path issues, which consist of following a path of choices – finding precise answers to well-structured challenges. Human problem-solving, on the other hand, encompasses challenges involving ill-structured settings, as well as the design of problem-solving methods themselves. These are insight problems, and insight is an important aspect of intelligence that computer science has yet to solve. For these reasons, as stated by Herbert L. Roitblat (2020):

> The current AI systems are heavily dependent on representations. A human engineer must discover a problem and simplify the solution into distinct steps, a set of input data and expected outcomes, or a set of rewards and actions. Only then can an AI algorithm be designed to solve that problem. What we are lacking is not algorithms that can solve complicated problems, but algorithms that can seek out and discover new problems and develop their solutions without help from humans.

It has also been demonstrated how artificial general intelligence (AGI) might be attainable and why a robopocalypse is neither imminent nor plausible. And, because AI computers cannot tackle problems that need insights, divergent thinking, commonsense/knowledge, and creativity, they will continue to lag behind humans for some time; thus, they will never spell the end of human race and human work in the healthcare industry as deceased theoretical physicist Stephen Hawking had fatalistically predicted. The least thing that the integration of AI healthcare and medicine in general is to facilitate physician-patient encounters. The role of safeguarding this ancient relationship between the physician and the patient falls under the mandate of all university teaching hospitals in Africa.

Opportunities and challenges of integrating AI into the university teaching hospitals

Opportunities

Excellent university teaching hospitals and the healthcare systems in Africa are expected ethically to be distinguished by their integral provision of medical services to the most vulnerable, the poor and marginalized. One method to make this mark a reality is to adopt a preferential option for the poor that targets the most vulnerable segments of society and the African patient-centred healthcare that encourages medical and healthcare professionals to prioritize the human aspect of medicine. This goal is even more easily achievable with the usage of AI in healthcare and of its integration in the university teaching hospitals' curriculum (Pope Benedict XVI, 2011). AI has now permeated every aspect of learning in almost all higher educational institutions and of society including teaching and public services in Africa, respectively. For instance, today the application of AI in the university teaching hospitals in Africa and the healthcare system, if well integrated and used, has the potential to prepare medical professional graduates who will in turn not only be able to safeguard the physician-patient relationship but also to transform patient care and significantly minimize the cost of running health facilities in Africa.

On the other hand, we all know that the new AI-driven medical technologies are capable of being powerful instruments for medical diagnostic and treatment efficiency as well as cost-effectiveness, but also for destruction and racial bias as we shall explain later. From a moral standpoint they can offer either a service or a disservice, provide wrong diagnosis as well as discrimination of patients. Integrating AI into the curriculum of university teaching hospitals in Africa can bring about various opportunities that can enhance medical and health education, medical research and community service, particularly the patient care. Here we can cite key opportunities.

Improving medical diagnosis and treatment

Healthcare providers project that the integration of AI in medical sector will improve medical diagnoses and treatment as well increases healthcare quality in the university teaching hospitals. AI-powered diagnostic tools can assist medical students in accurately diagnosing diseases and planning treatments. Integrating the use of AI-driven tools such as CT-scan and MRI into the curriculum can actually familiarize medical students with their usage, potentially leading to earlier detection and more effective treatments, particularly in resource-constrained university teaching hospitals in Africa.

Lowing of expenses and improving administrative efficiency

Secondly, the integration of AI in medical education curriculum of the university teaching hospitals lowers expenses and improves treatment strategies. It helps in cost reduction and administrative efficiency. AI-driven automation can indeed streamline administrative tasks, optimize resource allocation, and reduce healthcare costs. Teaching hospitals in Africa can educate students on the potential cost-saving benefits of AI adoption and how to implement AI-driven solutions effectively. Regarding access to specialized medical knowledge, AI can significantly help bridge the gap in access to specialized medical knowledge by providing educational resources and decision support systems. Medical and nursing students, most of them coming from remote rural areas in Africa, can easily learn from AI-driven platforms that offer insights and recommendations based on latest medical research and data.

Improving remote rural healthcare provisions via telemedicine

Telemedicine and remote healthcare were an ideal medical approach in rural Africa during the Covid-19 pandemic. Clinicians and nurses in Africa were able to provide good outpatient departmental services for human beings by supplying drug in the rural areas using social, medical and communicative robots. For example, the Republic of Rwanda was among the African countries which adopted the use of AI-driven robots to keep the surveillance on the borders to curb the spread of the Coronavirus. Rwanda also used AI-drones as medical supply services to supply drugs in the rural areas. The current population of Africa is 1,481,603,040 as of Monday, 12 February 2024, based on the latest United Nations estimates. Urban population is 44.7 %, while the rural population is 55.3 % (United Nations, 2024). This statistical fact points out how relevant telemedicine and remote healthcare are in the predominantly rural population in Africa. So, with the help of AI, university teaching hospitals in Africa could develop telemedicine solutions to enable remote consultations and healthcare delivery. Consequently, university teaching hospitals in Africa are challenged to seriously integrate telemedicine into their curriculum, teaching their students how to use AI-powered platforms to provide virtual care to patients in underserved areas. It is through these AI-driven medical services that African medical schools can contribute to the improvement of healthcare system efficiency and dramatically improves patient outcome prediction (Scherz, 2022).

Enhancing medical education in university medical schools

AI has the potential of enhancing medical education in various university teaching hospitals in Africa. Actually, the possibility of incorporating AI into the curriculum can provide medical students with exposure to cutting-edge technology and methodologies, preparing them for the future of medicine and healthcare. With the availability of these AI-powered medical tools, they can learn about AI algorithms, their applications in diagnostics, treatment planning, and patient care. AI also makes possible for governments and other healthcare providers to forecast future healthcare costs for specific patients using straightforward algorithms. Linked to this opportunity of integrating AI into university teaching hospitals' teaching function is the idea of individualized or personalized medicine (National Research Committee (US), 2011). AI algorithms have the potential to analyse patient data to tailor treatments based on individual characteristics and genetic preferences. In the continent with widespread poverty and inadequate medical services (John Paul II, 1995, no. 43), university teaching hospitals in Africa can teach their medical and nursing students about personalized medicine concepts and how AI can be utilized to optimize patient outcomes.

Our growing biomedical understanding of genetics and genomics, and how they drive health, disease and drug responses in each person, is enabling physicians and nurses to provide better disease prevention, more accurate diagnoses, safer drug prescriptions and more effective treatments for the many diseases and conditions that diminish our health. On the one hand, the advent of personalized medicine is indeed moving us closer to more precise, predictable and powerful healthcare that is customized for the individual patient. On the other hand, it can radically move the medical profession into depersonalization of the traditional physician-patient relationship as well as into the production of racially discriminating drugs and medical treatments in our hospitals and health centres.

Maintenance of the lives and rights of the marginalized poor in Africa

Using AI in promoting medical and health education, medical research and patient care in the university teaching hospitals and other healthcare facilities is consistent with many of the principles of Catholic social teaching, including giving the preferential option for the poor, upholding human rights, particularly the right to life and universal medical care cover, and having a holistic understanding of integral human development (Pope Paul VI, 1967, no. 21; 1971, no. 23). Through her various social-ethical considerations on the rights and duties of man as an *Imago Dei*, the Catholic Church constantly observes that every man has the right to life, to bodily integrity, and to the means which are suitable for the proper development of life; these are primarily food, clothing, shelter, rest, medical care, and finally the necessary social services. Therefore, a human being also has the right to security in cases of sickness, inability to work, widowhood, old age, unemployment, or in any other case in which he is deprived of the means of subsistence through no fault of his own (Pope John XXIII, 1963, no. 11). From the moral perspective of this social teaching of the Catholic Church, then, we can assertively say that any integration of AI into medical education curricula of the university medical schools in Africa is expected to further these rights of man, not to undermine them in any way.

Medical and healthcare in Africa should, therefore, be designed, communicated and used in ways that recognize individual patients' rights and promote the culture of life. The preservation of human life should be an utmost duty of each human person and of every institution involved in the medical and healthcare provisions in Africa. From the African anthropological and religious conception of life, human life is not merely something that must not be intentionally and directly be destroyed, but also respect must be shown for it by creating social and biomedical conditions necessary for its full and proper development: physically, culturally, morally and spiritually (Kiragu, 2022, pp. 218–219; Pope Leo XIII, 1891, no. 9). In fact, the culture of life in Africa is firmly embedded in our interpretation of the human person, who is not just matter or thing (*kinhu* – in my own Sukuma language) but an acting and moral person (*munhu* – in my own Sukuma language) with some rights and duties as well as interrelationships with God, with others and the universe (Wijsen & Tanner, 2000, 2002).

Facilitating healthcare analytics

The integration of AI into the curriculum of the university teaching hospital can facilitate the analysis of large datasets to identify patterns, trends, and correlations that can inform medical education, research and healthcare policies. It can also equip medical and nursing students with skills in healthcare analytics, enabling them to contribute to research projects and evidence-based decision-making in the medical profession.

Challenges

Obviously, as a product of science and technology, AI has the potential to generate significant means of improving not only the medical and health education, medical research and patient care in the African university teaching hospitals, but also of improving the quality of healthcare and human life if properly guided. AI and its ethical use in medicine and healthcare is a wonderful product of God-given human creativity and power. However, from the moral standpoint we must acknowledge and understand that AI as a technological product is not ethically neutral, because it establishes a technological framework that ends up conditioning medical and health education, medical research and patient care as well as habituating lifestyles and altering societal possibilities along lines determined by the interests of certain strong medical groups.

Judgements to deploy AI in university teaching hospitals and healthcare systems in Africa, although appearing merely utilitarian, are actually biomedical ethical judgements concerning the type of medical doctors and nurses we want to graduate and the healthcare systems we would like to build. Because the use of AI appears to dominate not just liberal economics with the goal of maximizing profit, political life in view of fostering democracy, transforming society and education, we must also be cautious about its potentially detrimental effects on humans in general and on the ancient physician-patient encounter in medicine in particular (Pope Benedict XVI, 2011, nos. 68–78). Given that our paper is about the critical ethical considerations on the correlation between AI and physician-patient relationship in view of advocating for the role of university teaching hospitals in mitigating depersonalization of healthcare in Africa, let us now identify and investigate some dangers with the focus on those challenges which threaten the ancient medical ethical principle of the physician-patient relationship (Wahome & Nderitu, 2023, p. 18).

Danger of overreliance on AI

Overreliance on AI is the first potential ethical challenge connected with the integration of AI in the university teaching hospitals and healthcare in Africa. Overreliance on AI and extensive surveillance might result in the dehumanization of healthcare, with patients feeling as though they are being hunted down by existing healthcare personnel (O'Neill, 2019). This practically mean that when university medical school students and healthcare practitioners depend too much on AI, they may tend to regard patients as data points or collections of symptoms rather than multidimensional individuals with unique histories, needs and experiences. Put differently, they may tend to depersonalized medicine and patient's care. This, in turn, can lead to a major lack of empathy and understanding of the patient's point of view, and ultimately undermining the quality of treatment offered. A good example here is the application of virtual assistants in university teaching hospitals. AI virtual assistants are utilized in the context of physician-patient contact not only to communicate with patients and acquire information but also to provide basic medical advice.

AI-powered virtual assistants, or better say, digital assistants refer to application programmes that understand natural language voice commands and complete tasks for the user. Some of the typical tasks an AI-powered virtual assistant might perform include scheduling medical care appointments and managing email accounts. Although these AI tools can be useful in some cases, relying on them too extensively can result in depersonalized healthcare, objectified people, and a detached patient experience. In other words, training university medical school students in using AI in healthcare raises the ethical risk of man being 'technologized', rather than technology humanized. This risk is realized when 'technical capacity casts a dangerous spell: instead of delivering the tools that improve their care to human life, there is the risk of giving life to the logic of the devices that decide its value' (Pope Francis, 2019).

Anthropological and ethical issues

The idea of teaching university medical school students about algorithms which is applied in AI systems also have anthropological and ethical issues. Some of these ethical challenges involved include transparency, social inclusion, impartiality, reliability, accountability, bias, discrimination, and a variety of other unforeseen consequences (Pontifical

Academy for Life, 2024; Green, 2018; Delio, 2020). The algorithms utilized in AI systems are only as objective as the data used to train them. They are also only as racially neutral as the data scientist who created and uploaded them is. If the training data and/or data scientist is biased and racist, the AI system may perpetuate those biases and automating inequalities when making clinical decisions, leading to unfair and/or discriminating outcomes for particular patient populations. It actually becomes a high-tech tool which unfairly profiles patients and punishes the most vulnerable and marginalized in society (Eubanks, 2018). For example, if the AI-powered CT-Scan has been trained on data predominantly focused on European white women patients, it may be less accurate in medically diagnosing certain diseases in African women. The result is that patients may receive poor diagnosis and medical treatment as a result of their race, gender, or other factors.

Eventual loss of the ancient physician-patient privilege

The eventual loss of the traditional physician-patient relationship with its goal of enhancing the culture of life in healthcare is another possible risk of teaching and socializing university medical students with the use of AI in healthcare in Africa (Beauchamp & Childress, 2006). One of the vivid negative outcomes of the process of depersonalizing the doctor-patient relationship and the healthcare systems via the application of high-tech medical tools is that patients may begin to believe that if their doctors, nurses, and other health stakeholders are replaced or supplemented by AI-based medical and healthcare systems, they will become less compassionate and caring. This could not only violate the biomedical ethical norm of confidentiality, but it could also make patients feel less comfortable sharing sensitive information with their doctors, potentially leading to poorer health outcomes.

In the context of Africa, Africans extremely value physical human contact in all aspects of human connection and relationship. Africans consider human beings not merely as single compound substances made of body and soul (Aquinas, 1948), but as rational beings who consist of a bundle of relationships. They are free and intelligent subjects, with the capacity to relate with others, with the spirits, animals, plants, and with God. From the perspective of the traditional African ontology, there is a hierarchy in being. As the Source, Originator and the ultimate End of all creation, God is located at the apex of the pyramid. Ancestors and spirits are in second place in the pyramid, followed by human beings, animals and other living creatures. At the bottom of the pyramid are non-living beings. Altogether these constitute a single integral cosmos. This African ontology is therefore composed of two ontologically interrelated worlds: the *spiritual* (invisible) world and the *physical* (visible) world (Bujo, 1998, p. 197; Magesa, 1998, pp. 44–51). The divine invisible world being the sphere of God, the ancestors and the spirits, while the visible world being composed of creation, including rational humanity, animals, plants and inanimate beings. The Belgian Franciscan missionary in the Congo Placide Frans Tempels (1906–1977) referred to all these as 'forces of life', or 'vital forces' (Tempels, 1952, p. 41). This means, for Africans, reality is dynamic, and being is force. Being both the primary and the ultimate life-giving Power, the Divine Force is located at the top of the hierarchy of the universe. It refers to God the Creator and Sustainer, the Holy One. Although these two worlds are distinct, they are not separated from each other. They are ontologically intertwined.

Precisely in Black Africa, a human person cannot, therefore, be defined by the Cartesian principle of *cogito, ergo sum* (I think, therefore I am), which depends on thought and is important in western individualistic civilization. Rather, an African human is ontologically relational. He consists of a network of relationships which constitutes his identity and personality. The whole conception of the human as understood in conceptual west differs radically from the African conception of the human person. Thus, from the African anthropological standpoint, the above Cartesian principle is changed to become *cognatus sum/sumus, ergo sum/sumus* – I am/we are related; therefore, I am/we are (Bujo, 2009, p. 33). I am a relative, therefore I exist, or better, therefore we exist. In Africa, one is a person only in relation to other people, that is, the community.

It is in this regard that instead of obtaining medical services from AI-powered virtual assistants, an African patient would always prefer to see someone – a caring and compassionate physical human person – such as a kind and merciful doctor, a cheerful and caring nurse, or loving relative – performing and offering medical services to him or her. Truly, in an African community life does not come automatically as in the conceptual western sense because everything happens in a dialectic relationship. An African then identifies himself with spirits, ancestors, animals, plants, minerals, waters and fellow human beings. The late Cameroonian Jesuit Father Engelbert Mveng stated in Black Africa, a human being is a microcosm within the macrocosm (Mveng, 1985, p. 12). He is an acting individual person with rights and duties but always within the communal parameters. He freely exercises his individuality within the community and for the general flourishing of the community to which he belongs and is morally obligated to.

Ethics of data privacy and security

Training university medical students on how to use of AI in physician-patient interactions might also raise ethical questions regarding data ethics, particularly data privacy and security. As previously stated, people may be reluctant to disclosing and sharing personal health information with AI-based healthcare systems in various African university teaching hospitals due to a lack of trust in the protection of their private information. University teaching hospitals in Africa ought to teach their medical students that confidentiality is integral to maintaining human dignity and a prolife attitude. It is an ethical duty to privacy. It is concerned with the storage, security and use of personal information. In fact, since the ancient time of the Greek physician called Hippocrates (Augustyn, 2024), confidentiality in regard to patient medical information is considered as a cornerstone of the physician-patient relationship as it creates the atmosphere of trust that is essential for a healthy therapeutic relationship between the patient and physician (Beauchamp & Waiters, 1990, p. 307). Basically, commonly known as patient-physician privilege, confidentiality applies to private conversations between doctors and patients. The protection of information shared between these two is essential to guard patients' dignity against stigmatization and discrimination as well as the minimization of patients' autonomy. Therefore, in practical terms this means that university medical students ought to be taught that they are morally obligated to protect the confidentiality of their patients.

Inaccuracy of the value-based care paradigm

Yet another possible ethical danger related to the use of AI in healthcare is the so-called value-based care paradigm. This paradigm aims to increase healthcare quality while reducing expenses. Its supporters have established initiatives that employ data analytics to focus care to the most vulnerable patients (Mjåset et al., 2020). They argue that directing care toward these patients could considerably increase per capita costs and population health outcomes. However, the effectiveness of the value-based care paradigm is dependent on accurate patient identification. This is when AI comes into play. Once these vulnerable patients are identified as members of a population, the AI-driven healthcare system provides them with comprehensive care that includes a wide range of medical and social services managed by care managers. The very ethical problem of this system is that it changes from perceiving the patient as an individual (as in models based on the doctor-patient relationship) to seeing the patient as a population. With the triple goal of improving patient experience, population health, and healthcare spending (Berwick, Nolan & Whittington, 2008), the value-based care paradigm essentially seeks to address the risk factors that lead to disease rather than pay for expensive acute care, treating the root causes of problems.

The value-based care paradigm necessitates the use of AI in the African university teaching hospitals due to the necessity for data analysis, which not only depersonalizes healthcare but also pushes medical students, nurses and practising clinicians to perceive patients through the lens of AI technologies that strive to reduce medical expenses; thus to embrace a version of what Pope France calls the 'technocratic paradigm' (Pope Francis, 2015, nos. 106–108). The globalization of the technocratic paradigm entails objectifying patients rather than AI technology humanized (Pope Francis, 2015, no. 106). The truth is that tech-science, which has its origin in Galileo's experimental science, and which reached its climax with Isaac Newton (1642–1727), has given man enormous power and an astonishing dominion over people and the entire universe. However, nothing guarantees that medical professionals will always use AI-driven medical technologies and tools intelligently, ethically, and responsibly, particularly in healthcare with its historic objective of maintaining the sanctity and quality of human life. We only need to recollect the vast array of technology used by Nazi German doctors to murder millions of people, including six million Jewish people who died in the Holocaust. This historical fact needs to remind all university teaching hospitals in Africa, as Pope Francis suggests, that 'contemporary man has not been trained to use [technological and economic] power well', because 'our immense technological development has not been accompanied by a development in human responsibility, values and conscience' (Pope Francis, 2015, no. 105).

Bias against patients with chronic illness

This ethical challenge is associated with the use of AI-driven health-care systems in Africa. It can actually change how university teaching hospital medical students and physicians interact with the patient since they provide the parameters for how they decide who should be attended to first. This type of medical practice is controversial in light of the ideals of Catholic healthcare, which tries to preferentially accompany the afflicted poor, particularly those whose care may appear inefficient. It can also threaten to reinforce a cost-effectiveness-based notion of 'deserving-ness' that may generate bias against patients with chronic illness, against minorities and poor patients (Fleming et al., 2021, p. 217). In this sense, the use of AI in healthcare for cost-effectiveness sheds new light on well-known anthropological and ethical issues in AI ethics, such as racial bias in an algorithm used to manage population health and depersonalization in healthcare. This tendency may unintentionally support systemic racism in the healthcare system and encourage health policies and decision-making procedures that do not preferentially prioritize the needs of those patients who are most physically vulnerable, socially marginalized and economically disadvantaged. In this case, therefore, the preferential option for physician-patient relationship should be reaffirmed and safeguarded in all its force as a biomedical ethical response to the danger of depersonalization of the healthcare in Africa arising from the application of AI in the healthcare.

Quality-of-life-ethic versus sanctity-of-life-ethic

The idea of integrating AI in healthcare may indeed promote the quality of life of patients, but it cannot guarantee the sanctity of their lives. We comparatively doubt also the ability of AI-powered medical robots to value, promote and respect human life as do the rational-spirited physicians. That is why from the African holistic medicine and healing perspective, a healer (a physician) is referred to as a person who is recognized by the community. He must be a competent person who faithfully provides healthcare service using vegetable, animal and mineral substance and certain other methods based on the socio-cultural and religious background. He must also rely on the shared knowledge, attitudes, and beliefs that are prevalent in his community regarding physical, mental and social well-being and causation of disease and disability. More importantly, the African indigenous worldview emphasizes the inter-relatedness of healing, medicine and spirituality. This means, in Africa no healing can take place simply because the medicinal herbs administered to a sick person contain curative elements. Instead, healing is realized due to the interventions of the Supreme Being, the ancestors and even the living members of the patient (Tessema, 1980, p. 52). Healing and health are not individual concerns, but they are fundamentally communal in the broad sense of the term, including the surrounding physical environment. So, university teaching hospitals and their respective medical schools operating in African milieu are morally obligated to be culturally sensitive and inclusive as they go along with their traditional core functions of teaching, research and community engagement.

Reaffirming the preferential option for the physician-patient relationship in the age of AI

The technocratic paradigm, which regards nature as an insensate order, a cold body of facts, a simple 'given', an object of utility, and raw material that needs to be shaped into something useful, is undoubtedly prevalent in today's world. It has gained so much power that it would be challenging to function without it and even more challenging to use its resources without succumbing to its internal logic. AI is a byproduct of the technocratic paradigm and is present in every person's life, profession, and teaching institutions such as university teaching hospitals. For example, its integration in those healthcare institutions has undeniably facilitated quicker, more effective, and easier medical diagnostics and treatments, as we intimated above.

In spite of its potential opportunities, the application of AI-driven medical tools in healthcare in Africa possesses the danger of depersonalizing the traditional doctor-patient relationship; consequently, isolating patients from their communities which are deeply rooted in the African relational anthropology called *Ubuntu* (Green, 2018). Pope John Paul II observed: 'African cultures have an acute sense of solidarity and community life. In Africa, it is unthinkable to celebrate a feast without the participation of the whole village. Indeed, community life in African societies expresses the extended family. It is my ardent hope and prayer that Africa will always preserve this priceless cultural heritage and never succumb to the temptation to individualism, which is so alien to its best traditions' (John Paul II, 1995, no. 43). This fact then points out to the urgent need to safeguard the physical physician-patient relationship, in which we perceive and engage with a patient as a person. In this sense, African university teaching hospitals have an ethical imperative to find a rich balance between the ethically prudent use of AI technology in healthcare and the necessity for human relationships and empathy in patient encounters. This is an African encounter ethics that conforms to the evangelical imperative of being our brother's keeper. As Pope Francis suggests, 'The Gospel tells us constantly to run the risk of a face-to-face encounter with others, with their physical presence which challenges us, with their pain and their pleas, with their joy which infects us in our close and continuous interactions' (Pope Francis, 2013, no. 88; Pope J. Stephen, 2019; Mescher, 2020).

In fact, from the African traditional religion perspective, a disease is always an indication that something in human relations is terribly wrong. A disease can actually bring people to take the community dimension seriously. The Kenyan philosopher and theologian John Mbiti (1931–2019) rightly suggested: 'Only in terms of the other people does individual become conscious of his own being… When he suffers, he does not suffer alone but the corporate group. Whatever happens to the individual happens to the whole group, and whatever happens to the whole group happens to the individual, the individual can only say, "I am because we are, and since we are, therefore I am"' (Mbiti, 1990, pp. 108–109). In this regard, the healing of the sick person is considered to be truly effective and holistic if it heals and restores not the physical condition of the individual but also his moral-spiritual, psycho-emotional, social and ecological conditions. This practically implies that the physician deals with the complete person and provides treatment for physical, spiritual, social, ecological and psychological symptoms. Thus, we cannot easily let AI in the healthcare undermines the noble art of African traditional anthropocentric medicines and healing – the sum total of all knowledge and practices explicably in diagnosis, prevention and curing of physical, mental or social imbalance.

In light of the foregoing arguments, university teaching hospitals and medical centres in Africa should be keenly mindful of the possible consequences of depersonalization in healthcare and seek to ensure that ethical AI is utilized to supplement human physicians. AI should not be used to replace patient medical care. And, because the employment of AI in healthcare cannot be avoided today, the ethical paradigm of lifelong learning, training programmes, and collaborative robots must be adopted in all the university teaching hospitals. According to this paradigm, AI technology should benefit and serve man, even if some of the so-called rotten jobs in healthcare would be eliminated as a result of the use of AI in healthcare. Medical students should know and understand that AI ought always to be at the service of humanity; it should be anthropocentric. So, if we want human healthcare medical graduates and medical robots with AI to collaborate in harmony, the medical machines must be designed with human behaviour in mind. The reverse is ethically not true. In fact, top management of the university teaching hospitals and leaders in society have the freedom to regulate and direct the use of AI technology in healthcare; they must put it to the service of a healthier, more humane, more social, and more integrated approach to healthcare.

Ethical and anthropocentric AI in the healthcare system also necessitates that we do not undercut the socially based *Ubuntu* ethics of medical students' and doctors' encounters with patients. The physician-patient encounter's *Ubuntu* ethical dimension promotes human interrelationships and unity. It emphasizes human qualities, such as community and social relations so that patients feel fully connected to their respective local communities. As noted above, an African, in light of this *Ubuntu* moral principle, prefers normally to view the suffering of others with the heart. This patient-physical encounter with his relatives and physicians is expected ultimately to lead to long-term companionship with the patient, drawing people deeper into community. This model of patient-doctor-relative encounter is an appropriate paradigm for African biomedical ethics – an ethic that emphasizes the traditional African truism that the practice of medicine, as an art of healing, is based on a physician-doctor encounter with the suffering Other, which leads what we call humanizing presence that constitutes a solidarity initiative for integration and closeness with the patients and their families (Mambo, 1996, p. 176). It also leads to personalized medical attention and an ongoing responsibility, caring, and accompaniment through illness (Nicholson, 2021; Pellegrino & Thomasma, 1982). Therefore, to humanize healthcare we must respect the fact that each person is unique and unrepeatable and responds differently to life crises.

The technocratic paradigm, which Pope Francis refers to as a way of engaging the suffering other and the world as objects, material for manipulation, and devoid of spiritual and metaphysical meanings beyond the subject's own goals and desires, contrasts with seeing the suffering other through the lens of the *Ubuntu* ethic of physician-patient encounter (Pope Francis, 2015, nos. 101–123). As stated above, even healthcare institutions like university teaching hospitals in Africa as elsewhere run the risk of succumbing to the AI-technocratic worldview. Healthcare systems are susceptible to the materialistic business mentality that is preoccupied with cost-effective administration, statistics, plans, and assessments, with the hospitals as the primary beneficiaries rather than the patients. Patients, who ought basically to be the object of preference for medical attention, love, sympathy, mercy, and compassion, can turn into manipulable statistics.

False intimacy, objectification and commodification of the body as well as social isolation are some striking examples of the emotional harm brought on by the usage of medical devices with AI that have the ability to communicate with patients and provide assistance (Saez & Reimer, 2024). For instance, when a patient develops an intimate relationship with an AI-humanoid robot doctor, this may result in patient 'thingification' and racial inequality (Liao, 2020, p. 284). The formative consequences of repeated action/practice in the development of virtue or vice are discussed by virtue ethicists (MacIntyre, 1984). Similarly, AI-humanoid robot physician-patient encounter practices, similar to the technocratic paradigm, can feature reductionist thinking of the patient, particularly the reduction of patient to data points in medicine and healthcare in general (Scherz, 2019). As future medical practitioners, medical students in various African university teaching hospitals and who have been influenced by the technocratic paradigm will no longer treat patients as individuals in a community, but rather as individuals in a population. AI essentially cannot function without objectification and reductionism which ultimately ends in depersonalization in healthcare.

Mitigating depersonalization in healthcare: Ubuntu synergy in medical education

Before we explore the specific role of university teaching hospitals in promoting Ubuntu synergy in medical education with the goal of preventing depersonalization in healthcare, we felt it would be useful to first offer a list of existing university teaching hospitals and medical schools in Africa East as a case study.

Table 1. List of University Medical Schools in East Africa

Country	Medical school	Public/private
Tanzania	Bugando Medical Centre: Referral Consultant and University Teaching Hospital	Private
	Muhimbili University of Health and Allied Sciences	Public
	Kilimanjaro Christian Medical University Medical College	Private
	Herbert Kariuki University Teaching Hospital	Private
	St. Francis Ifakara University Teaching Hospital	Private
Uganda	Mbarara University School of Medicine	Public
	Makere University: Medical School	Public
	Gulu University School of Medicine	Public
	Uganda Martyrs University School of Medicine	Private
	IHK Postgraduate Medical School	Private
Kenya	University of Nairobi: Medical School	Public
	Kenyatta Teaching, Referral and Hospital	Public
	Moi University: Medical School	Public
	Mater Misericordiae Hospital: Medical School	Private
	The Aga Khan University Hospital	Private
Rwanda	University of Rwanda School of Medicine	Public
	University of Gitwe School of Medicine	Private
	University of Global Health Equity	Private
	Adventist School of Medicine of East-Central Africa	Private

Based on their vision statements, we may conclude that they are all committed to promoting excellence in teaching, research, and developing health professionals. In light of their respective visions, one might wonder how African university teaching hospitals and medical centres can help promote *Ubuntu*-centred healthcare in order to combat depersonalization in healthcare caused by AI applications in medical diagnostic and treatment procedures, as well as patient care. *Ubuntu*-centred healthcare refers to African holistic healthcare ethics based on relational anthropology. It is a healthcare ethic that emphasizes African communitarian ideals including interconnectivity, community, and humaneness. If these ideals are truly embraced and become integrated into the curriculum of medical education in all university teaching hospitals, they can greatly contribute to mitigating depersonalization in healthcare, particularly in the context of AI. Here are some ways in which African university teaching hospitals help to reaffirm the traditional physician-patient relationship while additionally minimizing depersonalization by prioritizing *Ubuntu*-centred healthcare in age of AI.

Cultural sensitivity and social inclusion as a moral imperative

The first step in addressing depersonalization in healthcare is to educate medical students on the moral importance of being culturally sensitive and socially inclusive. University teaching hospitals and medical schools are to be advised and encouraged to incorporate *Ubuntu* concepts into medical education, emphasizing the necessity of understanding patients' socio-cultural contexts. By establishing a culturally sensitive and socially inclusive atmosphere, medical professional graduates can actually better interact with patients, eventually develop patient-centred care, and mitigate the possible risk of depersonalization linked with AI integration in healthcare. University medical schools should teach medical students the value of patient-centred care and encourage future healthcare professionals to prioritize the human part of medicine over the AI-technological aspect of medicine. This effectively indicates that medical training programmes should always incorporate communication skills development, empathy training, and ethical considerations to ensure that medical students comprehend the long-term biomedical ethical relevance of the doctor-patient interaction in the age of AI.

Medical training programmes should also recognize that what is theoretically taught includes not only how to conduct a medical diagnosis and treatment, but also how to be compassionate, wise, courageous, and patient-centred. As previously said, every patient in Africa societies wishes to be attended and treated by a physician or nurse who is informed, kind, friendly and merciful. Honesty, truthfulness, integrity, kindness, love, compassion, and respect are among the *Ubuntu* principles that physicians, nurses, and healthcare assistants in Africa are required to acquire, practice, and eventually apply in their medical profession. Such values allow an African patient to reveal personal information and the type of illness required by a trusted doctor to recommend effective diagnosis, treatment, and care. These principles also allow doctors, nurses, and other healthcare practitioners to best use their medical and health professional competence to restore the patient's health (Coxill, 1990).

Nurturing and promoting the culture of life among medial students

The second way to mitigate depersonalization in African healthcare in the age of AI is to teach medical students in university teaching hospitals about the indispensability of the culture of life – the culture that emerges when respect for human life is accepted as foundational and absolute, and its application extends to all aspects of personal, family, and social life. The Cameroonian philosopher and theologian Martin Nkafu Nkemnkia defines the culture of life as 'the effort towards a greater humanization, a greater order in the universe, and it is the process through which one can interpret the aspiration and orientation of men and mankind where trying to give meaning to existential problems and clarify his positions in the world and history. Culture is achieved both on a formal level that is the analysis of the social and historical phenomena and on an ethical and artistic level, through the daily experience of life' (Nkemnkia, 1999, p. 168). According to Nkemnkia, the culture of life is equal to vitalogy. This is because life is an eternal principle which everyone yearns for. To live means to possess a vital force, to conserve oneself in it and be bound permanently to his force without which nothing can exist (Nkemnkia, 1999, p. 168). As Placide Tempels asserts, 'in Bantu thought they speak, act and live as if for them beings were forces. Force is a necessary attribute of beings: Force is the nature of being, force is being and being is force' (Tempels, 1952, p. 44).

And, because life is so important to Africans, university teaching hospitals should integrate patient-centred AI technologies into medical education and the healthcare profession. They must guarantee that students grasp the capabilities and limitations of artificial intelligence in healthcare. Indeed, by integrating AI applications in medical and ethical training programmes, medical students gain firsthand experience in working with technology while also learning to balance its use with personalized patient care and to uphold the African moral traditions of abundant life (Magesa, 1998, p. 175).

Emphasis on biomedical ethical training and reflective
medical practice

Another way to combat personalization in African healthcare is to ensure that university medical school offer biomedical ethical training and reflective medical practice. Considered rightly as mandatory continuous professional development strategies, these biomedical ethical trainings that incorporate Ubuntu values such as the importance of shared decision-making between patients and medical professionals should help medical students navigate the challenges associated with AI in healthcare. On the one hand, we think that this specific kind of ethical training should aim to ensure that medical students prioritize patient welfare, preserve the patient's life, autonomy, dignity, and privacy, and adhere to *Ubuntu* ethical norms that emphasize holistic treatment and health. *Ubuntu*-centred holistic healthcare generally considers not only patients' physical health, but also their social, emotional, and spiritual well-being, as well as the needs of their respective families and communities (Antus, 2017, p. 218; Bujo, 1998, p. 184). All of these aspects of holistic health imply taking personal responsibility for each sickness and being aware when professional medical help is required. Thus, university teaching hospitals should include African holistic care principles into their separate curricula, encouraging medical students and healthcare personnel to consider patients' larger needs beyond clinical issues.

Similarly, reflective medical practice should be encouraged among medical students in university teaching hospitals, which would encourage them to critically evaluate their personal interactions with patients, AI technology, and healthcare systems, ultimately leading to a better understanding of the impact of depersonalization in African healthcare.

Conducting research on ethical and anthropocentric AI in African contexts

The fourth strategy for reducing depersonalization in healthcare and strengthening the physician-patient interaction is to encourage university teaching hospitals to perform research on ethical AI applications in African contexts. They can really lead medical research initiative that focus on the development and application of AI technologies that are culturally sensitive, socio-economically inclusive, and contextually relevant. These medical research efforts can assist ensure that AI tools protect doctor-patient care while also respecting *Ubuntu* principles and contributing positively to African holistic healthcare without compromising and eroding the human touch.

Encouraging community engagement and transdisciplinary approach

It is our strong conviction that through community participation and collaboration, African university teaching hospitals and medical centres can make a substantial contribution to mitigating depersonalization in healthcare in the age of AI. Community service is a traditional part of each university. This function of the university teaching hospitals aims to build strong partnerships with local communities by actively incorporating them in African holistic healthcare decisions and practices. Indeed, by actively engaging with African local communities, university teaching hospitals and their medical students as healthcare providers can better experience, identify, understand, and judge the needs, values, and preferences of the people they serve, reinforcing a patient-centred paradigm that aligns with *Ubuntu* principles of relatedness with all creatures, interconnectedness, community, and humaneness (Kiragu, 2022, pp. 231–235; Magesa, 2014, pp. 89–98). They can also markedly contribute to confront depersonalization in healthcare in Africa by stressing on transdisciplinary teamwork, networking, and interpersonal skills.

On the one hand, university teaching hospitals could stimulate transdisciplinary collaboration, bringing together students from various healthcare professions such as medicine, nursing, pharmacy, biomedical ethics, medical sociology, medical law, and moral theology. Actually, as the teaching method that moves beyond just teaching across disciplines using common themes, topics, or issues that thread through different courses, transdisciplinary requires collaboration between disciplines to create a cohesive curriculum in which students collaborate to solve multifaceted problems. So, this kind of transdisciplinary approach to medical and healthcare education supports a holistic approach to patient care and helps students recognize the specializations and unique contributions of different healthcare providers in preventing depersonalization.

On the other hand, by emphasizing the development of strong interpersonal skills and networking among students and healthcare professionals, African university teaching hospitals can prioritize the development of strategies for establishing meaningful doctor-patient relationships. This will help to counteract the above-mentioned potential dehumanizing consequences of AI in healthcare.

Establish centres of excellence in Ubuntu-centred biomedical sciences

This concept of developing centres of excellence in biomedical sciences through international collaboration can also aid in the establishment of a high-quality, competitive, and skilled workforce in East African university teaching hospitals and medical centres for social and economic development in AI age. The African Development Bank (AfDB) allocated $98 million in 2015 to build four biomedical scientific centres of excellence in East Africa (Waruru, 2015). These centres were to be set up at universities in Tanzania, Uganda, Rwanda, and Kenya. They were expected to be the top regional institutions for training medical professionals in non-communicable diseases, such as nephrology, urology, oncology, cardiovascular diseases, biomedical engineering, e-health, and telemedicine (the delivery of health services via mobile phone applications).

In this international collaboration, Tanzania will host the East Africa Heart Institute, while Rwanda will create the East Africa Biomedical Engineering Institute, which will include e-health. Kenya will host the East Africa Kidney Institute, while Uganda will house the East Africa Oncology Institute. However, in order to carry out this project, each teaching university in Tanzania, Rwanda, Uganda, and Kenya may choose any university or medical teaching centre with whom to engage for knowledge transfer and best practice benchmarking. University partners will help with faculty development, curriculum and programme design, best practice creation, research, and publication.

Furthermore, these linked centres of excellence in East Africa will provide ethical leadership in postgraduate education, training, and research services to meet the region's growing demand for specialized human-centred medicare. In Kenya, for example, the Kenyatta University teaching hospital has already established collaboration, networking, and knowledge transfer agreements with the Institute of Urology and Nephrology in Barcelona, Spain, and Seattle University in the United States.

Conclusion

We can conclusively argue that university teaching hospitals in Africa are well placed in preserving the ancient tradition of the physician-patient relationship and in ensuring ethical AI integration in the healthcare while minimizing negative effects of AI. They can significantly do so by giving primacy to the *Ubuntu*-centred healthcare by incorporating African cultural values in medical education curriculum. The contents of that curriculum should evolve and revolve around the development of guidelines and protocols that prioritize patient holistic well-being, confidentiality, autonomy, and culture of life as well as preferential option for the doctor-patient encounter. University teaching hospitals can also do by fostering community engagement, prioritizing medical research on AI applications in African contexts, and ensuring that AI applications align with African ethical considerations and respect for human life and dignity.

By doing so, university teaching hospitals can contribute to a healthcare system and medical research that not only preserves the essential human connection between healthcare providers and their patients but also leverages AI technology. Put differently, by inculcating the *Ubuntu* values in medical students as future healthcare professionals, university teaching hospitals in African can ensure that ethical AI complements rather than replaces human interaction in patient care. Therefore, we urge all university teaching hospitals in Africa to lead the way in ensuring that AI technologies are ethically integrated into healthcare practices and encour.

References

Antus, E. (2017). Bioethics in theological perspective. *Journal of the Society of Christian Ethics, 38*(1), 220–225.

Aquinas, T. (1948). *Summa Theologiae* (5 Vols. Fathers of the English Dominican Province, Trans.). Benzinger Brothers.

Augustyn, A. (2024). Hippocratic oath. In *Encyclopaedia Britannica.* https://www.britannica.com/topic/Hippocratic-oath

Beauchamp, T., & Childress, J. (2006). *Principles of biomedical ethics* (6th ed.). Oxford University Press.

Beauchamp, T., & Waiters, L. (1990). *Contemporary issues in bioethics* (3rd ed.). Wadsworth Publishing Company.

Berwick, D., Nolan, T., & Whittington, J. (2008). The triple aim: Care, health, and cost. *Health Affairs, 27*(3), 759–769.

Bujo, B. (1998). *The ethical dimension of the community: The African model and the dialogue between North and South.* Paulines Publications Africa.

Bujo, B. (2009). *Plea for change of models for marriage.* Paulines Publications Africa.

Coxill, W. (1990). *Abundant life in changing Africa.* Congo Belge Press.

Delio, I. (2020). *Re-enhancing the earth: Why AI needs religion.* Orbis Books.

Eubanks, V. (2018). *Automating inequality: How high-tech tools profile, police, and punish the poor.* St. Martin's Press.

Fleming, M. D., Shim, J. K., Yen, I., Thompson-Lastad, A., & Burke, N. J. (2021). Patient engagement, chronic illness, and the subject of health care reform. *Medical Anthropology, 40*(3), 214–227.

Green, B. P. (2018). Ethical reflections on artificial intelligence. *Scientia et Fides, 6*(2), 9–31.

Guardini, R. (1965/1998). *Das Ende der Neuzeit* (9th ed.). Würzburg. English: *The end of the modern world.* Wilmington.

Kiragu, T. W. (2022). *Holistic healthcare ethics and culture of life: Towards a new approach to healing in the catholic Archdiocese of Nyeri, Kenya.* CUEA Press.

Liao, M. S. (2020). *Ethics of artificial intelligence.* Oxford University Press.

MacIntyre, A. (1984). *After virtue: A study in moral theory* (2nd ed.) University of Notre Dame Press.

Magesa, L. (1998). *African religion: The moral traditions of abundant life.* Paulines Publications Africa.

Magesa, L. (2014). *What is not sacred? African spirituality.* Acton Publishers.

Mambo, O. (1996). Practicing medicine across cultures: Conception of health communication and consulting practice. In K. Motshabi & M. Steyn (Eds.), *Cultural synergy in South Africa* (pp. 176–186). Knowledge Resources.

Mbiti, J. S. (1990). *African religion and philosophy* (2nd ed.). Heinemann.

Mescher, M. (2020). *The ethics of encounter.* Orbis Books.

Mjåset, C., Ikram, U., Nagra, N. S., & Feeley, T. W. (2020). Value-based health care in four different health care systems. *NEJM Catalyst Innovations in Care Delivery*, pp. 1–23. https://catalyst.nejm.org/doi/full/10.1056/CAT.20.0530

Mveng, E. (1985). *L'Afrique dans l'Englise: Paroles d'un croyant (Africa in the church: Words of a believer).* Editions L'Harmattan.

National Research Council (US) Committee on a Framework for Developing a New Taxonomy of Disease. (2011). *Toward precision medicine: Building a knowledge network for biomedical research and a new taxonomy of disease.* https://doi.org/10.17226/1384.

Nicholson, P. (2021). Made known in the breaking of bread: Accompaniment and the practice of medicine. *Linacre Quarterly, 88*(3), 281–290.

Nkemnkia, M. N. (1999). *African vitalogy: A step forward in African thinking.* Paulines Publications.

O'Neill, K. L. (2019). *Hunted: Predation and Pentecostalism in Guatemala.* University of Chicago Press.

Pellegrino, E. D., & Thomasma, D. C. (1982). *A philosophical basis of medical practice: Toward a philosophy and ethic of the healing professions.* Oxford University Press.

Pontifical Academy for Life. (2024), *What is the matter with AI ethics? An introduction to the Rome call for AI ethics.* https://www.romecall.org

Pope Francis. (2015). Encyclical letter *Laudato Si'* on care for our common home (24 May 2015). *Acta Apostolicae Sedis, 107*(2015), 847–945.

Pope Francis. (2019). *To participants in the plenary assembly of the pontifical academy for life (25 February 2019).* https://www.vatican.va/content/francesco/en/speeches/2019/february/documents/papa-francesco_20190225_plenaria-accademia-vita.html

Pope Benedict XVI. (2011). Post-Synodal Apostolic exhortation *Africae Munus,* on the church in Africa in service to reconciliation, justice and peace (19 November 2011). *Acta Apostolicae Sedis, 104*(2012), 239–314.

Pope John XXIII. (1963). Encyclical letter *Pacem in Terris,* on peace on earth (11 April 1963). *Acta Apostolicae Sedis, 55*(1963), 257–304.

Pope John Paul II. (1995). Post-Synodal Apostolic exhortation *Ecclesia in Africa,* on the church in Africa and its evangelizing mission: Towards the year 2000 (14 September 1995). *Acta Apostolicae Sedis, 88*(1996), 5–82.

Pope Leo XIII. (1891). Encyclical letter *Rerum Novarum,* on condition of workers (15 May 1891): *Acta Leonis* 11:97–114. *Acta Sanctae Sedis, 23*(1892), 641–670.

Pope Paul VI. (1967). Encyclical letter *Populorum Progressio,* on the development of peoples (26 March 1967), no. 21. *Acta Apostolicae Sedis, 59*(1967), 257–299.

Pope Paul VI. (1971). Apostolic letter *Octogesima Adveniens,* on the new social problems (14 May 1971). *Acta Apostolicae Sedis, 63*(1971), 401–441.

Pope, S. J. (2019). Integral human development: From paternalism to accompaniment. *Theological Studies, 80*(1), 123–147.

Roitblat, H. L. (2020). *Algorithms are not enough: Creating general artificial intelligence.* MIT Press.

Roitblat, H. L. (2024). *AI is no match for the quirks of human intelligence.* https://thereader.mitpress.mit.edu/ai-insight-problems-quirks-human-intelligence/?utmsource=pocket&utmmedium=email

Saez, G., & Riemer, A. R. *et al.* (2024). Objectification in heterosexual romantic relationships: Examining relationship satisfaction of female objectification recipients and male objectifying perpetrators. https://core.ac.uk/download/pd!/188142039.pdf

Scherz, P. (2019). *Science and Christian ethics.* Cambridge University Press.

Scherz, P. (2022). Data ethics, AI, and accompaniment: The dangers of depersonalization in Catholic health care. *Theological Studies, 83*(2), 271–292.

Tempels, P. F. (1952). *Bantu philosophy* (C. King, Trans.). Présence Africaine.

Tessema, S. (1980). Traditional medicine: Past growth and future development in Eastern Africa. *East Africa Medical Journal, 57*(1), 51–56.

United Nations. (2024). *Population of Africa.* https://www.worldometers.info/world-population/

United States Conference of Catholic Bishops. (2018). *Ethical and religious directives from Catholic health care services* (6th ed.). United States Conference of Catholic Bishops.

Wahome, J., & Nderitu, S. (2023, June 16, Friday). Artificial intelligence can help to end corruption and other ills. *The Standard.*

Waruru, M. (2015, October 9). Four East Africa medical centres of excellence underway. *University World News Africa Edition.* https://www.universityworldnews.com/post.php?story=2015100980919608

Wijsen, F., & Tanner, R. (2000). *Seeking a good life: Religion and society in Usukuma – Tanzania 1945–1995.* Paulines Publications Africa.

Wijsen, F., & Tanner, R. (2002). *I am just a Sukuma: Globalization and identity construction in Northwest Tanzania.* Rodopi.

Chapter 9

Digital revolution, new-age pedagogies, and social transformation: Explorations in teaching/learning experiences in Indian higher education

SANDRA JOSEPH AND KASHISH DUA

Abstract: Concerns of this chapter relate to a comparatively small but ever-growing population of teachers and students in India who have limited or no access to technology. It specifically understands how, in the case of India, the impact of technology on pedagogy for cultural inclusivity is largely under-addressed. Taking cognisance of these gaps, it aims to understand how technology can impact pedagogy to promote cultural inclusivity. It examines important documents promulgated by apex regulatory bodies of higher education, namely, the Ministry of Education which assesses institutions annually through the National Institutional Ranking Framework (NIRF) and the National Assessment and Accreditation Council (NAAC) under the aegis of the University Grants Commission, which calls for a Self-Study Report (SSR) once in 5 years. These documents available in the public domain have been studied to ascertain how the State and Higher Education Institutions (HEIs) are adapting themselves to use technology in classrooms in view of achieving social transformation. It attempts to understand the intersection of digital revolution with new-age pedagogical frameworks specifically to address diverse cultural backgrounds of students in HEIs.

The chapter narrows down its focus, identifying highly ranked institutions by examining parameters of 'Teaching-Learning and Evaluation', which pertains to practices of adapting to technology, pedagogical approaches, and cultural inclusion. The concluding section explores the potential of bringing about social transformation if policies encourage the use of digital revolution to implement theoretical frameworks like 'Culturally Responsive Teaching' (CRT) as per the requirements of Indian classrooms.

Keywords: Indian higher education, digital revolution, new-age pedagogies, culturally responsive teaching, culturally relevant pedagogy, social transformation

India is characterized by the convergence of various ethnicities, languages, religions, and traditions, making it one of the most culturally diverse countries in the world. This cultural tapestry is deeply woven into its social fabric and reflects prominently in its educational institutions. Classrooms in India, especially in Higher Education Institutions (HEIs) serve as microcosms of the broader society bringing together students from diverse socio-economic backgrounds, linguistic communities, and religious affiliations. Any effort at fostering an inclusive environment requires embracing the cultural diversity of the country. It also holds the possibility to promote cross-cultural understanding, empathy and social justice.

The global digital transformation, which took shape in 2014 is rapidly changing the socio-economic landscape of India. Digital revolution is observed to be driven by various factors that include advancements in technology, government/State initiatives, increasing internet penetration, and changing consumer behaviour. One of the most significant aspects of digital revolution in India has been the exponential growth in the internet and mobile penetration. As per popular discourse, the easy availability of 'affordable' smartphones and 'affordable' internet data plans, has brought millions of Indians online. This also includes its vast population in rural areas. According to the Internet and Mobile Association of India (IAMAI) and KANTAR's 'Internet in India Report 2023', there are 821 million Internet users in India. This makes India one of the largest online markets facilitating access to information and services. It has fuelled the rise of various digital platforms and services catering to diverse needs. These digital platforms and services cut across several sectors such as e-commerce, finance, healthcare, entertainment, and education.

While there has been a rise in online learning platforms that present a democratized image of the online educational space, latest data about internet usage raises some serious social concerns. Mainstream media celebrated the growth in internet users in India as per the 2023 study of IAMAI and KANTAR (ABP News Bureau, 2024). However, it missed highlighting how 45 % of the population still does not access the internet; and out of the active users, only 3 % of usage is directed towards online learning. Based on the all-India sample of IAMAI and KANTAR, 23 % of people found the Internet too difficult to comprehend and use, 21 % were not allowed to use the Internet and 16 % did not own devices like computers and phones at home to access the internet.

Scholars have extensively examined these social realities and the digital divide, including the effectiveness of online learning environments. (Bista, Chan, & Allen, 2021; Das, 2022).

Culturally responsive teaching in India

The theory and practice of 'Culturally Responsive Teaching' are understood to emerge from the work of Gloria Ladson-Billings, an African American scholar whose idea of 'Culturally Relevant Pedagogy' (CRP) took shape during her experience as a fifth-grade student in a segregated Philadelphia school. On one occasion, her teacher went beyond the history curriculum and discussed the successful black Americans whose mention was nowhere to be found in textbooks. This moment made Ladson-Billings realize the significance of the methods through which aspects like 'race and ethnicity' were taught and 'who' taught these ideas. Her work primarily interrogates the traditional methods of teaching ideas of race and ethnicity in the United States of America. However, her argument of connecting classroom instruction with the cultural backgrounds and experiences of students, particularly those of marginalized groups, holds the radical potential of being useful for societies outside the country. It is in her work that ideas of academic success intersected with notions of 'cultural competence' and 'critical consciousness'. She proposed that to achieve a positive teacher-student relationship and enhance student engagement, emphasis needs to be placed on pedagogical practices. They should build upon the students' experiences and strengths. Her work argues that Culturally Responsive Teaching can empower students. It can teach them to critically examine power structures and inequalities and become catalysts of transformation in their communities.

Ladson-Billings' ideas are taken forward by Geneva Gay in her book, *Culturally Responsive Teaching: Theory, Research, and Practice* (2018). Gay provides pragmatic strategies for educators and urges them to address systemic inequalities and create opportunities for students to succeed, irrespective of their cultural backgrounds. Each section of her book ends with notes on practical possibilities that offer insights into implementing Culturally Responsive Teaching in real-life classroom scenarios. The significance of her book lies in recognizing the 'multidimensionality' of culturally responsive teachers. She states that for teachers to be culturally responsive they should bring about social and academic empowerment of students by setting high expectations for them, shaping curriculum based on students' strength to ultimately change educational institutions and society for better, and free students from pedagogies that are steeped in existing oppressive structures. These requirements as foregrounded in Gay's work indicate the need for teachers' training programmes that can help them develop not just strategies for Culturally Responsive Teaching but also the right mindset for it.

The scholarship in the context of India remains limited to multicultural education and classroom diversity in general. While some scholars address issues of linguistic diversity in primary education in India (Jhingran, 2009; Mohanty et al., 2009), others deal with teacher education reform in elementary education to engage with increasing student diversity (Kumar, 2014; Kumari et al., 2019). The realities of Indian Higher Education Institutions with their relatively high cultural diversity and largely homogenous curriculum reflective of dominant cultures and ideologies receive attention for requirements of curricular changes (Sabharwal, 2020), issues of stereotyping of student identities and language policies (Chandras, 2021), and perception of diversity among faculty in Indian HEIs (Thaddeus & Ganesan, 2019). Engagement with the specific paradigm of 'Culturally Responsive Teaching' in Indian Higher Education Institutions lacks a substantial pragmatic approach and serious scholarship.

Often centrally designed curricula are taught in HEIs whose compositions differ from each other significantly and are largely detached from student realities. Despite revisions and efforts to keep curricula in sync with the changing times and heightened awareness of social hierarchies, many disciplines still cater to representations of the Global North, the Caste system that is peculiar to the Indian scenario, and generally of the upper-and middle-class cultures. These unilaterally designed curricula exclude students whose caste, class, regional, and linguistic diversities lie outside the domain of dominant cultures that find representation. The onus to break away from these dominant ideologies, to make students aware of cultures other than the hegemonic ones, and to train them to critically engage with structural and social hierarchies lies with teachers. Ensuring the cultural relevance of a curriculum that does not represent classroom diversity can be achieved through pedagogical practices devised by individual teachers based on their contexts. This chapter inquires the usefulness of technology in assisting pedagogies that are geared toward Culturally Responsive Teaching. The first step is to examine if stipulated parameters clearly indicate and comprehensively portend how highly ranked colleges are using technology for pedagogical and assessment purposes and if any of these are utilizing it to cater to concerns of cultural representation and social transformation.

Examining Self-Study Reports of the top-ranked colleges which offer a robust academic framework for understanding implementation, challenges, and implications of Culturally Responsive Teaching practices within the Indian higher education context, facilitates its exploration within institutions known for their academic excellence, diverse student populations, and institutional best practices. It is also important to note that two of the five ranking parameters are 'Teaching, Learning and Resources' and 'Outreach and Inclusivity' which indicate that the colleges have institutional practices in place that might provide insights into some successful practices of the use of technology and progressive pedagogical practices.

Some observations

An important document that assesses pedagogies of holistic learning is the NAAC's requirement of submitting a Self-Study Report. Criterion 2 requires colleges to report on the assessment of 'Teaching-Learning and Evaluation' practices. It reviews the effectiveness of teaching methodologies, curriculum design, and assessment frameworks employed by respective institutions. The questions within this criterion stress the requirement for a student-centric learning environment focusing on HEIs to encourage active participation, critical thinking, and creativity among students.

Furthermore, it evaluates the coherence between pedagogical practices and educational objectives. It also assesses the availability of required resources and infrastructure to strengthen effective teaching and learning endeavours. What remains central to this criterion is the scrutiny of student assessment mechanisms for their fairness, transparency, and efficacy in evaluating learning outcomes accurately. This is a resource for how HEIs present their best practices in teaching-learning and assessment. The objective and subjective information available through these reports published in the public domain are also supplemented with additional information in supporting documents allowing the HEIs to go beyond the space limitations of the NAAC proforma. This self-presented data work as samples of what pedagogical practices look like in the HEIs that are recognized for their excellence by the Ministry of Education, India. This also opens up avenues to study the potential, lacunae, and the road to implementing culturally responsive teaching in India.

Methodological approach

To begin with, the preliminary study of the latest self-study proforma and its questions for colleges shows that it generally includes multiple sections, some of which seek information on the following criteria:

- how HEIs cater to student diversity (section 2.2)
- details of the teaching-learning process (2.3), and
- evaluation process and reforms undertaken by the HEIs (2.5).

However, upon closer examination, it can be noted that these sections that hold the potential of unravelling how HEIs respond to socio-cultural diversity of classrooms are defined by limited factors and perspectives. Section 2.2 restricts analysis of the diversity of students by asking for information on special programmes for slow and advanced learners. This restriction of diversity to learning levels does not necessitate engagement with socio-economic factors that often contribute to varied levels of learning. The section on teaching-learning process (2.3) asks for:

- documentation of student-centric methods, such as experiential learning, participative learning, and problem-solving methodologies used by the HEIs for enhancing learning experiences.

While this allows space for HEIs to give descriptive details of their pedagogical frameworks that cater to student diversity it does not qualify characteristics of student-centric teaching-learning methods. The second sub-section within 2.3 requires information on how ICT-enabled tools are used by teachers in HEIs to ensure an effective teaching-learning process. An open-ended question without specifications on what effective teaching-learning entails, does not particularly focus on cultural diversity, yet opens up possibility of reflecting on new-age pedagogies that are culturally responsive.

The relevant aspect of Criterion 2 pertains to the evaluation process and reforms undertaken by the HEIs. However, it concerns itself only with transparency of the process and mechanisms in place to deal with student grievances leaving no scope for HEIs to think about or reflect on evaluation processes that can facilitate cultural inclusivity of students.

Taking these factors into consideration, a qualitative analysis of the latest available self-study reports and supporting documents of the top-ranking institutions was undertaken. It attempted to explore if, despite the Self-Study Report proforma's lack of focus on intersections of technology and pedagogical frameworks that align with features of culturally responsive teaching, the representation of teaching-learning practices by colleges contain information that reflects efforts at using technology-driven pedagogical practices to ensure representation of student diversity and inculcation of critical skills that encourage students to question social hierarchies deeply entrenched in various aspects of the Indian milieu. It also explored how and to what effect concerns about use of technology and student cultural diversity find representation in the reports. What follows are some generalized key observations about the information submitted.

On analysing the information submitted by one such HEI, it can be observed that the institution emphasizes its role as a public-funded institution to respect diversity and aim at having inclusive classrooms. It also foregrounds the institution's commitment to catering to needs of disabled students through establishment of specialized centres responsible for providing ICT support including assistive software for students with visual disabilities. Under the question of the teaching-learning process, the documentation of courses that focus on student-centric approaches includes details of projects undertaken for courses such as 'Techniques of Ethnographic Filmmaking', 'Historian's Craft', 'GIS and Remote Sensing' and courses taught by the education department. The report also mentions contribution of the Robotics Society in providing students with project-based learning experiences.

In the section that particularly asks for information on the use of ICT-enabled tools to make teaching-learning process effective, the report of the concerned top-ranking HEI, focuses on internet availability through Wi-Fi access in classrooms and laboratories; availability of Google Suite, now known as Google Workspace, a collection of cloud computing, productivity, and collaboration tools, software, and online products; access to laptops on request; library management software and the use of presentation programmes such as PowerPoint by teachers in classrooms. The report also includes use of student record management online applications like 'acad ME' and Learning Management Systems such as Google Classroom to ensure transparency and ease in the evaluation process.

While at the time when another leading HEI submitted its Self-Study Report, the proforma asked for strategies adopted by the institution to improve access for students belonging to groups labelled in the proforma as 'SC/ST', 'OBC', 'Women', 'Differently abled', 'Minority community' and 'any other'. In this section, apart from State policies that govern admissions and fee structures, the report mentioned the functioning of cells and societies like 'The Equal Opportunity Cell', the 'North East Cell', 'Friend's Corner', and the 'National Service Scheme' that work toward non-discrimination based on disability, the integration of students from North Eastern States into the wider community, smooth transitioning of foreign national students and students from states, respectively.

Under the section on use of technologies and facilities by teachers for effective teaching, the concerned Self-Study Reports of more than one top-ranking HEI include infrastructural sufficiency in terms of Wi-Fi access, LCD projectors, ICT-enabled classrooms, and laboratories, and an automated college library. However, some HEIs studied here document more details about pedagogy by listing various teaching-learning methods like presentation programmes, demonstrations, screening of documentary and educational films, group presentations, and use of models. Connections are also drawn between the introduction of these methods and increased sense of confidence, communication skills, and personality of students. In a separate section on innovative teaching methods, the reports list the use of e-resources, presentation programmes, group projects, field trips, film screenings, expert lectures, internships, and innovation projects.

The report of yet another institution conceptualizes student diversity in terms of learning levels as per the requirement of the report, students from other states, and students belonging to what the institution's response categorizes as 'backward community'. It highlights the role of bridge courses, use of the college website, work of alumni and current students to encourage student enrolments from diverse backgrounds. The institution's response to its student-centric teaching methods focuses on participatory learning, tutoring, interactive pedagogies, and encouragement to take up extracurricular activities.

The report of a leading women's HEI much like the others sees bridge courses, remedial classes, and mentorship programmes as effective methods of catering to student diversity. Some additional measures included were value-added courses like, 'Effective English Communication', 'Aptitude Coaching', and 'Career Counselling' offered by the college's training division. The report also documents collaborations with organizations like Tata Consultancy Services to provide affirmative training to 'slow learners'. Furthermore, it reveals that there are additional opportunities for advanced learners and students are encouraged to pursue online learning through courses in SWAYAM[1] and NPTEL[2] to gain extra credits.

The report also highlights the institution's 'Study Abroad Programme' that assists students to gain extra credits, and specialized coaching classes to clear various professional exams by organizations like the Institute of Chartered Accountants of India, Association of Chartered Certified Accountants, Institute of Cost and Management Accountants of India and Institute of Company Secretaries of India. The documentation of student-centric teaching-learning methods underlines the institution's endeavour to provide holistic development and encourage participative learning. The response specifically identifies Andragogy and Heutagogy as the college's primary pedagogical methods. Like other institutions, it considers project work, memberships in various extracurricular clubs, and internships as ways of enhancing teaching-learning process.

The section on ICT-enabled tools is rather detailed. In addition to Wi-Fi connectivity and technologically enabled infrastructure, the report describes contributions of e-studio for recorded lectures, online resources for self-paced learning, and blended/flipped mode-based pedagogical practices. The response also delineates the incorporation of Learning Management Systems like MyKlassRoom/Moodle and video conferencing platforms like Zoom, Google Meet, GoToMeeting, etc. in the teaching-learning process of the college. In the report, attention is paid to the documentation of faculty training programmes on 'Digital

---

[1] SWAYAM is a programme initiated by the Government of India and provides free open online courses for university and college learners through an online platform.

[2] The National Programme on Technology-Enhanced Learning (NPTEL) is a government-funded Indian e-learning platform for university-level science, technology, engineering, and mathematics subjects. It is jointly developed by seven Indian Institutes of Technology and the Indian Institute of Science.

Teaching Techniques'. As per information provided, 60 faculty members received this training, and further trained 300 faculty members of the institution to facilitate 100 % usage of online platforms by the institution's teaching staff.

The report also records the use of open-source interactive presentation software like Mentimeter and Kahoot for virtual classes. Further, the report mentions use of Enterprise Resource Planning (ERP) software for students' attendance, sharing of internal assessment marks, lesson plans, and other academic information. The report also reflects integration of IT for automation of several administrative and academic processes to increase their efficiency and ensure timely completion. The supporting documents submitted with the report list many courses offered by various departments some of which include courses on social responsibility, Indian culture, Contemporary India, Cross-Cultural Management, etc. that engage with issues of communalism, caste movements, anti-caste politics, and international cultures.

The summary of Criterion 2 in another well-recognized HEI focuses on the institution's efforts at promoting social awareness among students, non-discriminatory admission procedures, bridge courses for 'slow learners', infrastructural facilities for disabled students, provisions of fee concessions, scholarships and other welfare schemes for students from 'financially weak and disadvantaged' backgrounds. In the section seeking expanded details, the report proforma asks for documentation of information on strategies adopted by the HEI to improve access to students belonging to different categories such 'SC/ST/OBC', 'Women', 'Persons with disabilities', 'economically weaker sections', and 'outstanding achievers in sports and extracurricular activities'. The HEI's response to this question identifies financial assistance for students from non-caste backgrounds, organization of sensitization workshops by a women's cell for female students, disabled-friendly infrastructure for students with disabilities, scholarships and awards for students from low-income groups and prizes for student achievers in sports and extracurricular activities. To cater to student diversity, the report of recognizes mentoring programmes, personalized attention and identification of special needs of students by teachers, and communication mediation through student class representatives.

The sub-section 2.4 on incremental academic growth of different categories of students and its assistance in improving performance of students is responded with a summary of the process in place which includes use of software for result review, review of academic progression by the college's Principal and relaying of findings and recommendations to teachers to devise and implement methods to provide extra support to students. The report contains a separate section on catering to needs of advanced learners (2.2.5) wherein the institution emphasizes library facilities like JSTOR and Inflibnet, encouragement to take up small-scale research projects, and collaboration with faculty members for conducting research work. The report includes a special section that seeks details of teaching-learning methods that go beyond traditional lecture methods and lists presentations, case studies, group discussions, project-based work, industrial visits, live projects, and internships. It also mentions provision of an e-campus programme for sharing online content used by faculty with the students.

A list of participatory learning activities used by the faculty is also recorded in the report which in addition to the methods already mentioned like use of e-campus, consists of blended learning through the use *ePathshala* software. The use of technology by faculty members receives exclusive space in the report which acknowledges the role of the Internal Quality Assurance Cell in promoting the use of latest ICT techniques and records the operation of the Education Multimedia Research Center in the college used to prepare lecture videos and transmit them globally. The institution's report engages with innovative teaching approaches and their impact on learning. Use of Internet, film screenings, use of presentation programmes, visual aids like graphs, and charts, and access to computer labs are some of the facilities mentioned here. The section which seeks information on efforts made to facilitate the faculty in handling computer-aided teaching/learning materials draws upon methods mentioned in other sections and reiterates the institution's endeavour to encourage faculty to attend seminars, conferences, and workshops; use presentation software to deliver lectures, access computer labs, and seminar rooms. The numbers of faculty members who underwent staff development programmes are recorded in the report and state that a good number of teachers attended refresher courses continuously; HRD programmes; orientation programmes; staff training conducted by the college; summer/winter school, workshops, and faculty development programmes, respectively.

Scope of culturally responsive new-age pedagogies in the Indian context

A close textual analysis of all the reports has been useful to note that the use of technology and sensitivity towards cultural diversity forms an important part of the everyday functioning of these institutions. Efforts and practices to make educational spaces more culturally inclusive can be observed through the provision of welfare schemes and the establishment of special cells and societies to provide group-specific support to students. The assessment criterion also brings up questions and concerns related to specially curated mechanisms to not just encourage admission of students from various socio-economic backgrounds but also a safe, non-discriminatory space for everyone. The incorporation of multiple questions on cultural diversity as the basis of assessment and gradation of HEIs in the reports at different points in time displays recognition of the multicultural fabric of the Indian society and the importance of inclusivity as key factors in the functioning of Indian HEIs.

The lists of participatory and experiential learning courses for students, group projects and presentations, faculty training programmes, and collaborations with other organizations to make learning in HEIs more student-centric, demonstrate nascent strategies adopted by institutions to respond to various needs of students. However, lack of enhanced teaching-learning, and limitation of student-centric approaches to identification and categorization of students as slow and advanced learners, leave out the possibility of narrowing down the attention to specific cultural diversities in terms of caste, class, religion, linguistic and gender identities of students. This limitation in the assessment questions restricts the scope for HEIs to address cultural disparities and create inclusive learning environments that resonate with students' diverse backgrounds and experiences.

Moreover, these existing strategies and methods do manage to encourage the admission of diverse students. However, they do not take the next step to make classroom space a platform that continuously provides opportunities for representation of each student's culture. They also lack in instituting special pedagogical practices to encourage academic engagements that are sensitive to the multicultural inputs each student can bring to the learning experience. These untapped areas exclude possibility of adopting teaching-learning methods that inspire students to engage in cultural exchange within the classroom and expand their understanding of various disciplines with a simultaneous building of a critically aware mindset that can question inherent social hierarchies.

Similarly, the reports lay substantial focus on use of technology and efforts to maximize impacts of digital revolution in the education sector. From online and ICT-assisted teaching-learning methods to automation of administrative procedures, the reports studied lay out multiple mechanisms in place that reflect an increasing and conscious determination to extract benefits of digital revolution for enhanced learning environments. The systems in place attempt to transcend temporal and spatial barriers to knowledge dissemination. Educational technology (EdTech) tools, like Learning Management Systems (LMS), are in use to democratize access to education while giving educators new avenues for instructional innovation. However, integration of technology into pedagogy especially in the context of India needs to transcend mere digitization of content. If a holistic education aimed at social transformation is to be achieved, use of technology should be imbued with pedagogical intent, aligning with principles of active learning, collaboration, and critical inquiry (Bates, 2015). Based on teaching methods and technology usage described in the reports, the final section suggests ways to blend efforts not only to merely assimilate students hailing from diverse cultural milieus but also to celebrate their diversity by making better use of opportunities offered by digital revolution. This involves creating teaching approaches that match the principles of Culturally Responsive Teaching.

Integrating culturally responsive teaching and technology: A roadmap for promoting social transformation through HEIs

A theoretical paradigm that took shape in American society marred by racism and white domination, Culturally Responsive Teaching has shown a remarkable positive impact on creating classrooms that consciously tap into students' cultural diversity as effective ways of providing education that trains them to become global citizens with a social sensitivity that recognizes socio-cultural hierarchies and helps in challenging them.

There are several examples of successful implementation of culturally responsive teaching. In places like California, the development of culturally specific courses such as programmes based on ethnic studies has benefitted student learning and heightened their cultural awareness (Ethic Studies Model Curriculum, 2022). Reports such as 'Effective Teacher Professional Development' (2017) examine the effective strategies for professional development of teachers. It delineates and testifies to the benefits of introducing culturally responsive teaching methods at the level of teachers' professional development. Gay's 2002 article on special education engages with the significance of culturally responsive teaching in special education and provides an understanding of approaches that can make professional development of teachers more effective. Community-based education initiatives have also been the subject of study by Ladson-Billings (2022), and Garcia and Guerra (2004). Ladson-Billings' book gives details of successful teachers who have implemented culturally responsive teaching methodologies and explores their experiences in diverse communities to draw important insights. Garcia and Guerra's article also focuses on community-based methods that help in creating culturally responsive classrooms.

The benefits of culturally responsive teaching have also been studied for how they impact the social-emotional learning of students and work on their well-being. The works of Howard (2019) and Milner IV (2010) engage with the effects of race and culture on the learning and well-being of students, and the function played by teacher education in preparing teachers to address the social-emotional needs of youth, respectively. The social system in India is also infused with socio-cultural, ethnic, and racial discrimination. Legal reformations to protect historically oppressed groups have not necessarily translated into significant social changes. Education spaces hold immense potential to subvert these hegemonical structures. It can foster learning environments that disseminate knowledge not just to create an efficient workforce but to create a generation of citizens who are more sensitized to cultural differences, richness of experience and knowledge held by diverse cultures, and the importance of critical and socio-political consciousness. One of the ways to achieve this can be integration of technology and Culturally Responsive Teaching and the development of subjective new-age pedagogical methods that suit varied kinds of classrooms.

Based on the study of the top-ranking institutions' reports, the following suggestive strategies can be used to bring about social transformation by utilizing digital revolution to implement pedagogies aligned with values of culturally responsive teaching.

Faculty development in culturally responsive teaching and technology integration

The criteria studied from the reports, indicate a commitment towards capacity building and training of teachers. The specialized training centres and HEIs need to provide the teaching staff with professional development opportunities that focus on integration of technology and Culturally Responsive Teaching principles. Workshops, symposia, webinars, and online courses can bring together teachers dedicated to creating socially conscious pedagogies. These programmes can equip educators with knowledge and tools to effectively utilize technology in promoting equity in education.

Culturally relevant curriculum design

Institutions mention the role of their teachers in curriculum development activities such as syllabi revision. Involvement of teachers in these primary decisions can act as a fertile ground to sow seeds of sociocultural consciousness. Institutions that create their curriculum or play roles in curriculum development can work on learning modules that go beyond the dominant cultural representations. These modules can reap the benefit of vast digital databases and archives such as those marginalized communities that often get excluded from the curricula. They can access information through internet and online library resources to integrate examples, case studies, and narratives from cultures to which their student population belongs. Through contextualization of curriculum subject matter within the students' cultural frameworks, teachers can improve relevance, engagement, and retention of learning outcomes of courses.

Multimedia supplementary resources

The HEIs emphasized usefulness of audio-visual material in enhancing teaching-learning process in their respective Self-Study Reports. What is required is for the institutions and government policies to specifically evolve methods that create and curate multimedia cultural resources. These resources can act as supplementary materials to teach various courses. Cross-cultural understanding among students can be facilitated by developing online repositories of videos, films, and audio recordings that represent diverse cultural perspectives, languages, and traditions prevalent in India.

Use of digital cultural archives

The Self-Study Reports examined, state the use of ICT tools like laptops, projectors, and W-Fi by teachers in classrooms. What is lacking are guidelines to optimize their use to celebrate diverse cultural composition of classrooms. Teachers can be trained to look for digital exhibits, virtual museums, and online collections featuring contributions from varied communities. The incorporation of these in everyday pedagogical practices can allow students to learn different disciplines through cultures that do not find representation in their core curriculum.

Use of technology-enhanced language learning

Availability of laptops in the HEIs, mobile and Internet penetration, and active use by students open up avenues for teachers to use innovative methods to teach language and communication-based courses. HEIs can encourage use of language learning applications and develop interactive language labs to help students become proficient in various languages. The use of resources that incorporate culturally authentic language materials and interactive tasks designed for students can help them develop cultural literacy.

Encouragement of digital collaborative projects and assignments

The accreditation criteria value innovation and reforms in assessment methods used by HEIs. This concern can be furthered to benefit culturally responsive practices of assessment. Both at policy levels and subjective practices, students can be encouraged to indulge in digital storytelling through multimedia presentations, blog posts, and podcasts by tailoring their assessment questions in such a way that they get inspired to reflect on their heritage, cultural identities and lived experiences while responding to the learnings from curriculum. Courses in social sciences and humanities can empower students to use digital storytelling platforms and promote self-expression. They can be encouraged to connect with their cultures and their community elders. Based on these methods of learning and other forms of research they can be motivated to share folklore, personal narratives, and cultural insights.

Another method that has already taken shape in at least the HEIs studied here is that of collaborative projects. Efforts can be made to encourage students to work with their peers who come from cultural backgrounds different from their own and engage in cross-cultural exchange by collaborating on online projects. The use of project management tools, virtual teamwork platforms, and collaborative document editing like Google Documents holds the capacity to enable students to foster intercultural understanding and teamwork skills.

Conclusion

The preceding sections in this chapter highlight the gaps in Indian Higher Education Institutions' efforts to facilitate inclusive and transformative learning environments through integrating technology. The process of examining the Self-Study Reports of top-ranking HEIs revealed several themes that were common to them. It showed both progress and areas for improvement in HEI's efforts at promoting social awareness, supporting diverse student populations, and enhancing teaching-learning practices through use of technology.

This analysis helped in understanding that while such reports demonstrate important efforts toward inclusivity and innovation in higher education, the two do not intersect. The examination shows that there are still challenges in place and opportunities for improvement. The preceding sections reveal the need for a more nuanced approach to addressing specific cultural disparities and promoting cultural exchange within classrooms. HEIs in India must strive to develop curriculum modules that cater to diverse cultural backgrounds of students and integrate tools available as a result of digital revolution that specifically aim at facilitating cross-cultural understanding.

In conclusion, this chapter argues that integration of technology and Culturally Responsive Teaching principles holds tremendous potential for promoting social transformation in higher education in the context of India. By implementing pedagogies based on principles of Culturally Responsive Teaching and using digital tools, Indian HEIs can create learning environments that empower students to challenge social hierarchies. These practices can also help celebrate cultural diversity throughout educational journeys of students and help them become global citizens. These new-age pedagogies can also equip students with critical skills essential for navigating a world that is increasingly becoming interconnected. As HEIs in India evolve and adapt to the changing world of technology brought forth by digital revolution and a world marred by intolerance to difference, it is important to make inclusive practices that foster equity, diversity, and social justice an integral part of higher education.

References

ABP News Bureau. (2024, February 27). Over 800 million internet users in India, 707 million actively used OTTs in 2023: IAMAI report. *ABP Live*. Accessed 2 April 2024, from https://news.abplive.com/technology/internet-in-india-report-2023-iamai-kantar-ott-onl ine-users-data-state-1667795

Bates, A. W. (2015). *Teaching in a digital age: Guidelines for designing teaching and learning.* BCcampus.

Chandras, J. S. (2021). Student identity in the Indian university: Language and Educational Stereotypes in Higher Education. *Journal of Belonging, Identity, Language, and Diversity (J-BILD), 2021,* 25–41.

Darling-Hammond, L., Hyler, M. E., & Gardner, M. (2017). *Effective teacher professional development.* Learning Policy Institute.

Ethnic studies model curriculum. (2022). The California Department of Education Sacramento.

Garcia, S. B., & Guerra, P. L. (2004). Deconstructing deficit thinking: Working with educators to create more equitable learning environments. *Education and Urban Society, 36*(2), 150–168.

Gay, G. (2002). Culturally responsive teaching in special education for ethnically diverse students: Setting the stage. *International Journal of Qualitative Studies in Education, 15*(6), 613–629.

Howard, T. C. (2019). *Why race and culture matter in schools: Closing the achievement gap in America's classrooms.* Teachers College Press.

Internet in India 2023. KANTAR and Internet and Mobile Association of India. Accessed 2 April 2024, from https://uat.indiadigitalsummit.in/sites/default/files/thought-leadership/pdf/Kantar_iamai_Report_20_Page_V3_FINAL_web_0.pdf

Jhingran, D. (2009). Hundreds of home languages in the country and many in most classrooms: Coping with diversity in primary education in India. In T. Skutnabb-Kangas, R. Phillipson, A. K. Mohanty, & M. Panda (Eds.), *Social justice through multilingual education*. Multilingual Matters, 263–282.

Kumar, S. (2014). Inclusive classroom and social diversity in India: Myths and challenges. *Journal of Indian Research*, 2(1), 126–140.

Kumari, P., Nayan, R., Aggarwal, S. P., & Baswani, G. (2019). Rethinking teacher education programmes for inclusive classrooms: Issues and challenges in India. *International Journal of Information and Education Technology*, 9(2), 143–148.

Ladson-Billings, G. (2022). *The dreamkeepers: Successful teachers of African American children*. John Wiley & Sons.

Ladson-Billings, G., & Tate, W. F. (1995). Toward a critical race theory of education. *Teachers College Record*, 97(1), 47–68.

Milner IV, H. R. (2010). What does teacher education have to do with teaching? Implications for diversity studies. *Journal of Teacher Education*, 61(1–2), 118–131.

Mohanty, A. K., Mishra, M. K., Reddy, N. U., & Ramesh, G. (2009). Overcoming the language barrier for tribal children: Multilingual education in Andhra Pradesh and Orissa, India. In T. Skutnabb-Kangas, R. Phillipson, A. K. Mohanty, & M. Panda (Eds.), *Social justice through multilingual education* (pp. 283–298). Multilingual Matters.

Sabharwal, N. S. (2020). Student diversity and discrimination in Indian higher education: Curricula transformation for civic learning. In A. E. Mazawi & M. Stack (Eds.), *Course syllabi in faculties of education: Bodies of knowledge and their discontents, international and comparative perspectives* (pp. 170–186). Bloomsbury Academic.

Chapter 10

Towards digital transition in higher education: E-service-learning and artificial intelligence

IRENE CULCASI[1] AND MARIA CINQUE[2]

Abstract: The exponential acceleration of technological progress places us at the beginning of a new era. From generation to generation, world-changing technological innovations grow and Artificial Intelligence (AI) is one of them. The boundaries of learning extend beyond traditional classrooms and Higher Education faces new challenges and opportunities. The present chapter aims at exploring the promising news application of Service-Learning through technological interactions, also known as e-Service-Learning (e-SL). This experiential educational proposal has been cited by UNESCO (2021) as an innovative tool through which to address the complex challenges of our society, while enriching learning, fostering civic responsibility and strengthening community engagement. The idea of embedding digital tools in SL is promising but it opens up to a debate on the intricate relationship between technology, education, and societal impact. In particular, the new frontiers of Artificial Intelligence (AI) applied to the educational sector need to be discussed. A scenario in which AI benefits' will be widely distributed is likely, but it will not happen automatically and requires a careful reflection on how to integrate the triad of academic learning, digital technologies and civic engagement. e-SL could be a practical exemplification of the holistic educational vision of the future.

Keywords: artificial intelligence, AI literacy, digital literacy, e-service-learning, higher education

---

[1]   The author is credited with writing sections 1, 2, 3, 4, and 5.
[2]   Shared authorship of section 4 is attributed to the author.

Introduction

The exponential acceleration of technological progress places us at the beginning of a new era. From generation to generation, world-changing technological innovations grow and Artificial Intelligence (AI) is one of them. Since the term was coined in 1956, AI, as a discipline, has had a series of periods of great enthusiasm and other ones of reduced interest, so-called AI winters. Machine Learning (ML) is the technology behind the most promising aspect of AI, whose architecture is inspired by the neuronal network of the human brain. These networks are organized in layers and make predictions that are more accurate the more data they are powered by, to the point that many refer to data as the 'new oil' (Di Michele, 2023, p. 27). If the potential of AI is many, equally many are the questions and critical issues that its development imposes. From an educational point of view, according to the European Commission, teachers and institutions have an important responsibility:

> Due to the constant exposure of young people to the digital universe, those involved in education and training have an important task to stay abreast of an ever-changing environment and equip young people with the critical thinking skills required to exercise judgment, [and] analyze complex realities [...]. Education thus has a crucial role to play in helping young people strengthen the competences needed to successfully navigate the digital world they encounter on a daily basis. (European Commission, 2022, p. 8)

Also, the recent document on AI in Higher Education (Gimpel et al., 2024) emphasizes the need for universities to re-evaluate and update the competencies university students should acquire, while adapting to the changing landscape. Consequently, universities should also provide training programmes for teachers and staff to integrate technologies into various aspects of the educational system. Indeed, specific knowledge areas, skills, and attitudes (e.g. new competency area is AI management or AI innovation) are emerging; therefore, there is a corresponding necessity for Higher Education institution (HEi) for reconsidering its methodologies and pedagogical approaches for transforming both learning opportunities (with deeply connection with AI technologies) and teaching offers.

The aim of this contribution is to explore digital literacy in relation to the advancement of AI (AI literacy), considering a significant link with the e-Service-Learning (e-SL) pedagogical approach as a way to promote it. Indeed, as AI-powered educational technologies (AI-EdTech) become increasingly dominant in the instructional sector, teachers and institutions are faced with critical decisions on how to integrate them effectively. e-SL links the learning dimension to the community through a solidarity service, in a digital empowerment perspective; it enables students to integrate the use of technologies to become involved in their community, to critically reflect on the experience, and to learn on a personal, social and academic level (Aramburuzabala et al., 2024).

Artificial intelligence and new challenges for Higher Education institutions

AI is the name of the branch of computer science that deals with the development of techniques capable of simulating (not recreating) the cognitive abilities of human beings, such as logical thinking, planning, creativity and learning. From 2010 AI has had a broad impact thanks to significantly improved processing power, access to huge amounts of data and the implementation of new types of statistical models. Nowadays, AI has already expanded the limits of what can be achieved with machines and has led to changes across most industry sectors (Gimpel et al., 2024). Nevertheless, we need to remember that AI is not intelligent, if we consider intelligence as the ability to understand the world. Indeed, machines do not even understand elementary concepts such as cause and effect. Moreover, AI cannot make decisions because it is simply a statistical model that processes data. Conversely, if intelligence is defined as the ability to solve complex problems, then AI is already more intelligent than humans in specific types of activities. Another consideration goes against the widely diffused belief that technologies are ethically neutral because they can be good or bad depending on how they are used. As Di Michele suggests (2023, p. 107) in this way 'we ignore all the ethically relevant decisions that precede the moment when a tool is actually used, such as the design and development phase'. As an example, software programmers' lack of awareness of their own biases can lead to discriminatory effects. In addition, since AI relies on data, if a given minority is underrepresented in terms of data, AI inevitably reflects that discrimination. This poses a first dilemma: should we keep the data as it is or should we manipulate it by removing, for example, sexist or racist stereotypes to offer a socially acceptable result that nevertheless denies the existence of such problems in our society? (Di Michele, 2023).

From an educational point of view, 'future-proof graduates need to be able to identify and navigate AI's bright and dark sides to contribute to the responsible and value-creating development and use of AI' (Gimpel et al., 2024, p. 12). Given the achievements of AI, as it is well known, some universities have tried to ban the use of Generative AI (Gen AI), currently the most prominent example of machine learning. Gen AI enables the creation of digital content: it can be used to structure, write or revise text, produce images, synthesize speech, create videos and develop software code; GPT (Generative Pre-trained Transformer) models are among those that have captured the most interest. The reasons for the ban concern both plagiarism issues and the concern that the automation of content creation will reduce the analytical and critical thinking in the approach of complex topics (Di Michele, 2023, p. 180). For example, Darvishi et al. (2024) conducted a randomized controlled experiment that explored the impact of AI assistance with writing feedback (such as rule-based suggestion detection and semantic similarity) on student agency in the context of peer feedback. The study suggests that students tended to rely on AI assistance rather than actively learning from it, thus without the AI's guidance students didn't provide feedback of the same quality (Darvishi et al., 2024).

On the contrary, other studies (e.g. Zawacki-Richter et al., 2019) stresses that AI has a lot of educational potential in increasing education levels. Also, the study of Habib et al. (2024) exploring the impact of Gen AI on university student creative thinking skills and, in particular, their divergent thinking skills, underline that AI has the potential to significantly support creative thinking, but there are also negative impacts on creativity and creative confidence.

Assuming that it would be technically feasible to ban AI, another possible way is to introduce it to students in depth, thus giving them the tools to navigate a world in which AI will create much of the content they will see (Di Michele, 2023). According to Panciroli and Rivoltella (2023), it is necessary not to make the mistake of thinking that AI represents only a risk to be defended from because in today's complex societies without the support of algorithms, it would be very difficult to live. The use of AI in education aims to support and empower students through intelligent tutoring systems, smart classrooms, personalized learning experiences, immediate and targeted feedback, and immersive learning technologies (Zawacki-Richter et al., 2019). AI could be particularly helpful to address the challenges of limited resources in education, such as ones of the remote schools or areas, by creating opportunities (e.g. virtual learning environment simulating real-world scenarios) who may not have access (Onesi-Ozigagun et al., 2024).

The main challenge is to create forms of participation which allow young people to learn and practice critical digital and AI literacy. Therefore, its implementation should be approached with deep-rooted pedagogical perspectives that can guide teachers in finding the right balance between AI use assistance and students' active participation in their own learning. As AI continues to evolve, it is crucial to maintain a critical approach to ensure that it can generate benefits for both students and educators, while minimizing its risks. Indeed, other main challenges to consider are (Onesi-Ozigagun et al., 2024):

- Data privacy and security: HEi have to safeguard student sensitive data by implementing robust data protection measures (e.g. data anonymization, access controls etc.).
- Algorithmic bias: HEi have to consider that AI systems can amplify existing inequalities in education if specific biases are not addressed; thus, testing and ongoing monitoring and evaluation of AI systems are necessary to mitigate eventual inaccuracies.
- Teacher training and support: HEi have to provide necessary training opportunities for teachers on how to use AI tools because their role is crucial in guiding and supporting students.

Thus, for educational institutions the dual challenges arise of how to develop critical thinking towards technologies (Media Literacy Education) and how to promote a culture of AI in order to empower individuals in ethical knowledge and use of its languages and logic.

Promoting digital literacy and AI literacy

Promoting digital literacy through formal and non-formal education has been underlined as a crucial goal by different official entities such as the Council of Europe (2019), also because 'students often lack the ability to engage in critical thinking or reflect on the ethical dimensions of their online actions' (European Commission, 2022, p. 24). Although there is an increasing number of regional, national and international policies in Europe, there is still no common agreement about what the minimum levels are in order to consider a person digitally literate (Tinmaz et al., 2022).

This results in a serious knowledge gap about the global state of digital literacy skills of youth and adults (Jones & Procter, 2023). However, it should be considered that defining digital literacy is a challenge because of its instability: it changes as technologies and contemporary societies change (Bulfin & McGraw, 2015).

The UNESCO Digital Literacy Global Framework project (2018, p. 6) defines digital literacy as: 'the ability to access, manage, understand, integrate, communicate, evaluate, create and disseminate information safely and appropriately through digital technologies. It includes competences that are variously referred to as information literacy and media literacy, computer and ICT literacy.'

This definition encompasses the sum of related literacies, which are increasingly referred to as Digital Competence. However, the difference between 'literacy' and 'competence' is debated and competence denotes a deeper development (Jones & Procter, 2023). According to Bulfin and McGraw (2015), digital literacy cannot be conceived deterministically or instrumentally since this would result in seeing the meaning of literacy and technologies in merely technical or functional terms; such a view would also see literacy and technologies as neutral concepts, taking them out of the social, cultural, political and economic contexts that play an intrinsic part in their development, use, and critical understanding. This is why the two authors refer to the three-dimensional (3D) model developed by Green (1988), which affirms a holistic and integrated vision of literacy, by distinguishing it into three different dimensions (that Bulfin and McGraw adapted, 2015):

1. Operational literacy: is presented as an operational dimension and encompasses the development of skills in being able to handle tools or processes. From an educational point of view this dimension encourages teachers in promoting functional abilities.

2. Cultural literacy: is about knowing how to make meaning in context and includes values, motivations, passions, beliefs and ideology that come together in practice. From an educational point of view this dimension encourages teachers in creating authentic learning opportunities, connected to students' experiences and knowledge.

3. Critical literacy: involves an awareness that all literacies are a form of empowerment and power and focus on the social construction around a literacy that makes it more relevant than others. From

an educational point of view this dimension encourages teachers in promoting critical engagement and full comprehension about the implications of using dominant digital literacies, while understanding how to ensure that all individuals are able to participate.

According to Jones and Procter (2023), the 3D model and its dimensions sits in the frame of a situated conception of literacy, including knowledge, skills, attitudes and values.

Referring to AI competencies, Gimpel et al. (2024) distinguish two key or basic competencies and others advanced competencies. The AI basic competencies are AI literacy and AI reflection and should be considered alongside the five areas of digital competencies described by the DigComp 2.2 Framework: information and data literacy, communication and collaboration, digital content creation, safety, and problem-solving. Specifically:

- AI literacy: 'focuses on the dynamics between AI systems and human users. Examples are the knowledge to understand where and how the usage of AI may help humans, skills to efficiently give input to AI tools for high-quality results, and attitudes to critically inspect the outputs of AI tools, including appropriate reliance and not suffering from phenomena like automation bias' (Gimpel et al., 2024, p. 18);

- AI reflection: 'involves understanding how AI impacts society, adhering to legal standards, and navigating the moral complexities it presents. It is about being provided with the relevant knowledge to recognize the responsibilities that come with AI use, including issues of privacy, bias, and fairness. Further, it expands on the necessary skills to take responsibility and the attitudes to implement them correctly. This competency is essential for ensuring AI is used in a way that is beneficial and respectful to society' (Gimpel et al., 2024, p. 18).

AI advanced competencies depend on the context because they are specific to certain sectors and roles. Indeed, they are also called professional competencies.

As AI continues to advance, its role in education will become more prominent (Onesi-Ozigagun et al., 2024). Higher education institutions have different options for integrating AI in their curricula, resulting in specific types of activities focusing on AI as knowledge, skill or attitude (Table 1). Furthermore, De la Higuera (2019) identifies five fundamental pillars for building an AI curriculum: *Data awarness* (which is about acquiring the consciousness of being in a data-driven world in which media are not only tools – that is, devices – but also social and economic logics of which platforms are only the terminal part); *Uncertainty and Randomness* (which is about managing to acquire probabilistic reasoning and statistics); *Coding and Computational Thinking* (which is about the ability to use programming languages and manipulate large amounts of data); *Critical Thinking* (which is about gaining a real understanding of how technology works); and *Post-AI Humanism* (which is about understanding the areas of human beings, such as creativity and experience, that are characterized by interaction with AI).

Table 1. Events types for AI curricula integration in HEi

AI as:	Types of activities			
Knowledge	AI (ring) Lecture	AI Seminar	AI Guest Lecture	AI case study
Skill	AI-Lab	Project-based AI course	AI Hackathon	AI Certificate Programme
Attitude	AI Debate and Panel discussion	AI Networking event	AI Mentoring Programme	AI Fair/Open day

Source: Gimpel et al. (2024, p. 22).

In general, effective approaches to encourage digital and AI literacy include 'learning by doing' and interactive student-centred methods that provide students with the possibility to play an active role in their own learning journey supported by their faculty. Furthermore, since digital literacy and AI literacy are the sum of knowledge, skills and attitudes that students need to become informed and active participants, there is a clear connection between them and citizenship education and skills. In particular, as the social and cultural context in which we navigate nowadays transcends the differentiation between what we do online and offline – to the extent that we talk about an 'onlife' dimension (Floridi, 2014) – the construct of digital citizenship itself is no longer divisible between offline and online citizenship, but is an internal dimension of the unique citizenship we exercise (Panciroli & Rivoltella, 2023).

(e-)Service-learning

Service-Learning (SL) – also labelled e-Service-Learning (e-SL) when it is applied in relation with technologies – is a pedagogical approach centred on the Dewey principle of 'learning by doing' and in the Freire concept of action and reflection through educational *praxis*. This pedagogical approach connects the citizenship dimension with the learning dimension, giving students the possibility to learn while they serve their community through a solidarity activity that is strongly connected to their curricula. Specifically, e-SL has been explained as an experiential educational proposal that enables students to integrate the use of technologies to become involved in their community, to critically reflect on the experience, and to learn on a personal, social and academic level (Aramburuzabala et al., 2024). Thus, e-SL links the learning dimension to the community through a specific service activity, in a digital empowerment perspective.

Research in educational technology highlights that effective learning outcomes are achieved when the three types of educational interactions – 'student-content', 'student-student' and 'student-learner' – are meaningfully integrated (Bernard et al., 2009). Consequently, teachers must identify suitable digital tools and adopt instructional methods that promote interaction within the digital realm. This approach requires moving away from traditional, transmissive teaching methods towards designing active learning pathways facilitated by technology (Cinque & Culcasi, 2021). Also in implementing e-SL it is central to identify the appropriate digital tools to promote reflection, co-design, action and participation in and with the community. Indeed, e-SL provides an experiential practice where students engage in civic inquiry, reflection, and action through technology, collaborating with the community (Albanesi et al., 2020).

The innovative aspect of the SL is that it can be applied in any field since by inviting students to interface with real problems in their own community, the pedagogical proposal requires that students, depending on what they study, can co-design with the community partner and teachers a specific type of response and thus learn thanks to and through the community service they plan. In their systematic literature review, Culcasi and Fontana Venegas (2023) point out that SL positively impacts students beyond technical/hard skills, enhancing soft skills in social, personal, methodological, and digital areas (Culcasi & Fontana Venegas, 2023).

As noted by Stefaniak (2020) the number of studies exploring e-SL as a pedagogical strategy in online education has significantly increased. Specifically, in the e-SL literature technology could be considered as:

- a feature of the educational environment;
- an interaction element in the execution of the SL project.

If we consider technology as a contextual element of the educational environment in which we practice e-SL, the categorization of Waldner et al. (2012) is particularly useful; the authors define four types of SL including three hybrid models (Hybrid type I, II and III), classified based on whether the instruction and service components were conducted in-person or online. This classification underscores the flexibility and adaptability of e-SL in meeting the diverse needs of modern education, especially in times of crisis.

Furthermore, in the context of e-SL, digital technologies can be also incorporated in various ways, ranging from e-SL Hybrid Type I (SL fully on-site and teaching fully online) to Extreme e-SL (100 % online). For example, García-Gutiérrez et al. (2020) identified two main modes of interaction based on the role of technology in the SL project. The first mode, relationship-based e-SL, sees technology as an instrumental tool that facilitates and optimizes project development. The second mode, service-based e-SL, includes technology as both the learning objective and the service goal. However, García-Gutiérrez et al. (2020) did not account for the diverse roles of technology and digital devices or the varying levels of students' digital, personal, and social skills. To address this gap, Culcasi and her colleagues (2022) proposed an expanded model that categorizes technological interactions in e-SL into four types, considering both the roles of technology and the skill levels of students:

1. *Instrumental Channel-Type 1 Technological Interaction*: technology is the medium to implement the SL project when it would not have been used if it were not for a state of necessity. As such, the students do not need any particular technological expertise, while their personal and social skills are paramount.

2. *Integrated Channel-Type 2 Technological Interaction*: technology remains a medium, but its inclusion results from an intentional

design decision. As such, it requires students to be digitally literate to provide the service for the community.

3. *Instrumental Objective-Type 3 Technological Interaction:* technology is the goal for the SL project; it requires students to implement existing ICT tools in community service but does not involve the creation of new technological tools.

4. *Integrated Objective-Type 4 Technological Interaction:* technology is the objective of the SL project and includes creating new digital tools. Thus, students need advanced technological skills, while their personal and social skills may be minimal.

It is interesting to notice that, although the present model (Culcasi et al., 2022) has been proposed during the pandemic, it still works in a post-pandemic phase, offering higher education institutions a new frame seeking to foster meaningful engagement, collaborative learning, and impactful community involvement through technology.

A specific link between e-SL and AI, even before contextual or type of interaction in applying the SL projects, can occur at the level of identified societal needs. As mentioned, the SL invites students to take an active involvement in relevant social issues or needs that they can address through the skills they are acquiring in their educational journey. In this sense the link between e-SL and AI can be interesting when we pose the problem of how we can ensure that machines operate in line with values of justice and progress and generate a positive impact without leaving anyone behind. This means learning how to better interact with AI itself (Di Michele, 2023). An example of an e-SL project in this specific area could involve a group of e-technology engineering graduate students who are studying programming, engaging in the design of a new technology or application by highlighting unethical practices and creating an online awareness campaign about the need to develop ethics-centred guidelines and policies. From a learning and service perspective such students could play an essential role as communicators from their respective area of expertise, working on both technical and soft skills. Questioning ourselves how an artificial organism can 'behave ethically' recognizes asking what kind of intentionality one wants to give to the machine. These questions are part of the AI Literacy and in an example such as the one above, makes it well clear how educational systems can deal with AI not only in an instrumental sense but in a critical thematic sense (Panciroli & Rivoltella, 2023).

Furthermore, given the multidisciplinary nature of AI, the wide range of stakeholders and the countless aspects of the technology life cycle to be considered – from the time a new technology solution is identified to the time it is developed, implemented, and retired – it must necessarily be a joint effort in which all disciplines have to play their part. In this process, to ensure that technologies benefit everyone, it is not possible to expect a single discipline to achieve such a large goal. The great potential and power that come with AI require a greater sense of collective responsibility, and only if we have a clear idea of what the societal and individual needs are will we be able to design or open debates on how to design and implement the appropriate tools to ensure that AI works in line with our values. For this reason, according to Di Michele (2023) this is a unique moment to reflect on who we are, what kind of society we want and what are our most urgent goals.

Thus, to work critically on AI as a social issue, Di Michele offers a specific 'Map for the responsible adoption of AI' (Figure 1) for navigating and examining the key issues to be addressed through the AI lifecycle, considering different possible actors (the professional, the user and the community at large). We believe that this map could be useful to reflect together with students on the complexity of AI in terms of impact and widespread responsibility, and then, be able to design specific e-SL projects, depending on the area of expertise, also in a multidisciplinary perspective. Specifically, in this Map, depending on the group involved and for each stage of the AI life cycle, there are different types of questions. These will take on different meanings depending on whether they are evaluated according to their impact on individuals, communities, or society at large. The actors are first outlined below, and then the main stages of the life cycle from AI are explained.

The interested parties are:

- the professionals how develop the new technologies, such as technicians or engineers;
- the end users of the technology, that is, any individual or company that wants to delegate the performance of a specific task to an AI model (for example, a company that decides to use a software to select candidates for a competition);
- the community at large because how technology can be used and regulated is certainly a collective issue even if it is still rarely part of the public debate.

All these actors, at different levels, make a series of decisions that have strong ethical connotations through the AI' life cycle which can be divided into three main phases:

1. the *what phase* concerns the identification, definition of new opportunities related to society's priorities. In this phase we should ask ourselves: 'What problems do we want to solve?' or 'What principles should not be violated?' or 'What are the minimum levels of security?' or 'What combination of artificial and human intelligence can most effectively promote individual and societal goals and values?'. Such questions are complex and, in some cases, required value- and principle-focused answers, and in other cases governance-focused approaches;

2. the *how phase* concerns the design and development of the technology. In this phase we should ask ourselves: 'How we can ensure that algorithms do not discriminate against groups?' or 'How we can protect our privacy?';

3. The *where phase* occurs when the technology becomes available to final users and when we consider whether or not to adopt a new technological solution.

With respect to these stages and questions in the AI life cycle, an example of an e-SL project could involve a group of students in Sustainability management and Corporate Social Responsibility in creating focus groups about the relationship between AI and climate change, and then build guidelines for companies to adopt the least polluting solutions that reduce noxious emissions. Another e-SL example might involve a team of architecture students dealing with the relationship between the physical environment and the introduction of new technologies. Indeed, as the introduction of cars changed the landscape substantially, this could also happen for the introduction of new technologies. A further example of an e-SL project could involve a group of education students working to promote more inclusive solutions by collecting and disseminating cases where people with disabilities or vulnerable people have found themselves excluded from technologies, highlighting the barriers of access to the digital world.

These examples lead us to understand how from 'what' to 'where' phases, ethically relevant choices need to be made. As educators, the best tool we have is education, and the use of maps such as the one proposed gives us a fundamental resource to start thinking about the many issues that need to be addressed and to ensure that everyone is feeling responsible.

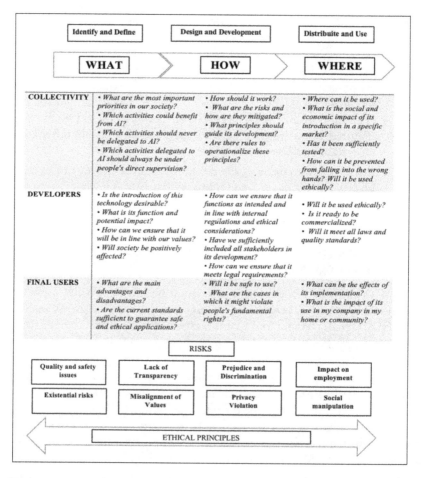

Figure 1. A map for responsible adoption of AI
Source: Di Michele (2023, p. 273)

Conclusion

The exponential technological innovation constantly offers us exciting new solutions, but as we continue to develop new technologies, we should increasingly remember that the ultimate goal is not innovation per se, but what is beneficial to humanity and enhances the human experience (Di Michele, 2023). A scenario in which AI benefits' will be widely distributed is likely, but it will not happen automatically and requires our effort on three main goals (Panciroli & Rivoltella, 2023):

- Educate Artificial Intelligence
- Educate about Artificial Intelligence
- Educate with Artificial Intelligence

These three new directions are located within the international literature on AI applied to education that calls for a new definition of Educational Technology (Panciroli & Macauda, 2021). Service-Learning or e-Service-Learning has been cited by UNESCO (2021) as an innovative tool through which to address the complex challenges of our society, while enriching learning, fostering civic responsibility and strengthening community engagement. We believe it can be a powerful pedagogical tool to work on these three main areas. In addition, because of its cross-disciplinary character in addressing social issues within communities, SL results in creating new perspectives for dialogue, sinking even very complex challenges from various angles. For example, at the present historical period, philosophy as discipline could help to better understand values and changes taking place in our society, to question the status quo, to evaluate options and consider pros and cons, and for this reason it could be the basis of any interdisciplinary SL project. According to Elam and Reich (2022), each discipline should bring its own contribution to the understanding of the topic, which means developing educational interventions on AI beyond Computer Science, including the humanities, the arts, and the social sciences. The challenge is to move from knowledge to participation and to enable the exercise of one's citizenship by putting oneself in an increasingly responsibility role in supporting others in the processes of digital literacy (Rath, 2017). Indeed, it is not a matter of relegating these issues to specific subjects, nor is it a matter of understanding digital and AI literacy according to a merely instrumental logic, but of creating an education aimed at introducing students to a digital culture.

Future research should empirically investigate the impact of e-SL on AI literacy by specifying its dimensions of knowledge, skills, attitudes and values.

References

Albanesi, C., Culcasi, I., & Zunszain, P. (Eds.). (2020). *Practical guide on e-service-learning in response to COVID-19.* European Association of Service-Learning in Higher Education [EASHLE]. https://www.eoslhe. eu/wp-content/uploads/2020/10/Practical-guide-on-e-Service-Learning_ web.pdf

Aramburuzabala, P., Culcasi, I., & Cerrillo, R. (2024). Service-learning and digital empowerment: The potential for the digital education transition in higher education. *Sustainability, 16,* 2448. https://doi.org/10.3390/su1 6062448; https://www.mdpi.com/2071-1050/16/6/2448

Bernard, R. M., Abrami, Ph. C., Borokhovski, E., Wade, C. S., Tamim, R. M., Surkes, M. A., & Bethel, E. C. (2009). A meta-analysis of three types of interaction treatments in distance education. *Review of Educational Research, 79*(3), 1243–1289.

Bulfin, S., & McGraw, K. (2015). Digital literacy in theory, policy and practice: Old concerns, new opportunities. In M. Henderson & G. Romeo (Eds.), *Digital literacy in theory, policy and practice: Old concerns, new opportunities* (pp. 266–281). Cambridge University Press.

Cinque, M., & Culcasi, I. (2021). L'impatto della pandemia sull'istruzione superiore: limiti e opportunità dell'e-Service-Learning. *Quaderni di Pedagogia della Scuola, 1,* 113–126.

Council of Europe. (2019). *Developing and promoting digital citizenship education.* Recommendation adopted on 21 November 2020. https:// rm.coe.int/developing-and-promoting-digital-citizenship-education/168 0a236c0

Culcasi, I., & Paz Fontana Venegas, R. (2023). Service-learning and soft skills in higher education: A systematic literature review. *Form@re – Open Journal Per La Formazione in Rete, 23*(2), 24–43. https://doi.org/10.36253/ form-14639. ISSN 1825-7321 (online).

Culcasi, I., Russo, C., & Cinque, M. (2022). E-service-learning in higher education: Modelization of technological interactions and measurement of soft skills development. *Journal of Higher Education Outreach and Engagement, 26*(3), 39–56. ISSN: 15346102.

Darvishi, A., Khosravi, H., Sadiq, S., Gasevic, D., & Siemens, G. (2024). Impact of AI assistance on student agency. *Computer & Education, 2010,* 104967. https://doi.org/10.1016/j.compedu.2023.104967

De la Higuera, C. (2019). A report about education, training, teachers and learning artificial intelligence: Overview of key issues. *Education Compute Science*, *11*, 1–11. http://www.k4all.org/wp-content/uploads/2019/11/Teaching_AI-report_09072019.pdf

Di Michele, M. (2023). *Intelligenza Artificiale. Etica, rischi e opportunità di una tecnologia rivoluzionaria*. Diarkos editore.

Elam, M., & Reich, R. (2022). *Stanford HAI Artificial Intelligence Bill of Rights. A white paper for Stanford's institute for human-centered artificial intelligence*. https://hai.stanford.edu/sites/default/files/2022-03/HAI%20Policy%20White%20Paper%20-%20Stanford%20HAI%20Artificial%20Intelligence%20Bill%20of%20Rights.pdf

European Commission. (2022). *Final report of the Commission expert group on tackling disinformation and promoting digital literacy through education and training*. European Union. ISBN 978-92-76-55140-9. https://doi.org/10.2766/0486.

Floridi, L. (2014). *La quarta rivoluzione. Come l'infosfera sta trasformando il mondo*. Raffaello Cortina.

García-Gutiérrez, J., Ruiz-Corbella, M., & Del Pozo, A. (2020). Innovación y aprendizaje- servicio virtual: Elementos para una reflexión basada en la experiencia. *RIDAS: Revista Iberoamericana de Aprendizaje Servicio, 9*, 62–80. https://doi.org/10.1344/RIDAS2020.9.4

Gimpel, H., Gutheil, N., Mayer, V., Bandtel M., Büttgen, M., Decker, S., Eymann, T., Feulner, S., Kaya, M. F., Kufner, M., Kühl, N., Lämmermann L., Mädche, A., Ruiner, C., Schoop, M., & Urbach, N. (2024). *(Generative) AI competencies for future-proof graduates. Inspiration for Higher Education institutions*. University of Hohenheim. https://doi.org/10.5281/zenodo.10680210

Habib, S., Vogel T., Anli, X., & Thorne, E. (2024). How does generative artificial intelligence impact student creativity? *Journal of Creativity*, *31*(1), 100072. https://doi.org/10.1016/j.yjoc.2023.100072

Jones S. L., & Procter, R. (2023). Young peoples' perceptions of digital, media and information literacies across Europe: Gender differences, and the gaps between attitudes and abilities. *Technology, Pedagogy and Education*, pp. 1–22. https://doi.org/10.1080/1475939X.2023.2210152

Onesi-Ozigagun, O., Ololade, Y. J., Eyo-Udo, N. L., & Ogundipe, D. O. (2024). Revolutionizing education through AI: A comprehensive review of enhancing learning experiences. *International Journal of Applied Research in Social Sciences, 6*(4), 584–607. https://doi.org/10.51594/ijarss.v6i4.1011

Panciroli, C., & Macauda, A. (2021). Intelligenza artificiale in una prospettiva educativo-didattica. In C. Panciroli (Ed.), *Elementi di didattica post-digitale* (pp. 37–44). Bologna University Press.

Panciroli, C., & Rivoltella, P. C. (2023). *Pedagogia algoritmica. Per una riflessione educativa sull'Intelligenza Artificiale*. Scholé.

Rath, M. (2017). Media change and media literacy – Ethical implication of media education in the time of medialization. In L. Gómez Chova, A. López Martínez, I. Candel Torres (Eds.), *ICERI 2017 Proceedings* (pp. 8565–8571). IATED Academy.

Stefaniak, J. A. (2020). Systems view of supporting the transfer of learning through e-service-learning experiences in real-world contexts. *TechTrends, 64*, 561–569.

Tinmaz, H., Lee, Y. T., Fanea-Ivanovici, M., & Hasnan, B. (2022). A systematic review on digital literacy. *Smart Learning Environment, 9*(21). https://doi.org/10.1186/s40561-022-00204-y

UNESCO. (2018). *A draft report on a global framework of reference on digital literacy skills for indicator 4.4.2: Percentage of youth/adults who have achieved at least a minimum level of proficiency in digital literacy skills*. https://unesdoc.unesco.org/ark:/48223/pf0000265403

UNESCO. (2021). *Reimagining our futures together: A new social contract for education*. Report from the International Commission on the Futures of Education. https://unesdoc.unesco.org/ark:/48223/pf0000379707

Waldner, L., McGorry, S., & Widener, M. (2012). E-service-learning: The evolution of service learning to engage a growing online student population. *Journal of Higher Education Outreach and Engagement, 16*(2), 123–149.

Zawacki-Richter, O., Marín, V. I., Bond, M., & Gouberneur, F. (2019). Systematic review of research on artificial intelligence applications in higher education – where are the educators?. *International Journal of Educational Technology in Higher Education, 16*, 39. https://doi.org/10.1186/s41239-019-0171-0

Chapter 11

Universities and the digital divide: The capabilities approach from a Latin American perspective

ALEJANDRA MARINOVIC[1]

Abstract: Latin America suffers from strong inequalities in diverse dimensions, including income, education, race, and gender, which are entangled in multi-dimensional ways of poverty and exclusion. Universities can play a significant role in equalizing opportunities and improving the quality of life in the region, through their efforts toward education, research, and their contextual transfer and application, especially in least favoured frameworks. While the advance of technology offers numerous benefits, at the same time it is fostering, at an accelerating speed, a digital divide. Such a process has exacerbated socio-economic differences, which were particularly deepened during the pandemic when education had to happen through digital means. Sen and Nussbaum's capabilities approach for human development offers a useful normative framework to consider such gaps and derive guidelines for universities. This chapter explores the role of universities in confronting the digital divide, especially in Latin America, from this approach. We argue that the digital divide generates stronger social and ethical demands for universities at all levels of their activities, and all levels of the digital divide (access, skills and usage, and outcomes). At the same time, maintaining the focus of universities on the human person, and not on technology as an end, appears as a significant challenge for universities in the digital era.

Keywords: universities, digital divide, digital age, capabilities approach and Latin America

[1] The author thanks research assistant Raúl Villalobos for his excellent support and Gabriela Arriagada Bruneau for her valuable comments.

Introduction

The digital age finds Latin America in an educational crisis (Fer-reyra et al., 2017; World Bank et al., 2022) amidst what the United Nations has called a difficult gridlock. Latin America and the Carib-bean is the most unequal region of the world in terms of income; it is the region that experienced the sharpest drop in the Human Development Index (HDI) in 2020–2021 due to the coronavirus pan-demic and, while it significantly improved in 2022, it failed to reach pre-pandemic levels (UNDP, 2024). The region is also experiencing the most rapid rise in political polarization in the world and, accord-ing to Latinobarometro (2023) trust in institutions has decreased sig-nificantly to close to 20 %, with a similar trend in terms of generalized trust (WVS, 2023), all of which decrease the countries' ability to take collective action for the common good. In this preoccupant scenario, 61 % of people in Latin America[2] indicate to have high or very high confidence in universities (WVS, 2023), adding to their already high social responsibility.

One of the most salient challenges of the digital era is the impact on existing inequalities and the generation of new ones. The digital divide, defined generally as a division between people who have access to and use digital media and those who do not (Van Dijk, 2020), is receiv-ing increasing attention among researchers and policymakers, especially after the dire effects of the pandemic on inequalities (Mahler & Chris-toph, 2022), including in education (OECD, 2023).

Universities can play a significant role in facing the challenges of the information era, especially of generative artificial intelligence. This chap-ter explores the role of these higher education institutions in confronting the digital divide. It considers the matter from the ethical perspective of the capabilities approach (Nussbaum, 2011; Sen, 1992, 1999), which offers a base for normative arguments regarding the role of universities toward lower digital gaps.

The chapter is organized as follows. The first section offers a nor-mative framework to approach the digital divide in the context of mul-tidimensional inequality in Latin America; then, we discuss diverse

---

[2]   12 Latin American Countries are present in the 2017–2022 wave of the World Values Survey.

aspects of the digital divide and the levels in which it has manifested. The third and fourth sections lay out essential elements of characterization of the Latin American region; first, by offering indicators of the digital divide and comparing Latin America with other regions and within the region; and then contextualizing university education. The fifth section offers reflections regarding the role of universities in reducing digital inequality in Latin America. Section six discusses further elements of the role of universities in the digital era, based on the centrality of the human person. Finally, concluding remarks are offered.

Multidimensional inequality, education, and the digital divide: Normative elements

Inequalities are a complex phenomenon present in very diverse dimensions of people's lives. They are observed at numerous and intertwined levels: for example, differences between the income of developed and developing countries, as well as among people's ethnicity, religion, gender, sexual orientation, age, disability, spatial location, and class, to mention a few, which manifest within regions, societies, communities, and households. Gaps in newer areas are emerging, including access to and use of information and communication technologies (ICTs). A vast line of literature has shown that complex links exist among the numerous dimensions of inequality, especially that gaps tend to exacerbate each other for the poorest (UNDP, 2024). These gaps reverberate in inequalities that affect the quality of life and people's opportunities, including education, that are undesirable from a normative point of view (Marinovic, 2022).

To assess which, why, and to what degree inequalities are not desirable, we need a normative framework that incorporates the previous complexity. We propose to state our discussion from the perspective of the capabilities approach for human development (Nussbaum, 2011; Sen, 1992, 1999). This approach stems from the centrality of human dignity and offers a broad normative framework to conceptualize and evaluate individual well-being and social arrangements. Even if it is not a complete theory of justice, it does face questions of the balance between freedoms and equality (Walker & Unterhalter, 2007).

In the capabilities approach, Sen (1992, 1999) argues that human development should aim at increasing freedoms so that all human beings can pursue choices that they value. These freedoms have two fundamental aspects: freedom of personal well-being, constituted by functionings and capabilities, and freedom of agency, represented by the person's voice and autonomy. Functionings refer to the various things a person may value being and doing – such as being happy, adequately nourished, and in good health, as well as having self-respect and taking part in the life of the community. Capabilities are the various sets of functionings (beings and doings) that a person can achieve. Capabilities not only take functionings into account but the real freedom or opportunities each individual had available to choose and to achieve what he or she values, that is, the evaluation of equality must consider both the freedom in opportunities as much as observed choices. Finally, agency is related to what a person is free to do and achieve in pursuit of whatever goals or values he or she regards as relevant. In this approach, both freedom of personal well-being and freedom of agency are indispensable (UNDP, 2016, pp. 1–3).

Nussbaum (2011) and Sen (1992, 1999) highlight that the word capabilities is used in the plural in this approach because the most important elements for quality of life are multiple and distinct: health, physical integrity, education…, and irreducible. This approach poses the question: what is a person capable of doing and being? Therefore, it considers each human being as a good in itself. Education plays a central role in the capabilities approach; it is related to all three functionalities, capabilities, and freedoms, as we comment below.

Lozano et al. (2012, p. 134) indicate that functionings in education expand in a wide spectrum that goes from individual to social: (1) activities like reading or writing; (2) physical states, such as being able to be well-nourished and healthy; (3) mental situations, like being happy, or (4) social functionings, such as being integrated into society.

Concerning capabilities, Nussbaum (2011, pp. 33–34) argues that a decent society should provide at least some threshold of 10 central capabilities: (1) life, (2) bodily health, (3) bodily integrity, (4) sense, imagination, and thought, (5) emotions, (6) practical reason, (7) affiliation, (8) living with a concern for other species, (9) play, and (10) control over one's political and material environment. A society that does not guarantee the active cultivation of such key capabilities cannot be considered a just society. Notice that education can play a central role in developing these capabilities, especially those related to reason, thought, and control.

Terzi (2007) argues that education constitutes a capability in itself; furthermore, a basic one. She argues that the capability to be educated, broadly understood in terms of real opportunities both for informal learning and for formal schooling, can be considered a basic capability in two ways: (i) the absence or lack of this opportunity would essentially harm and disadvantage the individual, and (ii) since the capability to be educated plays a substantial role in the expansion of other capabilities, as well as future ones, it can be considered basic for the further reason that it is fundamental and foundational to the capabilities necessary to well-being, and hence to lead a good life (Terzi, 2007, p. 25). More particularly, Terzi (2007, p. 37) proposes seven basic capabilities for educational functioning: (1) literacy, (2) numeracy, (3) sociality and participation, (4) learning disposition, (5) physical activities, (6) science and technology, and (7) practical reason. She refers to the sixth capability as being able to understand natural phenomena, being knowledgeable about technology, and being able to use technological tools.

Walker (2006, pp. 128–129) has explored capabilities specifically related to higher education; she proposes eight of them: (1) practical reason, (2) educational resilience, (3) knowledge and imagination, (4) learning disposition, (5) social relations and social networks, (6) respect, dignity and recognition, (7) emotional integrity, and (8) bodily integrity. As we can observe, there are several coincidences with Terzi and Nussmbaum, such as practical reason and bodily integrity, but a stronger focus on resilience and social interactions appears.

Jointly with freedom of personal well-being, constituted by functionings and capabilities, Sen (1990) emphasizes having the freedom to choose one kind of life rather than another. The concept of agency is especially relevant for education, as it implies three levels of claims (Lozano et al., 2012, p. 134): the claim that it is possible to educate people to apply reason to personal decisions and preferences, the claim that it is possible to enhance people's capacities to reflect critically on the world and to envisage desirable changes, and the claim that capacities to accomplish such changes in practice can also be cultivated. That is to say, the goal of education from the perspective of the capabilities approach is to expand people's agency (empowerment) to enable them to be the authors of their own lives.

Under these claims, the ability to exercise freedom depends on the education we receive, and the latter plays diverse and essential roles (Sen, 1990). More education can help productivity, and therefore income; it can contribute to a better distribution of income; better-educated individuals and societies can put their resources to use in diverse ways of living; and, very importantly, education also helps in the intelligent choice between different types of lives that a person can lead. Inequalities concerning Sen's essential freedoms, manifested in inequalities of opportunities, and in particular related to education and income, affect people's life expectancy and access to basic services. Being more exposed to discrimination and exclusion can curtail a person's human rights and access to justice. In the socio-economic sphere, inequalities erode trust in institutions and governments, reduce cohesion, and feed diverse social tensions (Sen, 1990, 1992, 1999; UNDP, 2016).

The capabilities approach considers the possibility of differences among individuals, given that what they value can vary, as well as their context. However, it also provides criteria to evaluate when such differences constitute undesirable inequalities. Hence, the capabilities approach suggests that, under the extensive conditions of poverty, extreme economic inequality, exclusion, discrimination, and conflicts, such as in Latin America, the educational system –including universities – ought to contribute toward equality of opportunities and freedom of agency.

This approach also provides a useful framework for analysing possible actions in the presence of diverse inequalities, particularly the digital divide, since it tackles the question: equality of what? Though technology can be a significant factor toward equality, the lack of access and inequality of access and use constitute additional forces that create new dimensions of inequality and strain existing ones. Digital inclusion and fair use have become a key aspect in reaching the United Nations' Sustainable Development Goals, as its Secretary General indicated at the 2023 Internet Governance Forum (Guterres, 2023). Therefore, it might be impossible (or even not desirable, given possible differences in individual choices and values) to eliminate the digital divide, but the previous normative elements provide a basis to argue that it should be reduced when it negatively affects the freedoms of well-being and agency.

The digital divide: An evolving concept

Let us make further precisions regarding the definition of the digital gap. The most common definition, indicated at the beginning of this chapter, is the following: a division between people who have access and use of digital media and those who do not (Van Dijk, 2020, p. 1). Initially, the focus was on access, but further along, the quality of use has become increasingly more important. The OECD definition adds relevant aspects: it refers to the gap between individuals, households, businesses, and geographic areas at different socio-economic levels with regard both to their opportunities to access information and communication technologies (ICTs) and to their use of the Internet for a wide variety of activities (OECD, 2001, p. 5). Note that it refers not only to a divide among individuals, but it also considers collective differences and social spheres.

Definitions of the digital divide are still evolving, as technology and knowledge continue to change. For instance, the widespread emergence of generative artificial intelligence and the comprehension of the causes and consequences of the gap – which is not a unique divide, but many – are adding new elements to the concept. Lythreatis et al. (2022), in an extensive literature review, consider the digital divide as a phenomenon that refers to disparities in ICTs access, usage, and outcomes, where the latter adds a new layer to be considered. This view is being adopted by many researchers.

The elements laid out in the previous evolving definitions suggest that the digital divide is different from the impact of other technological changes. Van Dijk (2020) argues that it differs because of its speed and vast effects among countries, it touches every imaginable part of society and their activities, and its relevance in whether individuals are included or excluded from society in numerous domains, such as work, education, the market, communities, citizenship, politics, and culture. In this sense, being on the wrong side of the digital divide constitutes a major problem for individuals and communities.

For our next discussion regarding universities, it is also useful to keep in mind that the literature identifies three levels of the digital divide, according to their focus (Helsper, 2008, 2021; Lythreatis et al., 2022; OECD, 2001, 2023; Van Dijk, 2020).

Level 1 focuses on physical access. At this level of the digital divide, people have or do not have access to diverse ICTs. These include internet connectivity and speed, internet-enabled devices, related software and hardware, infrastructure, and data sources. This level represents the initial approach to the digital divide and soon became insufficient to characterize the impact of this technological revolution.

Level 2 emphasizes skills and usage. This level advances to the matter of quality of access: effective use of ICTs and digital literacy. It proposes that physical access is useless without the correct skills, knowledge, applications, and support. The divide refers to internet or social media use, digital literacy, and digital competencies.

Level 3 focuses on the outcomes. This level approaches the digital divide as a concept related to inequality effects. Extensive use of ICTs has called the attention of researchers and policymakers to two fundamental questions: (i) does the digital divide reduce or reinforce existing inequalities, and (ii) does it create new inequalities, in various domains: economic, social, political, cultural, educational, and personal development. At this level, the divide refers to the possibilities of exclusion of multidimensional benefits.

Measurements and analysis of the concept of the digital divide are far from exhausted in each of these three levels as they are still evolving, especially because of the significant differences among countries (such as developed and developing), social groups, and communities in terms of access, literacy, and outcomes. Amidst these difficulties, but essential to our discussion, the two following sections tackle the task of laying out primary elements of context for the Latin American region regarding the digital divide and the situation of higher education.

The digital divide in Latin America

Data and analysis of the digital divide in Latin America are still lacking. In this section, we offer key indicators that are instrumental to setting the context for our discussion, mostly of the level 1 digital divide (access), and some of levels 2 (skills and usage) and 3 (outcomes).

Internet access in Latin America has grown steadily, but it is significantly below developed countries. Access is widely different across regions and strongly related to income per capita (Figure 1). In addition, Latin America exhibits heterogeneity across countries. For instance, in 2021 Uruguay and Chile exhibit 90 % of the population using the internet, while Guatemala and Honduras are closer to 50 % (World Bank, n.d.).

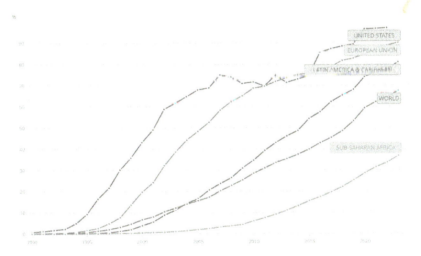

Figure 1. Individuals using the Internet (% of the population)
Source: World Bank Open Data

ICTs' access in Latin America is severely segregated by income, which has brought the outcome of deepening the profound inequality in the region since it creates and exacerbates exclusion; the potential for the Internet to serve as a social and political equalizing force in Latin America is hindered by its unequal access (Gray et al., 2017). Figure 2 offers data about this phenomenon from the United Nations Economic Commission for Latin America and the Caribbean ECLAC (CEPAL in Spanish). It shows that internet access is extremely disjointed by quintiles of income, indicating an additional dimension of the digital divide, this time within countries.

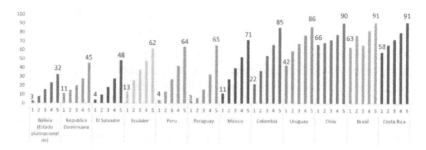

Figure 2. Household access to the Internet by income quintiles. 2018
Source: CEPAL (2020, p. 3)

Moreover, ECLAC reports that, in 2018, one-third of the regional population had no or limited access to the Internet due to their economic situation; 33 % of urban households were not connected, while in rural areas it is 77 %. Regarding age differences, 42 % of the population under 25 years of age, and 54 % of the population over 66 years of age were not connected (CEPAL, 2020). These figures suggest that the problem of basic access to ICTs in Latin America is far from being solved.

Regarding the capacity to use ITCs effectively (level 2 digital divide), it is important to bear in mind that Latin America is characterized by two important factors that create a further gap with developed countries. First, Latin America is a net importer of technology and has much fewer secure servers than developed countries (World Bank Open Data), exhibiting a strong dependence on the latter. Second, English is a foreign language for this region, posing an additional barrier to access, especially for the poor; for example, in Europe in 2023 the average English proficiency as a foreign language ranks in the 'high' category, while Latin America falls into 'low' (EF English Proficiency Index, 2023).

Data on usage in the region are scarce. The OECD database offers more detailed and frequent information. Four Latin American countries are members of the OECD: Chile, Colombia, Costa Rica, and Mexico. Comparing Latin American indicators of digital access and usage within the OECD context, it is possible to observe significant and sustained gaps. Figure 3 shows the average indicator of the four Latin American OECD members compared to the average of the 4 OECD members with the top indicators each year.

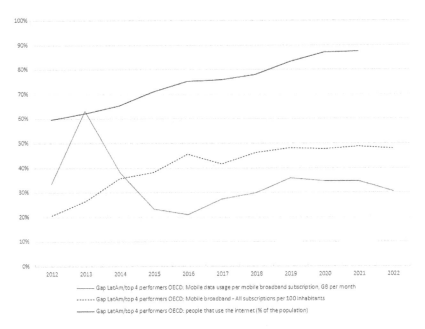

Figure 3. Digital Divide Indicators OECD: Latin American members v/s top performers
Source: own calculations using (OECD, n.d.)

Figure 3 indicates that the percentage of the population that uses the internet is similar, being that for the Latin American OECD members around 90 % of the average of the top 4 performers within this organization; this gap has been decreasing steadily over the last decade, reflecting a faster expansion of basic access in Latin America. However, if we consider the quality of this access in terms of speed (broadband) and data usage in gigabytes, the digital divide is much larger. In 2022, mobile broadband subscriptions per 100 inhabitants in the 4 Latin American OECD countries are less than half of that of the top 4 OECD performers, and mobile data usage in GB is a third of it. There are no indications that these gaps have decreased in the last 5 years.

The previous evidence suggests that the digital gap between Latin America and developed countries is large; furthermore, the region exhibits wide differences among countries, and economic inequalities are reinforced by the digital divide. Given, on the one hand, the great significance of the digital divide for human development discussed earlier from the perspective of the capabilities approach and, on the other, the size, extension, and evolution of the gap in its diverse dimensions, the role of the educational system and universities in reducing it becomes of pressing importance. To complement this scenario, the next section adds elements regarding the characteristics of education in the region, thus laying out our setup to discuss the role of universities in facing the digital gap.

Education in Latin America is unequal and lagging

Four in five sixth graders in Latin America and the Caribbean lack basic reading comprehension proficiency, according to The State of Global Learning Poverty by the World Bank and UNICEF, in collaboration with UNESCO. Latin America ranks in the second worst place in the world, only above Sub-Saharan Africa (World Bank et al., 2022). Access to tertiary education (Figure 4) has been growing steadily in the region but is still very far from the opportunities of more developed countries (World Bank, n.d.)

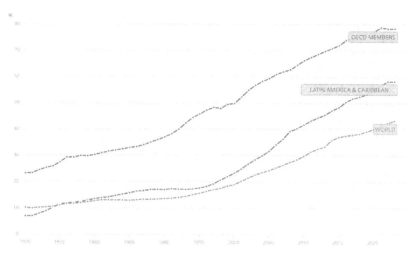

Figure 4. Enrolment in tertiary education
Source: World Bank Open Data

Ferreyra et al. (2017) pointed out that, even if enrolment has grown significantly over the last decades, only half of the students in Latin America and the Caribbean graduate on time. University education in Latin America exhibits a strong income return. Indeed, the same researchers report that a student with a higher education degree will earn more than twice as much as a student with a high school diploma. Even so, only 16 % of higher education students in Latin America and the Caribbean came from the poorest 50 % of the population in 2000, and 25 % in 2013. Countries in the region have developed numerous policies to increase enrolment of low and middle-income students, but these differences are still very significant. The high return to higher education in Latin America has also incentivized the creation of higher education institutions, both public and private. Ferreyra et al. (2017) indicate that by 2013 half of these institutions were private.

From these few elements, one can already perceive that the accelerated technological change that we are experiencing poses additional pressure on the digital divide regarding numerous aspects. Indeed, education constitutes an extremely relevant factor because more educated individuals are more likely to cope better with technology's complexity and will be more exposed to ITCs in their lives (Cruz-Jesus et al., 2016).

Having gathered the previous principal traits of Latin America regarding the digital divide and higher education, and presented earlier our proposed normative framework, we now tackle the role of universities.

The role of universities in reducing digital inequality: A Latin American perspective

For our arguments, it would be useful to consider in a simplified manner three essential university tasks: (i) Education of students, which includes challenges related to admissions and inclusion, lifelong learning, as well as offering relevant formation for the professional life of graduates amid a technological revolution. (ii) Research, understood as the development of knowledge in a wide range of disciplines and perspectives. (iii) Knowledge transmission and direct service to society, including the application of new technologies to social problems of the context and contributions to the discussion of new laws and public policies.

We have shown that this region exhibits a distinctive socio-economic structure and suffers from diverse dimensions of the digital divide. Technology has offered enormous benefits, but they are not captured with equality, either between Latin America and developed societies, or within countries of the region. The digital revolution has, at least, reinforced the already large inequalities in a multidimensional configuration. The trust that universities receive from the population and the capacity to influence the countries' performance place them in a privileged position to contribute against added digital inequality and, hence, give them the associated responsibility.

We have argued that inequality is a multidimensional phenomenon particularly present in Latin America. Our previous discussion shows that it manifests also in education. The advancement of digital technology, while offering significant benefits, has contributed to deepening existing gaps, creating further obstacles to individuals' human development and to society's flourishment. The capabilities approach provides a useful normative framework to address this multidimensional problem in the university arena, especially because of human development at its core, the multiplicity of human goods reflected in functionalities, capabilities, and freedoms, and its focus on individual and collective agency.

These elements constitute a useful terrain and framework to offer reflections regarding the role of universities in reducing digital inequality from a Latin American perspective. From the viewpoint of the capabilities approach and having identified three broad university tasks (education, research, and knowledge transmission) and three levels of the digital divide (focus on access, skills and usage, and outcomes), we organize our reflections for the regional context according to these dimensions. Our recommendations regarding the role of universities in reducing digital inequality in Latin America are as follows.

University task 1: education
- Level 1 digital divide. Being far from reaching universal access to ICTs in Latin America, universities should promote (i) access to and completion of higher education, which, in turn, facilitates digital access; (ii) direct access to ICT for students. Given the language obstacle, universities should facilitate the learning of English as a key tool for accessing ICTs.

- Level 2 digital divide. Facing a substantial gap in terms of skills and usage, universities ought to (i) educate and innovate in up-to-date digital skills; and (ii) offer knowledge, applications, and support for effective digital usage, including social media use, digital literacy, and digital competencies.
- Level 3 digital divide. A distinctive outcome of the digital revolution in the region is the exacerbation of already stringent socio-economic inequalities. Universities should reinforce (i) their potential equalizing role in society; and (ii) the freedom of agency of students, faculty, and the overall university community, for example, opening diverse opportunities and creating cooperation initiatives. Provide access to technology as a means in a universal perspective of human knowledge.

University task 2: research

- Level 1 digital divide. (i) Include technology in research, avoiding falling behind in digital access; (ii) build capacity for efficient, effective, and correct use of digital tools; (iii) foster technological advancement and innovation to improve better and faster access to digital technology.
- Level 2 digital divide. (i) Develop high-quality research about technology, research supported by technology and apply research to relevant society problems; (ii) generate opportunities of academic cooperation with developed countries to mitigate the technological gap; and (iii) innovate in skills and usage: universities are a most suitable place for the adoption and application of new technologies.
- Level 3 digital divide. (i) Contribute to the comprehension of the outcomes of the digital divide and pursue actions to reduce digital inequality; (ii) promote the ethical discussion of the effects of the digital revolution, including limitations, implications, and ethical considerations; and (iii) provide leadership in the understanding of the digital era.

University task 3: knowledge transmission

- Level 1 digital divide. Contribute to digital access in society at large.
- Level 2 digital divide. (i) Contribute to digital literacy in society at large; (ii) reinforce knowledge transmission to society, using all possible means to reach society at large.

- Level 3 digital divide. (i) Provide guidelines for the good use of digital tools; (ii) Contribute to the development of public policies regarding the digital revolution (innovation, rules, ethical aspects, …); and (iii) Collaborate with the government and civil society towards social cohesion in the digital era.

As we can see, universities can contribute vastly to improving the quality of life in the digital era. However, they should question continuously their sense in the face of the technological revolution, as it has shaken the meaning of the search for knowledge. The following section comments on this additional dimension of the role of universities.

Maintaining university focus on the human person in the digital era

Besides the previous elements, which have a regional focus, Universities in general should face an essential issue, which becomes even more important in the context of the digital age: to reflect on what it means to be human in the digital era, and even further, in the time of generative artificial intelligence. As argued from the perspective of the capabilities approach, University education should, more than ever, develop critical thinking and ethical discernment, as well as educate towards integrity, understood as a lifelong commitment to what is deemed valuable. In front of accelerated technological change, the sense of purpose of knowledge and human flourishing in a sustainable world must act as an indispensable moral compass for the work of universities (Juan Pablo II, 1990). Universities constitute principal spaces of scientific research for the progress of knowledge and society; they play a decisive role in economic social and cultural development, especially in a time with fast, constant, and far-reaching changes in science and technology (Francisco, 2017).

The latter reaches highlighted importance given that the digital era has come in the context of the technocratic paradigm, a one-dimensional paradigm where what is technologically feasible becomes good and power lies in those who own technology (Francisco, 2015, 2023). Under this perspective, technology becomes not only a means, an instrument, but a way of apprehending things, and, therefore, knowledge becomes technical feasibility. In addition, when the relationship with nature is mediated by technology under this paradigm, a technological imperative follows, an infinite desire for more, curtailing human freedom (Marinovic, 2023).

The risk of losing the sense of universities by abandoning the human person as a centre in the face of vertiginous technological changes would imply continually changing the points of reference for education (Congregación para la Educación Católica, 2021); it would curtail the capacity of universities to reflect on their actions toward the good and hinder university ethical discernment (Keenan, 2015). The loss of focus on the human person implies as well losing the capacity to judge and react to the digital divide.

Considering technology as a solution to every problem, and ignoring the relational dimension of human interactions, renders society less able to react against injustice (Francisco, 2020). In addition, following Newman's (2016) reasonings, the technocratic approach can also hinder teaching and learning by paring down a culture of dialogue and debate (Tierney, 2016), which represents a basic functionality of education. The capabilities approach, in accordance with several other normative frameworks such as virtue ethics, allows us to keep universities focused on the human person as an end, rather than technology, which is considered as a –very valuable – means.

Falling into the technocratic paradigm should also be avoided by universities by fostering all forms of knowledge, from a universal stance, to contribute not only to the students' professional and personal lives but also toward better citizenship and more excellent societies (Cortina, 2023; Mardones & Marinovic, 2021; Newman, 2016; Nussbaum, 2006). If universities lose sight of what matters for human flourishing, they will be unable to perceive and evaluate the effects of growing digital divides, which in turn would damage progressively development opportunities of individuals and societies.

Concluding remarks

Universities can play a significant role in alleviating the profound socio-economic inequalities that pierce Latin America. While the advance of technology brings numerous benefits, we have observed that, at the same time, it is fostering digital divides at an accelerating speed. Sen and Nussbaum's capabilities approach for human development offers a useful normative framework to consider such gaps and derive guidelines for universities. We claim that the digital divide generates stronger social and ethical demands for universities regarding all their activities at all levels of the digital divide. At the same time, maintaining the focus of universities on the human person, and not on technology as an end, appears as a significant challenge for universities in the digital era.

References

CEPAL. (2020). Universalizar el acceso a las tecnologías digitales para enfrentar los efectos del COVID-19. *Comisión Económica Para América Latina y El Caribe, Naciones Unidas, 7.*

Congregación para la Educación Católica. (2021). *Pacto Educativo Global.* Vademecum.

Cortina, A. (2023). La misión de las éticas aplicadas en las universidades del siglo XXI. *Humanitas: Revista de Antropología y Cultura Cristiana, 104.*

Cruz-Jesus, F., Vicente, M. R., Bacao, F., & Oliveira, T. (2016). The education-related digital divide: An analysis for the EU-28. *Computers in Human Behavior, 56,* 72–82. https://doi.org/10.1016/j.chb.2015.11.027

Ferreyra, M. M., Avitabile, C., Álvarez Botero, J., Haimovich Paz, F., & Urzúa, S. (2017). *At a crossroads: Higher education in Latin America and the Caribbean.* Directions in Development – Human Development. World Bank.

Francisco. (2015). *Carta Encíclica Laudato si' sobre el cuidado de la casa común.* Libreria Editrice Vaticana.

Francisco. (2017). *Constitución Apostólica Veritatis Gaudium sobre las Universidades y Facultades Eclesiásticas.* Libreria Editrice Vaticana.

Francisco. (2020). *Carta Encíclica Fratelli Tutti sobre la fraternidad y la amistad social.* Libreria Editrice Vaticana.

Francisco. (2023). *Laudate Deum: Exhortación Apostólica a todas las personas de buena voluntad, sobre la crisis climática.* Libreria Editrice Vaticana.

Gray, T. J., Gainous, J., & Wagner, K. M. (2017). Gender and the digital divide in Latin America. *Social Science Quarterly, 98*(1), 326–340.

Guterres, A. (2023, October 9). *UN Secretary-General's video message to the Internet Governance Forum.* Internet Governance Forum.

Helsper, E. J. (2008). *Digital inclusion: An analysis of social disadvantage and the information society.* Department for Communities and Local Government.

Helsper, E. J. (2021). *The digital disconnect: The causes and consequences of digital inequalities.* Sage Publications.

Juan Pablo II. (1990). *Constitución Apostólica Ex Corde Ecclesiae sobre las Universidades Católicas.* Libreria Editrice Vaticana.

Keenan, F. J. F. (2015). *University ethics: How colleges can build and benefit from a culture of ethics.* Rowman & Littlefield.

Latinobarometro. (2023). *Informe Latinobarómetro 2023: La recesión democrática de América Latina.* Corporación Latinobarometro.

Lozano, J. F., Boni, A., Peris, J., & Hueso, A. (2012). Competencies in Higher Education: A critical analysis from the capabilities approach – Competencies in Higher Education. *Journal of Philosophy of Education,* 46(1), 132–147. https://doi.org/10.1111/j.1467-9752.2011.00839.x

Lythreatis, S., Singh, S. K., & El-Kassar, A.-N. (2022). The digital divide: A review and future research agenda. *Technological Forecasting and Social Change, 175,* 121359. https://doi.org/10.1016/j.techfore.2021.121359

Mahler, D. G., & Christoph, L. (2022). The impact of COVID-19 on global inequality and poverty. *World Bank, 10198.*

Mardones, R., & Marinovic, A. (2021). Educating in politics, democracy and citizenship: The challenges of Chilean Catholic schools. In P. Imbarack & C. Madero Sj (Eds.), *Catholic education in Latin America* (pp. 73–91). Springer International Publishing. https://doi.org/10.1007/978-3-030-75059-6_6

Marinovic, A. (2022). Educación Católica y Desigualdad Socioeconómica en Chile. In *Educación ciudadana y enseñanza católica: La fraternidad como desiderátum* (pp. 203–245). Ediciones UC / CEPPE.

Marinovic, A. (2023). Fraternidad para el cuidado de la casa común. *Humanitas: revista de antropología y cultura cristiana, 28*(105), 466–471.

Newman, J. H. (2016). *La idea de una universidad* (1st ed.). Ediciones UC; JSTOR. https://doi.org/10.2307/j.ctt1h9cvnh

Nussbaum, M. C. (2006). Education and democratic citizenship: Capabilities and quality education. *Journal of Human Development, 7*(3), 385–395. https://doi.org/10.1080/14649880600815974

Nussbaum, M. C. (2011). *Creating capabilities: The human development approach.* Harvard University Press. https://doi.org/10.4159/harv ard.9780674061200

OECD. (n.d.). *OECD.Stat* [dataset]. https://stats.oecd.org/

OECD. (2001). *Understanding the digital divide* (OECD Digital Economy Papers 49). https://doi.org/10.1787/236405667766

OECD. (2023). *OECD digital education outlook 2023: Towards an effective digital education ecosystem.* https://doi.org/10.1787/c74f03de-en

Sen, A. (1990). Development as capability expansion. *The Community Development Reader, 41,* 58.

Sen, A. (1992). *Inequality reexamined* (1st ed.). Harvard University Press.

Sen, A. (1999). *Development as freedom.* Anchor Books.

Terzi, L. (2007). The capability to be educated. In *Amartya Sen's capability approach and social justice in education* (pp. 25–43). Palgrave Macmillan US.

Tierney, W. G. (2016). Portrait of higher education in the twenty-first century: John Henry Newman's 'The idea of a university'. *International Journal of Leadership in Education, 19*(1), 5–16. https://doi.org/10.1080/13603 124.2015.1096079

UNDP (Ed.). (2016). *Human development for everyone.*

UNDP. (2024). *Human Development Report 2023–24. Breaking the gridlock: Reimagining cooperation in a polarized world.*

Van Dijk, J. (2020). *The digital divide.* Polity.

Walker, M. (2006). *Higher Education pedagogies: A capabilities approach.* Open University Press.

Walker, M., & Unterhalter, E. (2007). The capability approach: Its potential for work in education. In *Amartya Sen's capability approach and social justice in education* (pp. 1–18). Palgrave Macmillan US.

World Bank. (n.d.). *World Bank open data* [dataset]. https://databank.worldbank.org/

World Bank et al. (2022). *The state of global learning poverty: 2022 update.*

WVS. (2023). *World values survey* [dataset].

Notes on Contributors

PEDRO PABLO ACHONDO MOYA is PhD in Territory, Space and Society, Universidad de Chile. Magister in Practical and Moral Theology. Institute of Geography, Pontificia Universidad Católica de Valparaíso, Chile.

MONTSERRAT ALOM BARTROLÍ is Director of the International Centre for Research and Decision Support (CIRAD), International Federation of Catholic Universities (IFCU), France. She is also Research Associate at the Institute of European Studies and Human Rights, Pontifical University of Salamanca (Spain). Research Associate at the CEPED-IRD, Université Paris Cité, France.

MARIA CINQUE is a full professor of Pedagogy of Inclusion and Group Methodologies at LUMSA University of Rome. She is the coordinator of the course for educators, Director of training courses for specialization in educational support activities for students with disabilities. From 2019 she is Director of the Postgraduate School 'Educare all'Incontro e alla Solidarietà' EIS of LUMSA University of Rome. She also teaches at Campus Bio-Medico University in Rome. She is Member of the scientific committee of the Uniservitate world programme from 2023 to date and member of the scientific committee of the Global Compact on Education for the Congregation for Catholic Education. Her main research interests focus on design of innovative learning environments, service-learning and soft skills, faculty development, technologies for teaching and learning and coaching and creativity.

IRENE CULCASI is a researcher and contract lecturer in Service-Learning at the LUMSA University of Rome, Italy. She holds a PhD in Contemporary Humanism (Education curriculum) from LUMSA University with a double degree from Pontificia Universidad Católica de Chile. She is coordinator of the research and projects area of the EIS-LUMSA Postgraduate School 'Educare all'Incontro e alla Solidarietà'. She is currently secretary of the European Association of Service-Learning in Higher Education (EASLHE), member of the European Observatory of Service-Learning in Higher Education (EOSLHE) and founder member of

Service-Learning in European schools and organizations Network (SLE-SON). She is also part of the Italian SL network and co-founder and vice president of Comparte, a non-profit organization working in the field of educational innovation and sustainability.

FRANCISCO DE FERARI CORREA is a PhD student in Human Rights, Universidad de Deusto. Master in Ethics for Social Construction, Universidad de Deusto. Degree in Philosophy, Universidad Alberto Hurtado. Director of community outreach at the Universidad Católica Silva Henríquez, Chile.

KASHISH DUA is an Assistant Professor of English at Jesus and Mary College, University of Delhi, India. She is currently a Fulbright-Nehru Doctoral Fellow (2023–2024), conducting research at the University of California, Berkeley, USA. Dua has edited a critical edition of William Shakespeare's *As You Like It*, published by Prentice Hall India (2019) and is co-editing *Vernacular Encounters: Politics and Possibilities*, scheduled for release in 2025. Dua's works have been published by Routledge, DK London, and Oxford University Press.

MAYTE GÓMEZ MARCOS is Assistant Professor of Statistics and Vice-Dean of the Faculty of Insurance, Law and Economics, and Associate Researcher at the Institute for European Studies and Human Rights at the Pontifical University of Salamanca. Previously, she was a lAssociate Lecturer at the Universitat Oberta de Catalunya and the Isabel I University of Castilla. Dr Gómez Marcos holds a degree in Economics and Business Studies from the University of Cádiz, a Masters in Project Management and Management from the University of Francisco de Vitoria and an Executive Master in Business Administration from the University of San Pablo CEU. She obtained her PhD in Applied Multivariate Statistics from the University of Salamanca, where she also received an International Mention. She has carried out research stays at Bernardo O'Higgins University in Santiago (Chile), Artesis Plantjin University College in Antwerp (Belgium) and Université de Lille (France). Her research interests include higher education, data science and multivariate statistics.

Prof. SANDRA JOSEPH is Principal of Jesus and Mary College, University of Delhi, New Delhi, India. Her experience in the field of teaching, research and practice in the discipline of Social Work spans over

30 years. She has to her credit a number of publications both international and national and is an editorial member for international refereed journals. In collaboration with the International Federation of Catholic Universities (IFCU) since 1998, she has completed four major cross-cultural research studies. She has to her credit several accolades and awards as a distinguished academician.

ALEJANDRA MARINOVIC is Assistant Professor of Applied Ethics at Pontificia Universidad Católica de Chile (UC). Her research focuses on social capital, citizenship education and socio-economic inequality. At Universidad Adolfo Ibáñez (2010–2021) she was Director of the MBA International Programme. She has extensive experience in the public sector (2000–2010), where she worked as an adviser to the Ministry of Finance of the Government of Chile and as Senior Economist at the Central Bank of Chile. She holds a PhD in Economics from Columbia University (New York), and a BA and MA in Economics from Pontificia Universidad Católica de Chile.

DR GEORGE MUTALEMWA is Senior Research Fellow at St. Augustine University of Tanzania, Director of Africa Peace and Development Network and Executive Secretary of the Association of Catholic Universities and Higher Institute of Africa and Madagascar. Mutalemwa created the People's Organisations Development Theory and University Revitalization Theory. He is the Founding Editor-in-Chief of the Journal of Sociology and Development and the moderator of 'Global Peace Studies for Sustainable Development in Africa'. He has served as Hoeffmann Lecturer for Intercultural Competences at the University of Vechta in Germany and as a Visiting Lecturer at the University of Innsbruck in Austria and at the Universidad Popular Autónoma del Estado de Puebla in Mexico.

MARIO TORRES JARRÍN is Director of the Institute of European Studies and Human Rights at the Pontifical University of Salamanca (Spain). Previously, he was Researcher Associate and Adjunct Lecturer at Friedrich Alexander University Erlangen-Nuremberg (Germany), Lecturer and Research Associate in the Faculty of Humanities at Stockholm University and Director at the European Institute of International Studies (Sweden). He has been Visiting Professor at Copenhagen Business School (Denmark), University of Bergen and University of Oslo (Norway), University Institute of Lisbon (Portugal), National University of Political Studies and Public Administration (Romania), University of

Salamanca (Spain), University of Economics and Anglo-American University (Czech Republic) and diplomatic academies in Europe, Asia and Americas. He holds a PhD in History, a master's in European Union Studies, and a BA in Business Studies from the University of Salamanca (Spain).

FERNANDO VERGARA HENRÍQUEZ is PhD in Philosophy, Universidad de Deusto. PhD in Education, Universidad de Barcelona. Degree in Philosophy, Pontificia Universidad Católica de Chile. Director of community outreach at the Universidad Academia de Humanismo Cristiano, Chile.

EMMANUEL WABANHU is Professor of Moral Theology at the Catholic University of Eastern Africa as well as a regular visiting Professor of Christian Moral Philosophy at the Consolata Institute of Philosophy in Nairobi, Kenya. He holds a PhD degree in Moral Theology/Business Ethics from the Katholieke Universiteit Leuven, Belgium. With the Paulines Publications Africa, he has published *The Shifting Ground of Doing Theology: Perspectives from Africa* (2017). With the Catholic University of Eastern Africa Press he has published *Methodologies and Techniques for Thesis Writing in Theology* (2021). He has coauthored *Bible and Orality in Africa: Interdisciplinary Approaches* (2021).

CECILIA CELESTE DANESI is researcher at the Institute of European Studies and Human Rights at the Pontifical University of Salamanca (Spain). She holds a PhD in Law and Artificial Intelligence from the University of Perugia (Italy) and University of Salamanca (Spain). Advisor at the Digital Caucus of ParlAmericas, the Future Challenges Commission of the Chilean Senate and the private and public sector on Ethical Governance of AI and regulation. Author of the book 'The empire of algorithms' and director of the journal 'Inteligencia Artificial, Tecnologías Emergentes y Derecho'. Co-chair of the group "AI Credentials" of the platform 'Women4EthicalAI' (UNESCO). Co-director of the Master Degree in Ethical Governance of AI (UPSA) and deputy director of the postgraduate course 'AI and Law' (UBA). Professor of the subject 'AI and Law' (UBA). Ambassador of the Women Economic Forum Argentina. G100 Argentina Country Chair AI & Data. TEDx Speaker.

CLAUDIA CHIAVARINO, psychologist and psychotherapist, PhD at the University of Birmingham (UK), is full professor of General Psychology, Psychometrics and Psychobiology at the Salesian University Institute of

Turin (IUSTO), where she holds a position as academic director and head of the Innovation and Research Center. Her research mainly focuses on cognitive and health psychology, including health-related digital technology applications to clinical, organizational and educational contexts.

ALESSIO ROCCHI is associate professor of General and Social Pedagogy at the Salesian University Institute of Turin (IUSTO), where he holds the position of CEO. Since 2022 he has been European coordinator of Salesian Institutions of higher education. His recent research focuses on the relationship between society, education, new technologies and their impact on the lives of young people, from a perspective inspired by critical human rights education.

ROBERTO SANTORO, socio-anthropologist, PhD at the University of Turin, is adjunct professor of Cultural Anthropology and General and Educational Sociology at the Salesian University Institute of Turin (IUSTO), where he holds a position as head of the Department of Educational Science. His research mainly focuses on Anthropology of Work, in particular Organizational Cultures in Third Sector-Non Profit Organizations.

CLAUDIO TARDITI, philosopher, PhD at the University of Turin, is Associate Professor of Philosophy of Education at the Salesian University Institute of Turin (IUSTO), where he holds a position as head of the Department of Communication. His main field of research is the phenomenological tradition, with particular focus on the phenomenological foundation of natural sciences and psychology. His recent research is focused on a phenomenological approach to AI.